OTHERWISE HOMELESS

Vehicle Living
and the Culture
of Homelessness

Michele Wakin

FIRST**FORUM**PRESS

A DIVISION OF LYNNE RIENNER PUBLISHERS, INC. • BOULDER & LONDON

Published in the United States of America in 2014 by
FirstForumPress
A division of Lynne Rienner Publishers, Inc.
1800 30th Street, Boulder, Colorado 80301
www.firstforumpress.com
www.rienner.com

and in the United Kingdom by
FirstForumPress
A division of Lynne Rienner Publishers, Inc.
3 Henrietta Street, Covent Garden, London WC2E 8LU

© 2014 by Lynne Rienner Publishers, Inc. All rights reserved

Library of Congress Cataloging-in-Publication Data
Wakin, Michele.
Otherwise homeless : vehicle living and the culture of homelessness / Michele Wakin.
Includes bibliographical references and index.
ISBN 978-1-935049-87-6 (hc : alk. paper)
 1. Homeless persons. 2. Homelessness—United States. 3. Homeless persons—Services for—United States. 4. Housing policy—United States. I. Title.
HV4505.W237 2014
362.5'920973—dc23   2013029326

British Cataloguing in Publication Data
A Cataloguing in Publication record for this book
is available from the British Library.

This book was produced from digital files prepared by the author
using the FirstForumComposer.

Printed and bound in the United States of America

 The paper used in this publication meets the requirements
of the American National Standard for Permanence of
Paper for Printed Library Materials Z39.48-1992.

5 4 3 2

For Victor and Viviana—
Home is where you are

Contents

List of Tables and Figures		*ix*
Acknowledgments		xi
1	Homes on Wheels	1
2	A Brief History of Homelessness and Vehicle Living	21
3	Navigating Vehicle Living	45
4	Negotiating Public Spaces	73
5	Service Provision and Programming	97
6	Vehicle Living vs. Unsheltered Homelessness	125
7	When Beggars Become Choosers	167
References		*177*
Index		*185*

Tables and Figures

Tables

2.1 The Decline of SRO Hotels and Housing Units in Skid Row Areas	31
2.2 Temporary Housing for Hurricane Katrina Victims	39
3.1 Vehicle Count Results, 2002–2004	48
3.2 Available Shelters for Homeless People in Santa Barbara, California	52

Figures

3.1 Primary Locations for People Living in Vehicles in Downtown Santa Barbara	46
3.2 Vehicle Types	47
6.1 Housing Affordability for SSI and Minimum Wage Earners	129
6.2 Three-City Comparison of Prioritized Special Needs Groups	130
6.3 City and County Housing Density	131
6.4 Sheltered/Unsheltered Breakdown by County	132
6.5 Locations of Unsheltered Homeless People in the 2007 PIT Count in Sonoma County	134

6.6 The Seven Subpopulations Required by HUD
     in the 2007 PIT Count in Sonoma County   134

6.7 Barriers to Securing Permanent Housing in the
     Survey Component of the 2007 PIT Count in
     Sonoma County   135

6.8 Locations of Unsheltered Homeless People in the
     Overall PIT Count and the Survey Component of
     the 2007 PIT Count in Santa Cruz County   145

6.9 The Seven Subpopulations Required by HUD
     in the 2007 PIT Count in Santa Cruz County   146

6.10 Reasons for Becoming Homeless and Barriers
     to Permanent Housing as Reported in the
     Survey Component of the 2007 PIT Count in
     Santa Cruz County   147

Acknowledgments

The most difficult part of writing this book was leaving so much unsaid. In conversations with Louie, one of my primary informants, he pushed me on the issue of personality. After reading an excerpt about himself, he said "that's all true but there's more to it than that," and I had to agree. I owe an immeasurable debt to the homeless community in Santa Barbara, California, for the laughter, personality, friendship, and insights they brought to this work. There is more to them than stories, more than vehicle living. They are unique individuals struggling for social legitimacy, and this book is designed to aid them in that struggle. I am grateful to inhabitants of the "jungle," including Ricky Goldsmith and Pres Ed, who invited me to my first jungle interview. I am grateful to Moms for making me feel at home in the shelter, an otherwise daunting place to spend my days. To my friends Crazy Ed, "the Onion," el Chapparro, Cuba, Martin, Lyn, Nancy, and most of all to Louie, my "street dad," I thank you for taking the time to show me "the Life," for answering my questions, and for looking out for my safety.

I also owe a great debt to the vibrant advocacy community in Santa Barbara. To Peter Marin and Glen Mowrer, your tireless work on behalf of homeless people has brought their concerns to the fore. You have given voice to the voiceless, and it has meant a better standard of living for some and the difference between life and death for others. To the McCune Foundation, the Fund for Santa Barbara, and the Mesa Lane gang (Chuck, Cath, Peter, Ken, John, Rob, Gary, Kathleen, Gayle, Lynelle, and other local providers and policymakers), thank you for sharing and thank you for listening. Thanks to the Casa Esperanza Board of Directors, New Beginnings, and sympathetic members of the Santa Barbara City Council and County Board of Supervisors. Without constant attention to the issue of homelessness, policy and advocacy would not advance as they have in recent years. These accomplishments, detailed herein, are a wonderful beginning.

The academic communities at the University of California–Santa Barbara and Bridgewater State University also deserve thanks for their support of this work. To Mitchell Duneier, for early encouragement, for being patient when I got things wrong, and for always being interested in methodological and theoretical discussions. To Don Zimmerman, for your mentorship in conversation analysis and ethnomethodology, and for being supportive when I chose to pursue a different path. Thanks to Bridgewater State University for supporting faculty travel in the pursuit of scholarship. Through this support, I was able to return to California twice and conduct comparative research in Santa Cruz and Sonoma counties. The Center for the Advancement of Research and Scholarship and the Office of Teaching and Learning also deserve thanks for supporting faculty scholarship through travel opportunities, book workshops, and the Summer Institute. To my colleagues in the Sociology Department, Patricia Fanning and Jodi Cohen in particular, thank you for your advice and encouragement. Finally, to the president of Bridgewater State University, Dana Mohler-Faria, thank you for granting me leave time to finish this book. Your visionary leadership is responsible for the university's involvement in regional efforts to end homelessness, and I am grateful for the opportunity to assist in this effort.

1
Homes on Wheels

Louie lives behind a woodpile in the industrial area next to the shelter. He is fresh out of prison after serving a five-year sentence for felony robbery, and the woodpile is the only place he feels safe. When it's really cold, Louie sleeps in his small car, a Toyota Celica packed with possessions and smelling of rot. Louie is tall—6'2"—and the car is uncomfortable for him so he rarely uses it as sleeping quarters. Occasionally, shelter staff coax him indoors with the promise of a cot in the corner, where Louie feels safer than he does in the middle of the floor.

Although his given name is Luis and he is Puerto Rican, he speaks no Spanish and everyone calls him Louie, Crazy Louie, or Louie the Lip. Tall, skinny, and mostly balding, Louie ties his hair into a little pony tail at the base of his neck. When things are going well, he is clean shaven and wears jeans and a button-down Hawaiian shirt or a T-shirt. When things are not going well, he is unkempt, unshaven, and wears a multi-colored joker's hat, complete with jingle bells on the ends. When things are really bad, Louie carries a hatchet, which he ordinarily hides in his car for protection. The hatchet is meant to warn people that Louie is not easy prey. He also uses it to even the score if more than one person tries to go after him. In particular, Louie worries about being "rat packed" by a group of Mexicans and Central Americans with whom he sometimes conflicts. As he says, "I can deal with the bean, it's the burrito I can't handle."

"I am no stranger to Santa Barbara," Louie told me. "I was one of the tree people in the 80s." In those days, there was no homeless shelter, so people congregated around one of the local landmarks, the Moreton Bay Fig Tree. "I met a lot of people, did a lot of stupid things. It was more adventurous then. I jumped a train once to go pick peyote in Texas. I picked in March though and it was colder than shit through Texas. You could make friends at the Fig Tree though. It's the same as people here, kind of like family." Louie was taken from his own family when he was eight years old and placed in a home for abused children. Surprisingly, he describes this as a nurturing experience "It was a small group of kids who couldn't go to regular schools, and I was pretty much everybody's best friend, I was always captain of the team."

Unfortunately, his comfort and status there were short-lived and Louie moved from the group home to foster care. By age 11, he says, "all of a sudden, I don't feel good about my situation. Now I got a foster dad that's abusing me and I'm basically more like a pet for them." He switched foster homes several times and got into trouble often: "I had issues, you know; I was not a happy person." His early experiences at the group home, he says, "helped establish my character because of the way the other kids made me feel. I had my dignity intact." Yet foster care eventually took a toll on Louie and he began to lose his ability to cope with adversity. "There was a point in time where I would take it all in and think that, you know, I could tough it out, you know, and stuff like that—and you hit bottom finally one day and find out you got nothin' in your tank. There's no past experience to say some day you'll get out of this because you say no, I've never been out of it, you know what I mean?"

By the time he was 27, Louie had been in and out of jail for petty crimes. Finally, he committed his most serious crime, "so there I was robbing a jewelry store across from the police department at noon on Friday. I didn't give a fuck—I'm at the point where I'm saying, *let's do this*." He describes his partner in crime getting cold feet when they were ready to rob the store. "He got scared and said 'it don't look good.' Well, it don't never look good when it could be the worst day of your life." Although it took the police a month to catch up with him, Louie was given ten years to life and was paroled after serving five. Prison was difficult for Louie, and in order to survive it, he competed with the other inmates by lifting weights. He pushed himself to the physical limit and continues to suffer chronic neck and back pain as a result. By the time I met him, Louie was taking three Vicodin to survive each day.

Soon after his release from prison, Louie applied for supplemental security income (SSI). "I've got to survive, you know; this outdoor shit is hell on my back." SSI benefits are intended for low income people who are over age 65, blind, or disabled, and Louie fell into the latter category. He initially submitted his application in April 1999, and it was denied twice because of insufficient proof of disability. To assist him in filing a third appeal, Louie contacted Channel Counties Legal Services Association, an agency specializing in civil cases for indigent clients.

With all of the paperwork finally in place, Louie was granted SSI in December 2000. He was deemed unable to work and therefore disabled because of "mental and physical impairments," including depression, personality disorder, Hepatitis B and C, and kidney and thyroid problems. Although recurrent substance abuse was also listed among his disabilities, this did not mean he could not receive SSI, merely that he needed to establish a representative payee who would agree to receive and disburse the money.[1] In March 2001, almost two years after he filed the initial application, Louie received a total of $8,421.34, representing the monthly payments he would have received since the date of his application, with deductions for general relief and employment payments he received during that time.

Louie's first purchase was a 1978 Toyota Dolphin motor home with 99,000 miles on it. He met its owner at a gas station in the shelter neighborhood and struck up a conversation with him. The man owned a home and used the Dolphin for vacations. It was in excellent shape, with the original upholstery and a sound engine and exterior. The toilet, shower, and stove were all in working order, and the interior had a collapsible kitchen table and a long bench that doubled as a sleeping area. It also had a smaller sleeping area above the driver's seat (cab).

Louie lived in the Dolphin for about four years, until he received a Section 8 voucher and moved into his own apartment. One of the main differences between living in his vehicle and living in an apartment was that Louie no longer had to worry about moving the vehicle or coming into contact with law enforcement. "They don't harass me now like they used to. I got tickets for everything. But don't get me wrong now, the Dolphin was better than the street. I can lay my stuff out here (in my apartment), I don't have to move it around, and with my medication there are many times where I really shouldn't be moving. You know what I mean?"

Louie's life experiences illustrate some of the reasons that homeless people use vehicles as a form of housing. First and foremost, vehicles allow for more safety, privacy, and autonomy than the shelters or the streets can provide. Living in a vehicle gave Louie the private space he needed to avoid the conflicts he faced on the street and to gain needed, uninterrupted rest. But vehicle living was not without its challenges, as purchasing and maintaining a vehicle also required managing resources and responsibilities. Louie's ability to manage financial resources, as well as legal and social responsibilities, is what kept him in his vehicle and eventually helped him transition to apartment living. Not all people who live in vehicles as permanent housing are able to manage these challenges and to purchase their vehicles legally or live in them on a long-term basis. Vehicles are not always used as a midway point between street and apartment living.

Vehicle living is one of many makeshift housing solutions used by homeless people to avoid the shelters and the streets. This book offers an in-depth ethnographic exploration of vehicle living in California and examines how it differs from other forms of makeshift housing. It treats public space as the contested ground on which the daily struggle for survival plays out. I focus on the regulatory practices used by police and city officials to curtail access to public spaces and the modes of resistance used by homeless people and advocates to argue for increased rights and privileges. The dynamic relationship between regulation and resistance is endemic to the experience of homelessness. This dynamic is the theoretical framework used to set vehicle living apart from other makeshifts, to examine how people living in vehicles negotiate public spaces, to explore how and why they resist shelters, and to underscore the importance of creating effective social policy that breaks the cycle of regulation and resistance.

The focus on public space is well-traveled ground, as "space wars" are a central part of the literature on homelessness and urban sociology (Dear and Wolch 1987; Duneier 1999), legal geography (Mitchell 2001), and the focus of national agencies like the National Law Center for Homelessness and Poverty and the National Coalition for the Homeless. The occupation of public spaces is also an emotionally charged issue, as NIMBY[2] battles demonstrate. Fitting vehicle living into this landscape shows that it is different from other forms of makeshift housing for homeless people, as most makeshifts do not allow for a long-standing or permanent claim to public space. Vehicles, by contrast, offer the possibility of legal ownership and a great deal of control over one's living environment. How does this affect the occupation of public spaces and the attention received from citizens and law enforcement?

Regulation is a way of putting homeless people literally and figuratively in their place by constraining their physical location and their behavior. "Strategies of authority" are one way of describing how homeless or other "unruly" people are managed. Talmadge Wright (1997, 183) describes four essential *authoritative regulation strategies* that exclude, repress, displace, or assimilate homeless people in terms of their occupation of public space and their participation in various forms of communication and protest. Authoritative regulation strategies also redefine social-physical spaces to favor their own interests (Wright 1997, 181). Homeless people who are unsheltered face regulation in the form of public space ordinances that target where they are and activities associated with a life in public (National Law Center on Homelessness and Poverty 2002). Examining what forms of regulation people living in vehicles encounter and how they manage them is one way of differentiating vehicle living from other makeshifts.

Resistance is a counter to regulation. It is a way of preserving choice and autonomy over living space. Homeless people have limited resources with which to pursue ongoing, organized resistance (Cress and Snow 1996). As a result, the most common forms of homeless resistance are designed to preserve a sense of self-worth or argue for services and provisions, including affordable housing and entitlement to public spaces. Immediate survival needs often overshadow ongoing, organized resistance. Vehicles offer unique resources for enacting resistance as they give homeless people a private, legally defensible space in which to conduct activities usually done in public. How does this affect their self-esteem, and how does it position them in the struggle for social legitimacy?

Negotiating an Interest in the Life

Crazy Ed: Hey Michele, that's Groucho, Groucho, that's Michele.

Louie: Ed thinks I sound like Groucho Marx. So anyhow, so what's the situation, you just interested in what, the Life?

Focusing on vehicle living was a choice I made according to interest as well as safety. On the streets and in the shelters, I was always, either explicitly or implicitly, beholden to someone to ensure that I was safe.[3] Vehicle living offered a more private, controlled environment in which to have conversations and conduct interviews. I spent over three years conducting ethnographic research among the homeless community and just over one year intensively researching vehicle living in Santa Barbara, California. I also conducted comparative research in Sonoma and Santa Cruz counties during the summers of 2006 and 2008 with a focus on policies for serving unsheltered homeless people, including those in vehicles.

For nine months of this research, I carried a digital audio recorder at all times and transcribed every night. This yielded an overwhelming amount of data. I also worried that I was relying on the recordings at the expense of actively listening (Lofland et al. 2006, 106). I switched to taking field notes and, later, to conducting semi-structured interviews, administering surveys, and conducting vehicle counts, for the remainder of this research. Discussed in more detail in subsequent chapters, these changes in methodology reflect an emerging research agenda that honed in specifically on the experience of vehicle living.

My approach combines macro-level concerns about the relationship between inequality and public space with the methodological mandate of Participatory Action Research (PAR); that research participants shape the research agenda, from start to finish (Foote Whyte, Greenwood, and Lazes 1991, 20). My role became increasingly advocacy oriented (Cole 1991), as I established and maintained rapport with several informants who aided in the process of data collection. Ethnographers who conduct advocacy research not only involve informants or community members, they play an active role in making social change happen. They advocate for the groups they research, write in forums to change public opinion, embarrass power brokers, and provide key information about a situation at opportune moments in the policy decision making forum (Fetterman 1991, 126).

Throughout the course of this research, I became actively involved in local-level policy through regular presentations to the Santa Barbara City Council and County Board of Supervisors and through involvement with nonprofit advocates and service providers. I also testified on behalf of homeless defendants at numerous municipal court trials in which they were cited for sleeping and camping. Data collected in service of this research were also used to justify the creation of the Safe Parking Program, which allowed safe nightly parking for people living in their vehicles. I ran this program as the Homeless Outreach Coordinator for ten months of this research, discussed in greater detail in Chapter 5. This experience illustrated the issues involved in creating policies and programs to serve homeless people and keep them off the streets.

To explore the issues involved in policing homeless people in public spaces, I conducted numerous ride-alongs with officers in Santa Barbara, Santa Cruz, and Sonoma counties. This was an essential step in understanding the opposite sides of the fight for public space. I also examined the point-in-time (PIT) counts in each of the three counties as a way of looking at how the federally mandated PIT is used to enumerate local homeless populations and design policies for serving them. This foray into federal and local policy helped formulate a more nuanced sense of regulatory mechanisms as both provisional and punitive.

My evolving role in the field was part of negotiating an interest in "the Life." Moving from buddy to advocate to service provider brought about fundamental changes in the way I viewed homeless people and the way they viewed me (Cole 1991; Jorgensen 1989, 55). This evolution also illuminated the regulation-resistance dynamic this book describes.

In the early stages of this work, it was difficult to maintain an "embodied presence" (Emerson 2001). I was always thinking about what I would bring back and present. That meant that in Erving Goffman's observation, I was playing a discrepant role, as "fink" or "informer" (Goffman 1959). Focusing on advocacy meant that rather than being a detached or even critical observer, I was actively involved in understanding and communicating aspects of vehicle living and homelessness that highlight issues of equity. I was also involved in shaping policy, turning observation into action. In the chapters that follow, I describe how vehicle living fits into the landscape of homelessness and explore how to direct policy and ethnography to increasing awareness and working toward social change.

Vehicle Living and Homelessness

Situating vehicle living along a continuum of housing solutions for homeless people underscores the fluidity of "homelessness" as a social category. According to the US Department of Housing and Urban Development (HUD), individuals living in their vehicles are officially part of the unsheltered homeless population. The high degree of variation within this category makes any attempt at enumeration difficult, as fixed definitions miss the myriad housing solutions and complex survival strategies that homeless people pursue. Yet definitions and enumeration drive federal funding, which in turn sets parameters for local policies and provisions.

Federally mandated PIT counts are a primary way of defining and measuring the homeless population and are required by HUD for any region seeking federal funding. According to HUD, unsheltered homeless people reside in "a place not meant for human habitation, such as cars, parks, sidewalks, abandoned buildings (on the street)" (US Department of Housing and Urban Development 2004). There is a high degree of overlap between those considered unsheltered and chronically homeless. The latter sleep in emergency or transitional shelters or in places not meant for human habitation. They must also have a disabling condition, meaning "a diagnosable substance use disorder, serious mental illness, developmental disability, or chronic physical illness or disability, including the co-occurrence of two or more of these conditions" (US Department of Housing and Urban Development 2004; 2008). The literally homeless are distinguished from the "precariously housed," who are doubled up or who pay a disproportionate amount of their income on rent. Homeless assistance is not directed toward the precariously housed.

The PIT count leaves out a laundry list of people in marginal housing, collectively referred to as the "hidden homeless" (Burt et al. 2001; Rossi 1989; Hallett 2012). Prostitutes staying in motel rooms paid for by clients, children in foster care or staying with relatives, people living in substandard buildings, doubled up with family or friends, staying in motels paid for with vouchers, or who are incarcerated, are not officially defined as homeless and are therefore not counted. In addition, homelessness is often not permanent but episodic, so snapshot counts do not measure homelessness over time or accurately reflect the number of individuals homeless in a given year (National Coalition for the Homeless 2009).[4] People living in their vehicles are counted among the unsheltered, yet it is difficult to determine which vehicles are being used as full-time housing and which are used as vacation vehicles. RVs are also designed as fully functional residences, calling into question their inclusion in the unsheltered homeless category.

The practical matter of counting unsheltered homeless people, locating inadequate nighttime residences, and accessing public and private places not designed for human habitation is daunting. The end result is that there is over and under counting (Hombs and Snyder 1982; Burt and Cohen 1989) and a heavy, albeit intentional, focus on those in shelters.[5] Many communities also tailor their counts of unsheltered homeless people to target those groups that are most visible or are considered a problem. People living in RVs are often overlooked, under counted, or targeted as problematic in annual PIT counts.[6] Designing effective policy is difficult without adequate statistical and ethnographic data. How Continuum of Care (CoC) regions conduct their PIT counts and use data to inform policy is a good measure of how effectively they serve unsheltered homeless people.

California is a prime location in which to examine vehicle living and unsheltered homelessness because of their prevalence. California is home to one in five homeless people nationwide, and over 60 percent of the statewide homeless population is unsheltered, including people in vehicles (US Department of Housing and Urban Development 2011). Understanding how vehicle living fits into the policy discussion of unsheltered homeless people highlights the complexity of needs and varying population demographics among the unsheltered. Homeless assistance has historically been directed toward meeting the needs of specific populations at the expense of others—and without acknowledging the constant influx of newly homeless people. Numbers and definitions of homeless people are difficult to generate with any precision, yet they figure centrally into policies that regulate the use of public space and govern service and shelter provisions.

Regulation

Criminalization and *shelterization*[7] are two of the primary regulation strategies used to contain homeless people by managing their physical location and their behavior. Regulation can be geared toward providing assistance and relief (Piven and Cloward 1993; Wright 1997), or it can be punitive. Punitive regulation excludes homeless people from public spaces and from political decision making, even for decisions that directly affect their welfare (Feldman 2004; Wright 1997). Policy decisions are shaped by negative reactions to homeless people in public spaces, turning anti-homeless ideology into concrete regulation strategies. Unless homeless people are able to garner a space of their own to which they can legally claim entitlement, they are vulnerable to various kinds of sanction.

Anti-homeless laws criminalize homeless people by targeting them as illegitimate users of public space. The most widespread forms of criminalization include the regulation of life-sustaining activities like sleeping; the selective enforcement of loitering, jaywalking, or open container laws; sweeps of city areas and the destruction of property; the enforcement of "quality of life" ordinances related to public activities and hygiene; and levying restrictions on providers of aid to homeless people (National Coalition for the Homeless 2007; National Law Center on Homelessness and Poverty 2002; 2009; Ellickson 2001; Kelling and Coles 1996). In principle, anti-homeless laws are designed to rid the streets of people who are seen as unclean, undeserving, and perhaps dangerous. In practice, they are expensive to enforce, address an immediate issue without offering a long-term solution, and create legal problems that can prevent homeless people from establishing employment or housing stability.

Criminalizing homeless people also violates several constitutional rights (National Law Center on Homelessness and Poverty 2009).[8] The fact that homeless people are targeted for legally defensible actions underscores the extent to which they are seen as non-citizens, not entitled to basic rights and provisions, and not adhering to the normative moral order (Feldman 2004). Law enforcement based on stigma results in homeless people being punished for some of the same activities that non-homeless people do with impunity. Vehicle living complicates anti-homeless laws because vehicles offer a physical barrier that allows occupants to perform activities in private and thereby avoid public scrutiny. Yet many of the vehicles and individuals in them are still visibly recognized as homeless and incur sanctions similar to what other homeless people face. This book examines and evaluates the difference between homeless people living in vehicles and those living in shelters and on the streets in terms of their ability to avoid criminalization and other forms of regulation.

Throughout this book, *shelterization* is used to refer to the set of ideas and regulatory mechanisms that suggest that homeless people belong in shelters. Access to shelter for homeless people depends, at minimum, on the availability of beds and on meeting the minimum entry requirements. Emergency shelters typically offer the least stringent entry requirements and the most rudimentary accommodations, and guests must submit to rules and regulations as a condition of their stay. Particularly in warm-weather states like California, emergency shelters are often only open during the coldest winter months, leaving homeless people unsheltered for the remainder of the year. Those who have a steady income through employment, SSI, or other sources, or those who are members of specific populations,[9] may have an easier time accessing shelter. Although the distinction between *emergency* and *transitional* shelter is not always clear, transitional shelters frequently offer better meals, more private sleeping accommodations, space for families, and services designed to meet the needs of specific populations (Wong, Park, and Nemon 2006). Because accessing these resources is often predicated on income, many homeless people are unable to move beyond emergency shelter.

Shelters are anathema to many homeless people because they are unsafe, unclean, and mandate submission to rules and regulations (Wagner 1993). Although not all shelters are the same in terms of surveillance, services, and approach (Friedman 1994), relatively few are designed to provide comfort and autonomy. Relinquishing personal belongings and being exposed to various kinds of surveillance and risk are part-and-parcel of most public shelters. Originally conceived of as an emergency measure, shelters have become a default setting that "warehouses" people in refuse or marginal city areas, offering few transitional opportunities (Baxter and Hopper 1981; Wolch and Dear 1993). Shelter conditions, as Leonard Feldman argues, "express a vision of the homeless as bare life, as beings stripped of human personhood and individual identity; they are to be kept alive but not given the resources and privacy for individuation" (Feldman 2004, 96) or community building. Homeless people who opt for private shelters depend on close relationships with and approval from staff, at the expense of building community with other homeless people (Dordick 1997). Shelters can also strip parental authority from homeless parents, as children understand shelter staff as authority figures to whom they and their parents must answer (Crowley 2003). As Elizabeth Joniak

(2005) also shows, conflict between staff and clients can exacerbate feelings of injustice and marginalization. Many homeless people prefer to remain on the streets to exercise control over their living situation and enjoy a degree of autonomy they could not attain in a shelter setting (Wagner 1993).

The irony of shelterization, at least in California, is that it offers about a five-month window during which homeless people can access indoor shelter. They are then on their own for the remainder of the year. Most develop makeshift living arrangements including beach huts, tents, "jungles" in wooded areas or along the railroad tracks, and vehicles. Once in these settings, they are subject to a range of anti-homeless ordinances that push them back toward shelter. This is particularly ironic for homeless people in vehicles, given the degree of self-sufficiency that they maintain. Criminalization and shelterization threaten vehicle living as a form of housing and suggest that the proper place for homeless people is in jail or an emergency shelter. Although one is punitive and the other, in principle, is rehabilitative, they are remarkably similar in terms of the restrictions they impose on homeless people. Being targeted for anti-homeless regulation means being recognized as a particular category of person and behaving in ways that are not sanctioned by authority. Access to shelter also depends on being recognized as a particular category of person and behaving in ways that *are* sanctioned by authority. So proper behavior is rewarded with squalid shelter, and improper behavior is punished with jail time, citation, or other sanctions. In either case, being homeless is the central feature of being targeted.

Avoiding regulation is something homeless people spend a lot of time on. In addition to locating and accessing services and provisions, it is one of the central activities in a homeless person's day (Hopper, Susser, and Conover 1985). For vehicle owners, acquiring and maintaining a vehicle to use as housing and avoiding police attention are tedious, time consuming activities but ones that allow them to preserve a sense of safety and autonomy and combat social stigma. This is a primary feature of what distinguishes vehicle living from other forms of homelessness.

Resistance

How do people without resources or social standing attempt to resist regulation? The most common forms of resistance to the regulation of homeless people include actions designed to maximize self-worth, to exercise free will, to protest unfair treatment, and to claim rights to public space. Acts of resistance by homeless people and their advocates are ways of contesting basic forms of regulation and arguing for increased rights and privileges or simply combating marginalization. Identity work and placemaking activities are two related ways in which homeless people contest regulation strategies that restrict behavior and location. Research on social action and social justice supports the idea that resistance strategies must also give voice to the thoughts and concerns of those under study and work to build alliances and encourage political participation (Lott and Webster 2006). This is an important component of homeless resistance, particularly since it relies so heavily on researchers and advocates for resources and support (Cress and Snow 1996).

Depending on outside resources and assistance is also a limitation in the sense that it leaves homeless people beholden to advocates for funding, for the legitimacy of an outside voice that can effectively use the legal and political language necessary to combat regulation, for an understanding of the needs and concerns of homeless people, and for the tireless energy needed to pursue anti-homeless regulation. For these reasons, without ouside advocacy, homeless resistance is often designed to address immediate survival, at the expense of arguing for social equity (Wright 1997).

One of the primary ways in which homeless people preserve a sense of self-worth is by trying to convince others that they are not as they appear. To understand how this works, David Snow and Leon Anderson (1987; 1993) distinguish between two basic forms of identity: (1) social identity, which is appearance- or behavior-based and is assigned by others; and (2) personal identity, which is claimed or asserted by the actor. This distinction has been explored in detail as it relates to social stigma and how a stigmatized person manages personal information in relationship to others (Goffman 1963). To gain a sense of social legitimacy, homeless people assert a positive personal identity to counter a degraded appearance or the visible signs of addiction, mental illness, and poverty. One of the primary ways this happens is verbal.

Homeless people use *identity talk* to explain their homeless status. It is either something they own and avow—"I'm an expert dumpster diver"—or something they distance themselves from: "I ain't no lazy bum." The more time homeless people spend on the street, the more difficult it is for them to deny their homeless status, with all of its negative connotations. In fact, they embrace the stereotypes and, in so doing, take ownership of the label (Becker 1971, 69–73). Identity talk gives homeless people agency in describing their own condition and is a way of asserting a positive personal identity. Yet it is a limited form of resistance due to its inability to challenge anti-homeless ideology and a degraded social identity. It also does not bridge the gap between homeless people and outsiders. In its various forms, identity talk often underscores for housed listeners the marginalization of homeless people.

Anti-homeless regulation focuses on appearance, behavior, and location as a collection of stigma-symbols that signify a homeless presence (Goffman 1963, 43). Despite the personal meanings and understandings homeless people ascribe to themselves, their activities, and their accoutrements, their biggest challenge lies in the ability to convince others that they are socially legitimate, "normal" people. Snow and Anderson's initial discussion of identity work includes the "procurement and arrangement of physical settings and props, cosmetic face work or the arrangement of personal appearance, selective association with other individuals and groups, and the verbal construction or assertion of personal identity" (1987, 1348). The first entries in this list are given short shrift because homeless people typically lack the resources to pursue or maintain them in the long-term. Vehicle owners therefore bring something new to the table. Those who legally own their vehicles represent a form of identity work that homeless people are usually not able to access or sustain: the procurement and arrangement of a legally owned physical setting.

Makeshift housing for homeless people includes huts (Phillips and Hamilton 1996; Wright 1997), abandoned subway tunnels (Morton 1995; Toth 1993), tent cities, shantytowns (Dordick 1997), jungles, and vehicles (Southard 1998). Sustaining makeshift housing means challenging the legal and social risks that threaten a life on the streets. Because they typically lack any formal, legal claim to the spaces they inhabit, most makeshift communities are easily displaced through "sweeps" or other forms of anti-homeless regulation (Ellickson 2001; Foscarinis 1996; Mitchell 2001; National Law Center on Homelessness and Poverty 1991). Regulation is particularly aggressive when homeless groups and individuals occupy a city's more prominent, lucrative spaces. As a result of the stigma associated with homeless people in public and the threat of regulation, we see the increasing spatial segregation of the poor and homeless into refuse areas or "service-dependent ghettos" (Dear and Wolch 1987; Wright 1997). Exploring this trend, Jennifer Wolch (1995) suggests that negative attitudes toward homelessness necessitate hiding in public spaces. When mere visibility can be grounds for harassment or arrest, homeless people go to great lengths to maintain a life on the streets. Avoiding shelters, developing alternative institutions, participating in social movement activities, and developing a sense of community with other homeless people, are all forms of resistance to regulation.

Although many of the vehicles that homeless people use as housing are designed to be lived in, they are still subject to anti-homeless regulation that targets appearance and behavior. This shows how regulation operates, by using the trappings of social identity to make assumptions about personal identity, and acting on these assumptions. As long as being homeless is considered a problem, being visibly, recognizably homeless means regulation. As Wright (1997, 70) describes, borrowing from Michel DeCerteau (1984),

> To be out of place is also to be without respect, and hence without the ability to summon the power, the resources, to change one's conditions. . . placemaking is a key element of resistance to the gaze that fragments, breaks up, dissociates the poor and homeless subject. Placemaking, in the form of autonomous collective street encampments, allows for the possibility of breaking the public gaze with attached authoritative judgments.

Wright shows that placemaking can lead to the redefinition of public spaces, allowing homeless people to build community and self-esteem (Wagner 1993; Wright 1997). In some cases, placemaking can lead to the acquisition of permanent housing (Wagner and Cohen 1991; Wright 1995; Wright and Vermund 1996). Placemaking is a counter to the idea that homeless people and the makeshifts they inhabit are illegitimate (Oyserman and Swim 2001; Veness 1993; Cuba and Hummon 1993). Vehicle living affords unique resources for performing identity work and conducting placemaking activities. Examining these resources provides a necessary counter to regulation strategies that exacerbate the immediate, emergency nature of homelessness and target a life in public.

Vehicle Living

Vehicles are part of a continuum of housing solutions that range from street to apartment to house. Vehicle living requires establishing an array of social networks, solving logistical problems, maintaining a degree of financial stability, and being a provider. To illustrate how vehicle living relates to homelessness, this book examines station and circumstance,[10] who RVers are, the logistics of vehicle living, and how it is received by police, business owners, citizens, and service providers. It also attempts to make sense of the thin line that separates RVs from other makeshift living arrangements. In so doing, rather than offering an overarching definition of homelessness, this analysis further problematizes how we understand the intersection between housing choice, identity, and public perception.

One of the primary reasons to focus on vehicle living is that, unlike the kinds of makeshift housing previously mentioned, vehicle living allows for the possibility of legal ownership. With ownership comes privacy, control over living space, freedom from shelter rules or the danger of the streets, protection from the elements and from various predators, and mobility. Despite these resources, those living in vehicles are still vulnerable to regulation strategies that target public appearance as problematic and punishable. Like homeless individuals who go to great lengths to pass as housed, those living in newer vehicles or passenger cars can blend in with tourists or motorists, and regardless of their personal history or appearance, avoid the *homeless* label. Most, however, exhibit the tell-tale signs associated with long-term use: parking in the same location, visible bedding, covered windows, tarpaulin on the roof, a patchy or unusual paint job, bicycles and other possessions clinging to the frame, worn tires, and other signs of residency. These tip-offs signal a homeless identity and often trigger regulation. But does permanent use mean that an individual is homeless?

Deciding whether or not someone who lives in a vehicle is homeless depends in part on what the individual thinks and in part on what others think; that is, on both personal and social identity (Snow and Anderson 1987; 1993). Not all people who live in their vehicles consider themselves homeless, but if neighbors, police, and city officials do, they are subject to various kinds of negative attention and regulation, including laws that restrict parking, mobility, and behavior inside the vehicle. The privacy that most vehicles afford offers a physical barrier for the individual so, technically speaking, it should not matter who the person is. Yet, as indicated earlier, the size of the vehicle and its age, appearance, and location can either hide or signal that occupants are homeless.

A lack of social legitimacy and personal entitlement are the most obvious parallels between homelessness and RV living. Recognizably homeless people on the street and in vehicles are symbols of failure. "Homeless" in Jason Wasserman and Jeffrey Clair's conception (2010, 139) "is a master status—an identity that permeates the entire life of the person who is homeless—and the negative judgments it carries become rigidly attached to understandings of who a person is, even sometimes in that person's own estimation." Regardless of what roles they play in the communities they are a part of, homeless people are objectified as broken windows in the sense that they themselves are reified as refuse (Marin 1995; Kelling and Coles 1996; Duneier 1999) and homelessness is seen as a personal failing. Viewing homeless people as an accepted albeit degraded part of society furthers their objectification (Blasi 1994; Marcuse 1988; Melnitzer 2007). Not only are they seen as illegitimate, non-citizens, but they lack access to the resources needed to challenge their situation and public perception of them in the long term (Feldman 2004; Cress and Snow 1996). In order to survive, they focus on immediate attainment at the expense of thinking about or planning for the future. Valorizing their survival strategies and homeless people as innovative bricoleurs (Snow et al. 1996) is dangerous because it reaffirms their position in the social hierarchy rather than focusing on social change. It is not only interesting that people living in vehicles have managed to use existing parking and travel laws to their advantage in fighting anti-homeless ordinances, but it is potentially useful in challenging practices of exclusion that threaten their existence.

Overview of the Book

This book offers an in-depth exploration of people who live in their RVs in Santa Barbara, California, and a comparative look at vehicle living and homelessness in California's Sonoma and Santa Cruz counties. Like many California cities, Santa Barbara's emergency shelters have exclusive entry requirements and are only open during the winter months. Homeless people therefore spend the duration of the year without shelter. RVs keep people out of the shelters and off of the streets, yet they are still not free of the stigma or the legal backlash that plagues homeless people. Understanding vehicle living sheds light on the complicated relationship between regulation and resistance as two sides in the battle over legitimacy and public space.

Chapter 2 provides a historical overview of vehicle living and homelessness and their eventual convergence. It tracks changes in vehicle living as it evolved from the auto camping popular in the early 1900s to the blighted trailer parks and luxury tourist vehicles of the mid- to latter part of the century. It also examines the differences in how homeless people have been understood over time, from the adventurous hobo in search of seasonal work to so-called skid row[11] denizens and later, families with children. These changes are viewed through public perception and policy as the arbiters of public space provisions. The chapter concludes by introducing Santa Barbara, California, as the primary area under study and offers an overview of homelessness and vehicle living within the city.

Chapters 3 and 4 focus on RV living, using ethnographic data to examine resistance and regulation, respectively. Chapter 3 explores how vehicle living compares with other available housing alternatives and the overlap between people living in their vehicles and those on the streets and in shelters and apartments. It describes the complex social ties that RVers must negotiate to be able to legally acquire their vehicles and maintain them. The chapter offers case studies of where people park, how they gain access to basic amenities, and their relationship to other RVers and to the local homeless community. Contrary to the stereotype that homeless people are dirty, uneducated, and without resources to provide for themselves and their families, Chapter 3 shows RVers as skilled negotiators, able to make the most of limited resources and to provide for themselves and others. In some cases, RV living facilitates the transition to permanent housing. Examining these issues sheds light on alternative housing solutions as a form of resistance.

Chapter 4 focuses on regulation and examines how vehicle owners resist anti-homeless ordinances that target the occupation of public space. Ethnographic data are used to illustrate these issues, which include interactions between police and homeless people in Santa Barbara, Santa Cruz, and Sonoma counties, and municipal court trial data in which vehicle owners are cited for violating parking and anti-sleeping ordinances. Police interactions with homeless people show the dilemma officers find themselves in when attempting to regulate public spaces. They also show how homeless individuals and groups become targets for enforcement. Municipal court cases are used to examine the efficacy of resistance strategies that target space and legality. The chapter concludes with the establishment of a program to serve people living in their vehicles, which is the subject of Chapter 5.

How does service provision for people living in vehicles compare with the creation of emergency shelters and services for other sectors of the unsheltered homeless population? Chapter 5 answers this question using ethnographic data to detail the creation of the Safe Parking Program for people living in their vehicles, a program that has garnered nationwide media attention (Chawkins 2008; Gutierrez and Drash 2008; Urbina 2006; Tietz 2012). It provides a view from the perspective of participant observer and offers a critical examination of the utility of programs for homeless people and of entry-level service provision. It examines some of the resources offered through organized programs and some of the barriers that keep homeless people away from them. Together, Chapters 4 and 5 examine the punitive and provisional sides of regulation.

Chapter 6 offers a comparative look at the unsheltered homeless populations in Santa Barbara, Santa Cruz, and Sonoma counties, focusing on the policies in place to document and serve them. It examines how the PIT counts in each county are calibrated with the ten-year plans to end homelessness and offers a qualitative profile of the unsheltered homeless population. In so doing, it places vehicle living into context amidst a housing market that is not affordable and in relation to a population that is difficult to enumerate or gather data on and that has complex service needs that make employment and the transition to housing a challenge. The chapter also examines the differences between unsheltered homeless people living in makeshifts, and those living in their vehicles, in terms of lifestyle as well as the resources and risks associated with both forms of housing. Finally, it examines practical and policy level solutions that would help unsheltered homeless people access entry-level housing and shelter.

The concluding chapter examines the complex relationship between housing choice and social legitimacy, specifically as related to the occupation of public spaces. It offers insight into how regulation can be understood and managed in relationship to homelessness and service provision. It also explores ways of breaking the cycle of regulation and resistance that condemns homeless people to a life on the margins. Conducting this exploration through an analysis of policy and grassroots movements allows for an evaluation of their efficacy in offering housing solutions that are acceptable, logical choices for homeless people.

Notes

[1] A representative payee is someone designated by a beneficiary of Social Security and appointed by the Social Security Administration. People who need representative payees are those deemed incapable of managing their money because of prior felony convictions, mental illness, or other stipulations. When a beneficiary receives supplemental security income, the payee receives and disburses the funds, and assists the beneficiary in managing the money.

When Louie realized that he would need to establish a representative payee, he was furious. "They think I can't handle myself. I've been handling my business for years!" Because of the trusting relationship Louie and I had established, he asked me to be his payee and I agreed. I acted in this capacity for four years so that he could continue to receive his benefits. After this point, he applied for and was granted the right to manage his own income.

[2] Dear (1992) offers a detailed exploration of how NIMBYism works and how it can be overcome. He outlines the main oppositional arguments that communities and individuals raise against locating shelters or other "unpopular projects" in their midst. These include the perceived threat to property values, personal security, and neighborhood amenities (Dear 1992, 4). Where facilities are located, as well as the perceived threat of the client population, are factors that have affected the siting of homeless shelters in communities nationwide.

[3] There are many examples of ethnographers' bravery in the field, of enduring harassment and winning arguments (Dordick 1997, 119–121). These

moments of pride signal to the ethnographer that she is able to handle herself in the field, that she is "in." There are fewer accounts of ethnographers taking chances that did not eventually pan out or that resulted in violence or bodily harm. Part of my reticence to conduct research in makeshifts stemmed from the fact that virtually all of the women who slept in unsheltered locations endured some form of abuse. Most women relied on men for protection, and in most cases, they were physically and/or romantically involved with them. Although unsheltered locations were the most interesting for me, ensuring my safety was also paramount. Visiting jungle locations was something I did sporadically and always with an understanding of the personal risk involved, as well as the risk for anyone who acted as protector.

[4] The methodology of homeless street counts is particularly fluid as communities conducting the counts often vary with respect to coverage area, volunteer support, and consistency across years. In addition to variation within one jurisdiction, there is also wide variation across areas such that some cities conduct street-by-street counts and others rely on reports from homeless service providers or experts in the field. HUD cautions against both of these strategies as they produce biased data. Only rarely do communities attempt to find people who are living in remote or hidden areas, leaving an untallied percentage uncounted and on the street. Chapter 6 offers a detailed overview of the point-in-time counts in three California counties, with a focus on methodology and planning efforts.

[5] The rise of the Homeless Management Information System (HMIS) to better track the use of homeless services has led to a focus on service provision and coordination, and overall enumeration. Homeless people who do not use shelters, who resist tracking through HMIS or other means, or who use day services, may be left out entirely. The dearth of information on unsheltered homeless people is particularly troubling in regions where they outnumber the sheltered homeless.

[6] In Link et al.'s 1995 study of the life-time and five-year prevalence of homelessness, "literal homelessness" includes a list of possible places one might live. Vehicles were found to be the most common place where homeless people reported staying (59.2 percent), followed by makeshift housing (24.6 percent). These results were found using telephone surveys and follow-up interviews, a more in-depth methodology than that used for PIT counts. In addition, because respondents were reporting prior rather than current experiences with homelessness, some of the stigma associated with "hidden" homelessness was minimized.

[7] The term *shelterization* was coined by sociologists researching homelessness in the 1930s and 1940s. It was used to characterize feelings of inefficacy, lethargy, and removal from schedule or responsibility that shelters were thought to inspire (Sutherland and Locke 1936). The current usage treats shelters as a form of regulation and explores the requirements for entering shelter and why homeless people would resist doing so.

[8] Anti-homeless laws are in potential violation of at least four Constitutional Amendments, three of which (I, IV, VIII) are part of the original Bill of Rights. First Amendment rights of free speech are violated when soliciting donations is considered legal, yet panhandling is not. The Fourth Amendment prohibits unreasonable search and seizure of property. This amendment is violated when law enforcement destroys and confiscates tents or

other belongings without notifying homeless residents or giving them a chance to claim their property. The Eighth Amendment, prohibiting cruel and unusual punishment, is violated when homeless people are cited for pursuing life-sustaining activities like sleeping, when no other alternatives are available. Finally, the Fourteenth Amendment equal protection clause prohibits the selective enforcement of laws to target homeless people. (See http://wiki.nlchp.org/display/Manual/Criminalization+Constitutional+and+Human+Rights+Framework and http://www.usconstitution.net/).

[9] The seven subpopulations specified by HUD for the annual PIT count are: chronically homeless persons, those who are severely mentally ill, those who have chronic substance abuse issues, veterans, persons with HIV/AIDS, victims of domestic violence, and unaccompanied youth (under 18). With the exclusion of unaccompanied youth, these primary need categories prioritize chronically homeless people and those with specific physical or mental issues and needs. People who are newly homeless and do not fit into these categories, although they may be easier to move into permanent housing, would not necessarily be prioritized for shelter.

[10] Hopper (2003) critiques the documentation of the surface appearance of homelessness alone; enumerating mere "station and circumstance." Instead he focuses on the underlying processes that bring to light the array of preventative mechanisms that keep people from becoming homeless. This book takes the opposite approach and examines the specifics of vehicle living as a way into exploring the ongoing struggle for space and entitlement. Connecting station and circumstance with the policies designed to serve unsheltered homeless people contextualizes vehicle living as a housing solution.

[11] The term "skid row" is commonly used to refer to urban areas where welfare hotels, employment services, and cheap amenities for homeless people could be found. The term originated in the 1800s and is associated with Seattle's waterfront area, where logs were dragged or "skidded" to sawmills to be processed into usable lumber. This usage underscores connection between migrant labor, transiency, and urban life that characterized these areas.

2
A Brief History of Homelessness and Vehicle Living

Both vehicle living and homelessness have undergone periods of relative acceptance from the 1920s to the present. During these times, they were understood as legitimate and were supported through public space provisions. Later in the twentieth century, both became synonymous with social blight. This chapter covers a wide range of vehicles used as housing, including trailers, the more permanent version of the motor home. Including a range of vehicles demonstrates the complex relationship between poverty, legitimacy, and housing choice. This chapter adds to the understanding of identity construction among homeless people by focusing on resources and public perception.

A Marxist reading of identity views the transformation of all activities and products into exchange-values, thereby reducing social relations to the social conduct of objects (Agnew 1982, 61). People evaluate themselves through their possessions and seek status through control of private space. Owning a home *and* vehicle is a far different and superior measure of status than using one's vehicle *as* a home. Examining the range of vehicle and housing choices over time, along with variations in the homeless community, puts vehicle living into perspective as an affordable housing choice that allows occupants to preserve a degree of control and autonomy that other settings do not offer. In so doing, it emphasizes poverty and housing choice as a continuum, in contrast with the treatment of homelessness as a monolithic social category.

From house cars to Winnebagos, vehicle living over time ranges in form and function. Perceptions of vehicle living also vary, from acceptance and public space provisions to heavily regulated RV parks. These shifts demonstrate a growing disapproval of the itinerance and mobility associated with vehicle living. Those who live in their vehicles must compromise by enjoying freedom and adventure but foregoing the comparative acceptance of traditional home ownership. In many cases, owners make a forced choice as they are unable to afford or are otherwise pushed out of their homes due to poverty, emergency, natural disaster, or any number of circumstances.

Homelessness has also undergone significant shifts in terms of the occupation of city spaces and less marked shifts in terms of public perception. Whereas homeless people today are seen as "down on their luck," in the early 1900s homelessness was considered to be an adventurous, albeit squalid, mode of existence. The combination of mobility and urban spatial permanence that skid row areas offered is far different than housing for homeless people later in the twentieth century. The "new" homeless include a greater volume and diversity of people, far more spatial dispersion, and the rise of the emergency shelter as a primary housing solution (Hoch and Slayton 1989).

The Early Years of Novelty and Adventure

In the early 1900s, automobiles were a novelty. Early vehicle living took the form of "auto camping"—literally, sleeping in one's car. Simplistic as it sounds by today's standards, auto camping combined independence and romanticism, offering an adventurous vacation or a means of supporting an itinerant career (White 2000). The two basic types of vehicle popular during this era were house cars and auto campers. The former was a larger, better appointed vehicle that was self-contained, with sleeping quarters as well as living space. The size of most house cars as well as the amenities they featured meant that they were owned primarily by wealthy tourists and were not affordable for middle-class Americans (Harmon 2001). Auto campers were smaller cars with tents or cots that could be assembled for sleeping, and were, like the Ford Model T, priced within reach of the average consumer. Auto campers typically camped on private property or in municipal lots that were established free of charge to encourage campers to spend money at local businesses (Hurley 2001).

This early support was tied to both social and economic standing, as people who went auto camping were considered honest people with money to spend. Acceptance of auto camping waned as people began to associate the camps with loose morals and the trash they left behind, particularly the tin cans that held their meals. The label "tin can tourists" stuck, and it served as synecdoche for campers as a social group. Although the Tin Can Tourists Association was established in 1919 to promote cleanliness and decency in the camps, turning the label into a source of pride, it still called to mind the hobo's can of beans (Thornburg 1991; Wallis 1991).[1]

Despite this unfortunate association, auto campers were a far cry from the hoboes of the early 1900s. Although both groups showed an interest in adventure and mobility, "hoboes" were more homogenous, comprised primarily of young, single white men who traveled surreptitiously by train in search of seasonal labor. Early sociological accounts of hoboes distinguish them from other types of homeless people. Borrowing from Alice Solenberger (1911); Ben Reitman, the "hobo doctor;" and St. John Tucker, president of the "Hobo College" in Chicago; Nels Anderson describes the hobo as "a migratory worker. A tramp is a migratory non-worker. A bum is a stationary non-worker" (Anderson 1923, 87). These categories are fluid however, as men tended to drift back and forth between them. In addition to the search for seasonal employment, the most striking feature of the hobo community was its unprecedented mobility (DePastino 2003, 65). Mobility was coupled with a great deal of autonomy over working conditions predicated by the high demand for migratory labor. Hoboes often refused jobs that did not meet their needs.

Hoboes typically moved through cycles of travel and rest, remaining stationary until their work ended and money ran out. They did not accumulate possessions but rather spent what they earned at whatever rate they pleased, allowing temporal as well as spatial mobility. It is this freedom from ongoing domestic and employment obligations that would become a signature feature of hobo culture. Auto campers, in comparison, got limited but thrilling glimpses of this lifestyle through their excursions, but always returned to the comforts of more traditional, permanent housing.

Chicago School sociologists associated the transiency of *hobohemia,* another name for skid row, with the dangers of urban living. The myriad stimuli encountered in cities was also seen as a demoralizing force, with consistency and social control at the heart of stability and moral order (Burgess 1925). Although not a central feature of concentric zone theory (an early theory explaining land use in the context of urban change and growth), Burgess mentions "zones of deterioration" as those that host areas of demoralization, promiscuity, and vice (Burgess 1925, 76). Mobility could be experienced in shorter, more controlled periods, but the constant itinerance of the hobo was likened to wanderlust or an unhealthy addiction (Park 1967, 158; Cresswell 2001) and was considered a threat and a danger. The proximity of hobohemia to railway stations underscored the heightened stimuli and transient nature of this environment.

Hobohemia offered "characteristic institutions" designed to serve the needs of the hobo and capitalizing on the rapid turnover and mobility of the area. These institutions included "cheap hotels, lodging-houses, flops, eating joints, outfitting shops, employment agencies, missions, radical bookstores, welfare agencies, economic and political institutions to minister to the needs, physical and spiritual, of the homeless man" (Anderson 1923, 15). Known by outsiders as "skid row" and more favorably by insiders as the "main stem" (Kusmer 2002, 160), these areas brought autonomy and community to the hobo lifestyle. They also attracted hustlers, or "jack rollers," who preyed on the recently employed or anyone with resources they could be separated from (Shaw 1966). Despite the dangers, vices, and unsanitary conditions that characterized skid row areas, they were a relatively stable part of the urban landscape. From Pioneer Square in Seattle to Chicago's West Madison Street, traveling hoboes had a place they could count on to serve their needs.

In the early 1900s many hoboes joined the Industrial Workers of the World (IWW) in an attempt to organize by industry and abolish the wage system, believing that

> The working class and the employing class have nothing in common. There can be no peace so long as hunger and want are found among millions of the working people and the few, who make up the employing class, have all the good things of life.
>
> Between these two classes a struggle must go on until the workers of the world organize as a class, take possession of the means of production, abolish the wage system, and live in harmony with the Earth (Industrial Workers of the World 1905).

The IWW saw in hobohemia a group of men working to protect their autonomy and free themselves from oppressive working conditions. Hoboes bought "red cards," which symbolized IWW membership and without which they risked being kicked off of freight trains or barred from employment. The International Brotherhood Welfare Association (IBWA) also attempted to bring about a change in employment for hoboes by offering them an educational alternative. It established Hobo Colleges, whose purpose was to "make us the masters of the machinery of production instead of its slaves." Similar to the IWW in scope and purpose, IBWA and its Hobo Colleges offered hot meals, dormitory lodgings, reading rooms, and job information (DePastino 2003, 106–108). Both organizations tapped into a revolutionary tendency common to the hobo lifestyle and inspired by the desire to escape the yoke of capitalism in the form of patterned labor, domesticity, and the accumulation of financial resources. These characteristics made the main stem ripe for political organizing.

Poverty and Struggle

The Great Depression changed the nation's understanding of poverty, as well as its understanding of auto camping and homelessness, making the first obsolete and the second more widespread. The link between makeshift camping, poverty, and the struggle to survive (White 2000) also became fixed in the public imagination during the 1930s. The "Hoovervilles" (named after President Herbert Hoover) that sprang up on city outskirts across the nation were makeshift camps of tents and vehicles, largely inhabited by the "nouveau poor" who were victims of Depression-era poverty. As David Thornburg (1991, 34) notes, "Not every town had its Hooverville, but almost every consciousness did." As a result, home ownership became an explicitly political goal that would restore the bonds of community and nationhood in an era of unparalleled homelessness (DePastino 2003, xxi). The sense of adventure and choice that accompanied early auto camping and hobo living was replaced by a feeling of necessity, desperation, and survival. Employment opportunities were scarce, and the once-thriving employment centers that populated skid row began to close their doors. Travel by train also became more restrictive, limiting the mobility of skid row residents. More people—approximately half of all vehicle owners by the late 1930s—began living in their vehicles on a full-time basis, and the families that vacationed in them did so as the only affordable alternative. Some individuals were pushed into vehicle living as a response to the emergency conditions that swept the Midwest and high plains areas.

From approximately 1930 to 1936, thousands of migrants from Oklahoma, Texas, Colorado, Kansas, and New Mexico moved west en masse to escape the "black blizzards" brought on by severe drought and unsustainable farming practices. The nation sympathized with the plight of families and struggling farmers as depicted in photographs by Dorothea Lange for the Federal Emergency Relief Administration, reports by UC Berkeley economist Paul Taylor, and in the novels *The Grapes of Wrath* and *Of Mice and Men* by John Steinbeck. These portrayals inspired sympathy because of the nation's feeling that white farmers were honest, hardworking victims of circumstance. Ironically, once the primarily white, Protestant immigrants settled in California, they found themselves working for Italian, Scandinavian, Portuguese,

Armenian, Japanese, or Hispanic growers and contractors (Gregory 1989, 165).

Although other states served as destinations for Dust Bowl migrants, California hosted approximately 24 percent of the 1,367,720 people who left the Southwest between 1910 and 1930 (Gregory 1989, 7). Paul Taylor's work shows that although farmers and farm workers were represented, many migrants were in fact blue-collar workers who were attracted to the promise of prosperity. While farmers were often stereotyped and resented by the communities they settled in, they inspired far more sympathy than their more itinerant hobo counterparts and the nonwhite victims of natural disasters in the twenty-first century. Many were also able to make the steady climb back to sustenance and a living wage, as the Depression gradually gave way to a new era of increased prosperity.

The aftermath of the Dust Bowl migration brought new and less restrictive laws governing intrastate travel and massive agricultural reform under the New Deal. Laws enacted in 1933, 1936, and 1939 that attempted to bar poor and indigent people from California were overturned, and farm workers, a previously ignored subset of the labor market, were rewarded with increased services thanks to the public's perception of them as honest and hardworking (Gregory 1989). Prior to this, basic rights and provisions, including the right to unionize, were overlooked for farm workers. These changes would impact the state's agricultural industry and relationship with homeless people and immigrants for years to come.

Overall, the 1930s were marked by an understanding of poverty and suffering never before experienced by working-class Americans and the nation as a whole. The decade also saw a growing class polarization that would eventually render hoboes and the skid row areas that housed them obsolete, along with a radical shift in the perception of leisure activities and camping in particular. Municipal parks closed during this era, and only federal forest lands were kept open for tourists. Auto camping rebounded in the mid- to late 1930s, but campers were still thought of by some as a 'parasitic class of wheeled hoboes' (Hurley 2001, 204). Traditional homeownership, by contrast, was considered an essential ingredient in the recipe for citizenship and social success (Hurley 2001, 210).

By the late 1930s, trailers were viewed as a more permanent form of shelter, and camps proliferated as a result (Harmon 2001). Along with the development of new parks came increasing citizen concerns about the drain on public resources that might be incurred through crowding, sanitation problems, and the need to school "migrant children." The fear of trailer living as environmentally and socially unhealthy continued to grow (Foster 1980, 277). Two things resulted from this fear: (1) camps were located in industrial areas or on inexpensive property, and (2) the image of trailers and trailer parks as a social menace became fixed in the public imagination (Harmon 2001).

Forms of auto camping in the late 1930s included tents and pop-up trailers. An estimated 400 companies were manufacturing 400,000 trailers per year (Burkhart, Noyes, and Arieff 2002). Units gradually became more streamlined, with variations known as the tear drop, ham can, and bread loaf, all to be towed behind the family car. In addition to better construction and improved roadways, automobiles made the trailer attractive for housing or vacation use (Clark and Wilcox 1938). Yet the shadow of poverty and subsistence lingered, and manufacturers struggled to rescue the image of trailers and autocampers as a threat to sedentary life and American morals. Many felt that campers' ties to the social system were simply "looser" (Thornburg 1991, 72). There was also an increasingly marked distinction between acceptable forms of trailer travel, including tourist excursions enjoyed by middle-class and wealthy families, and trailer living as a way of life. By the late 1930s published directories of trailer parks explicitly distinguish luxury from affordable parks, marking an implicit distinction between legitimate and questionable residents.

In response to concerns about the increasing number of trailers used as housing and the lack of separation according to vehicle or social class, parks became more regulated. Sewerage, electrical hook-ups, and trash disposal became customary in most parks, as did separate areas for people with children and pets. Length and width restrictions, parking permits, zoning restrictions, duration limits, fees, and taxation as personal rather than real property were also the norm. Many of the early legal cases attempting to impose new restrictions focus on whether or not the trailer should be classified as a dwelling or a vehicle. Although the former classification won out, whether or not an object is "determined by its use, the intention of the user, the perceptions of others, or its objective physical features" (Wallis 1991, 73) is still a key question. As trailer parks struggled for permanence and acceptance, hoboes attempted to solidify their place in the labor market. Like "trailerites," hoboes also bucked the trends of homeownership and wage labor.

The 1930s saw the hobo population impacted by governmental shifts in aid programs and assistance through the New Deal. The National Committee on Care of Transient and Homeless was created in 1932 to better coordinate service organizations and attempt to enumerate the homeless population. Part of the Federal Emergency Relief Act also entailed funding for homeless people through the Federal Transient Service (FTS) (Kusmer 2002). The transient centers founded through the FTS were designed to offer immediate assistance in the form of accommodations and did not require employment as a condition of service. The centers also provided health care, educational opportunities, and on-site employment. Despite their success in reducing the number of transients without shelter, budget cuts in 1935 forced many centers to close. Approximately 400,000 people were released from transient centers, causing a new wave of street transiency (Kusmer 2002).

Largely inspired by World War I veteran protests and demands for compensation, several additional programs were created to offer employment. The Civilian Conservation Corps (CCC), also known as President Franklin D. Roosevelt's "tree army," offered work and shelter for three million men between 1933 and 1942 (Maher 2008). Comprised of nine corps regions, the CCC offered vocational training and employment for able-bodied men between the ages of 17 and 28 who were willing to send $25 of their $30 weekly allotment home to their families. Impressive in scope, the CCC planted three billion trees, built 46,854 bridges, slowed soil erosion on forty million acres of farmland, and developed 800 new state parks (Flynn 2008; Maher 2008). More important, it offered support for upholding the ideals of work, family, and conservation that would act as a rehabilitative force for struggling men. Although Roosevelt fought for continued support of the CCC, funding ceased in 1942 as World War II required an ongoing influx of men and troops.

The New Deal brought about a shift in the way the nation viewed homelessness, with the "new" and more sympathetic homeless comprised of families with children, and the "old" homeless comprised of single men (Hoch and Slayton 1989). These changes occurred in tandem with increased prosperity and the virtual demise of seasonal agricultural and industrial labor. As a result, the skid row population began to diminish. Chicago's main stem saw a drop from 60,000 in 1907 to 12,000 in 1958 (Hoch and Slayton 1989, 92). There was also a shift in population from younger, transient laborers to an older and more stationary "home guard." Although many still sought work, inhabitants of skid row were stereotyped as alcoholics, accelerating demands for the renewal of central city areas. Shelters also began to replace skid row as the primary housing solution for homeless people, beginning a devastating trend of offering charitable services over employment or education and excluding homeless people from policy decisions affecting their welfare. The large-scale redevelopment of skid row areas, which would take place in the decades to come, also eroded the sense of community, autonomy, and privacy that characterized such neighborhoods.

From World War II to Counterculture

Despite the embrace of traditional home and family life that the New Deal reinforced, the onset of World War II brought a renewed acceptance of trailer living as a source of defense housing for military personnel. From 1940 to 1943, some 36,000 trailers were purchased by the federal government as stopgap housing (Foster 1980). In 1940 alone, the federal government ordered 6,500 trailers, approximately half of the annual output nationwide (Thornburg 1991, 144). These temporary homes and the parks that housed them offered only the most basic amenities, and communities still objected to having parks sited in their midst. Particularly in communities that housed wartime industry, rapid population increases and associated housing demands were controversial. The Bay Area alone saw an influx of 300,000 new residents from 1940 to 1943, many of whom worked in private and naval shipyards (Foster 1980). The federal government influenced siting decisions as new parks were located close to wartime industry and workers required on-site housing. The California legislature also allowed large cities to construct and operate municipal parks if a housing shortage existed, but this permission was terminated one year after the war's end, demonstrating the combined power of wartime emergency and severe housing shortage to override regulations and siting decisions (Foster 1980, 282).

Although traditional home ownership was the mainstay of social acceptance, trailers continued to be in high demand as permanent housing for veterans returning from war and raising families or benefiting from tuition subsidies authorized by the GI Bill of Rights. In fact, according to Andrew Hurley (2001, 212) it was not at all unusual to find trailer courts entirely filled with ex-GIs. Given the shortage of conventional housing, the federal government also requested that manufacturers increase production, a further indication of governmental control over the industry.

Trailers were particularly appealing forms of housing not only for GIs but also for migrant workers and working-class families who were unable to afford a full-sized suburban home. By the 1950s, many housing developments were mass produced, offering more affordable traditional homes. Yet even the liberal mortgage insurance programs sponsored by the Federal Housing Authority (FHA) and Veterans

Administration (VA) left a segment of the working class, particularly those in menial or non-union jobs, without conventional housing (Hurley 2001, 216). Those who could afford trailers began outfitting them with the same enthusiasm that brought an array of new gadgetry to the American kitchen and the suburban home. During this decade, trailers also became larger, ten-foot-wide units that moved once, from factory to park. As David Thornburg (1991) describes, by the 1950s the tow-behind trailer era was passing and the beginning of the mobile home era was at hand.

In 1952 the industry officially split, as the Trailer Coach Manufacturers Association was replaced by the Mobile Home Manufacturers Association and the Recreational Vehicle Institute, one focused on housing and the other on recreation and road worthiness. Although it had been coming for years, this distinction officially marked the difference between vehicles used as housing and those used for transportation and recreation, a distinction that needs some clarification. Mobile homes, despite their name, are not actually mobile but are a form of manufactured housing that moves once, from factory to site. Commonly called "trailers," these units vary greatly in size, with the larger "double-wides" resembling small but permanent homes. Motor homes, in contrast, are vehicles built onto bus, truck, or car chassis, and are meant for mobility. Despite the split, the reputation that both have as a downgraded form of housing informs how they are understood and regulated.

The large number of working-class families living in mobile homes during this era brought a widespread increase in the number and size of parks. Mobile home parks were met with skepticism by local communities, who considered them to be "a new kind of slum...offering all the bad features of the urban blight area" (Wallis 1991, 173). As a result, they were increasingly located away from central city areas to more remote, rural locations, which would also bring down land costs and loosen restrictions. Despite this marginalization, park residents, and families in particular, still touted the feeling of community that the parks fostered (Thornburg 1991; Counts and Counts 1992).

Hobohemia also underwent radical changes in the 1950s. Brought on by the mechanization of labor, the rise of the automobile as a primary means of transportation, and the political and cultural push toward homeownership, the mobility that characterized hobo life was now something that the nation enjoyed in a regular, more acceptable way. Without the lure of lucrative, seasonal work, and with increasing crackdowns on riding the rails, hoboes lost the mobility and a great deal of the romance that characterized their lifestyle. The population also aged as younger men were called to do low-skilled but physically demanding industrial labor.

Urban prosperity was on the rise in the 1950s and 1960s, leaving skid row areas largely vacant and leading to the demolition or redevelopment of single rent occupancy (SRO) hotels. As Charles Hoch and Robert Slayton argue (1989, 173), large-scale destruction of SRO units was a primary reason for the increased visibility of homeless people in cities nationwide (see Table 2.1).

Table 2.1: The Decline of SRO Hotels and Housing Units in Skid Row Areas

Denver (1976–1981)	45 hotels to less than 17
New York City (1975–1981)	Loss of 30,385 units/160 buildings
San Diego (1976–1984)	Loss of 1,247 units in 30 hotels
San Francisco (1975–1979)	Loss of 32,214 units
Seattle (1960–1981)	Loss of 15,000 units

Source: Hoch and Slayton 1989, 173.

The Housing Act of 1949 cleared the way for the wholesale conversion of downtown districts. Skid rows began to crumble, and residents struggled to compete in the mainstream housing market or submit to emergency shelters scattered throughout the city. At the same time, beat poets sought to romanticize skid row, particularly its disillusionment with the embrace of domestic life so prevalent in the 1950s. Yet critiquing the reigning domestic order did not dismantle it. Given the state of skid row at the time, such belated affinity only reinforced the traditional ideals of family and home ownership. The postwar economic boom brought a new understanding of hoboes and homeless people in general as anathema to what the country was striving for.

Skid row areas like Chicago's West Madison Street and the Bowery in New York City declined significantly in size during the postwar era (Kusmer 2002, 225). Businesses that were initially lucrative in hobohemia left the deteriorating skid row areas and they became islands of decay in major cities. Increasingly, remaining skid row residents were identified by sociologists as "disaffiliated" and not part of the team (Bahr 1970; 1973). The emphasis on the drunken, derelict nature of the skid row resident was also a prevalent theme (Bogue 1963; Bahr and Caplow 1973; Bahr 1970; Kusmer 2002). Although sociological studies show that many men had recently worked, desired work, and appreciated the autonomy of skid row lodging, they were still viewed as lazy no-accounts. One result of this pervasive stereotype is that rehabilitation programs like those initiated with New Deal legislation were essentially off the table. Skid row became a segregated area according to race and income and an immobile area without the vibrancy it once held. Aging residents relied on unstable work and government assistance to support themselves.

Adding to the sense of isolation and worthlessness that characterized skid row areas, police were also increasingly paying attention to skid row residents, making sure they did not bleed into more prominent areas of the city. Police attention took the form of large-scale "round ups" as well as daily ticketing and arrests. In Minneapolis in 1957, 44 percent of all persons arrested resided in the Gateway area, home to a proliferation of cheap lodging houses (Kusmer 2002, 234). Skid row became a magnet for law enforcement, and homeless people were seen as a nuisance, regardless of which area of the city they were found in. These trends continue to the present and inform the placement of shelters and services as well as the preference for makeshift living arrangements, including vehicles.

Innovations in camping by the late 1950s showed a propensity for either residential living in trailer courts or smaller, more mobile, more affordable units. Pickup campers, featuring a camper body or shell mounted on the truck's cargo area, proliferated in this era. The pickup camper was easy to drive, and the body could be removed when not in use, yet it was not seen as a family vehicle until the 1960s. Vans also became popular by the late 1950s and throughout the 1960s and 1970s, when sales took off. Vans were easy to drive, affordable, and had many features (including the "pop top") that were attractive to both families and singles. Along with more maneuverable vehicles, the Interstate Highway System, authorized in 1956, made nationwide travel even easier. Billed as part of defense spending, the Interstate Highway System was envisioned as facilitating coast-to-coast military operations and protecting the country from potential threats. Building the Interstate Highway System was a matter of governmental support as well as cultural buy-in.[2] In the 1950s and 1960s, the automobile was associated with freedom, adulthood, and sexuality. The country's love affair with road vehicles was popularized in movies like *The Long, Long Trailer* (1953), *The Wild One* (1954), and *Rebel Without a Cause* (1955).

Trailers were a mere subset of this fascination, portrayed as a quaint, if comical, mode of living.

Although trailers were restricted to parks and zoned out of most standard metropolitan statistical areas (Wallis 1991), they were increasingly recognized as a form of permanent housing, however downgraded. While trailer travel enjoyed a degree of legitimacy, road vehicles including vans, pickup campers, and RVs also soared in popularity from the late 1960s to early 1970s. Stratified according to price and size (White 2000), self-propelled homes on wheels could accommodate a range of individuals, families, and budgets. Winnebago, the industry leader during this era, became synonymous with the motor home. By the late 1960s, Winnebago adopted auto plant assembly line technology and accounted for over 50 percent of RV market sales, with units costing one-fifth of the price of other models. The Family Motor Coach Association and Kampgrounds of America (KOA) also formed in this decade, standardizing the coast-to-coast camping experience and providing a sense of community for RVers. Still popular in mainstream film and television, motor homes were also associated with the emerging counterculture of the 1960s and 1970s.

RVs, vans, and particularly "hippie buses" in the 1960s were associated with road trips, drugs, and alternative lifestyles. Popularized by Ken Kesey's infamous bus tours, vehicle living was seen as an extension of the counterculture revolution that characterized the decade. Painted in psychedelic colors, the bus inspired Tom Wolfe's book *The Electric Kool-Aid Acid Test* (1968). Kesey's own experimentation with drugs inspired his novel-*cum*-film *One Flew Over the Cuckoo's Nest* (1962). Associating vehicle living with drugs and experimentation solidified the growing discomfort with vehicle living that would grow in the years to come.

RVs were also controversial because of the oil crises in the 1970s, which not only made them more expensive to drive but also called into question their functionality. Their size was considered objectionable in national parks because of the damage they did to the natural environment. At the same time, President Richard Nixon recognized the mobile home as the only kind of housing affordable for moderate-income families and included them in the official count of new housing units being produced (Wallis 1991, 207). This new classification meant that the mobile home was regulated as housing in terms of construction, inspection, taxing, and financing, making it less affordable overall in comparison with traditional homes. Although motor homes did not enjoy the same permanence that mobile homes took advantage of, they were far less expensive to own and maintain. The market therefore became further polarized as those unable to afford the investment in a mobile home remained in their vehicles and on the road.

The 1980s and 1990s saw steady growth in the RV industry, with three basic variations: vans, motorized travel trailers, and buses (White 2000, 187). Industry leaders pursued diesel engines, reducing vehicle weight, and more aerodynamic design. They also explored innovations including slide-out or expandable living rooms, entertainment centers, sun roofs, GPS navigation, air conditioning, and other amenities. The RV market also changed during this time as owners were younger than in previous generations, with approximately 40 percent between ages 35–54 in 1997 versus only 20 percent in this age group a decade earlier (Wood 2002). This shows the growing niche RVs filled in the housing market. While the larger and more luxurious RVs became better appointed, mini RVs also became popular; and smaller, older units remained on the road, serving, for some, as an affordable form of permanent housing. With an industry sensitive to rising gas prices and economic recession, the purchase of new RVs is done in times of plenty by people who can afford the $40,000 to $400,000 for a new motor home. Currently, motor homes are continuing the trend toward "supersizing," with many reaching forty to forty-five feet and new models close to or exceeding the market value of a single-family home. Rentals have also become popular for those who want a vacation on wheels but do not want to make a commitment to RV living.

Responding to the Crisis: Developing Policy

Although the ranks of the homeless began steadily growing in the 1970s, it was only in the 1980s that homelessness became an epidemic social problem demanding a federal response. Beginning in 1981, Ronald Reagan's presidency was nothing short of devastating for homeless and low income people. During Reagan's first year in office, he cut the budget for public housing and Section 8 (a federal rent subsidy program) in half, to about $17.5 billion. By 1985 a vast low-cost housing shortfall, estimated at 3.3 billion units, left many people without affordable housing (Dreier 2004). A proponent of the "welfare queen" stereotype and the idea that homelessness is a choice, Reagan saw the homeless population grow to startling proportions. By the late 1980s it was clear that the federal government needed to present a comprehensive, uniform response to the rising tides of homeless people.

Relentless protest by the Community for Creative Non-Violence (and its leader, Mitch Snyder, in particular) and the Coalition for the Homeless drew attention to the need for immediate action. Small-scale marches and demonstrations combined with national events like "Hands Across America" and Comic Relief raised money and awareness. Yet as David Wagner and Jennifer Gilman (2012) point out, the call for emergency shelter was stronger than the demand for housing, underscoring the immediacy of the problem.

The first attempt at a federal response to homelessness finally came in 1987 when the Stewart B. McKinney Act, originally the Urgent Relief for the Homeless Act, was introduced in the House. It reached the Committee on Governmental Affairs, and a reluctant President Reagan signed the bill to provide "urgently needed assistance to protect and improve the lives and safety of the homeless, with a special emphasis on elderly persons, handicapped persons, and families with children" (Stewart B. McKinney Homeless Assistance Act of 1987; National Coalition for the Homeless 2006). Because the programs and services it encompassed were designed to deal with an emergency, they did not address the homeless population in its entirety, and they were implemented at the expense of long-term, permanent supports or sustainable infrastructure.

The late 1980s and 1990s brought an array of new provisions to McKinney, renamed the McKinney-Vento Homeless Assistance Act in 1999[3] and amended in 1988, 1990, 1992, and 1994. With the most sweeping changes in the 1990s, new programs focused on emergency care and expanded services to children and youth; those with mental health issues, AIDS, or addiction; dually diagnosed clients; veterans; and families. Targeting specific populations had the unintended effect of further stigmatizing homeless people or "cherry picking" to serve those most likely to succeed. At minimum, specialized institutions were separatist and confusing, leaving homeless people unsure of where to turn or left out entirely. Similarly, shelters were typically located in remote or dangerous locations, making it difficult to access needed services or to escape the spatial stigma of homelessness.

The first federal plan to end homelessness was penned during the George H.W. Bush administration and was submitted along with an implementation report and several programs focusing on food assistance and on services for those with severe mental illness. By 1995, under President Bill Clinton, funding for homeless assistance reached an all-time high of over $1 billion. Most important, under Clinton, the continuum of care (CoC) approach was crafted as an attempt to better coordinate services for homeless people. Often seen as a ladder, components of the CoC include intake and assessment, emergency shelter, transitional shelter, and specialized services such as alcohol and drug treatment (Burt et al. 2001, 13). Along with an increased focus on reporting and special attention to rural populations, which had previously been ignored, the CoC approach was a signature feature of the federal response to homelessness in the mid- to late 1990s.

The primary programmatic elements of the CoC, or linear residential treatment (LRT) model, are emergency, transitional, and permanent supportive housing. Differences between these three forms of shelter are increasingly important as communities attempt to create more transitional and permanent housing (Wong, Park, and Nemon 2006). Substantial program requirements and better and more available services are two of the distinguishing features that ideally set transitional and permanent housing apart from emergency shelter. In practice, the three types often blend such that even emergency shelters may have stringent program requirements, and services are not necessarily more available or advanced depending on program type. Section 8 housing, another option for qualifying homeless people, was significantly cut under Clinton, although renewal vouchers and certificates were funded (Bratt 2003). Unfortunately, the linear stepwise transition from street to apartment, as idealized through the CoC approach, rarely materialized, leaving the majority of chronically homeless people on the streets.

The replacement of Aid to Families with Dependent Children (AFDC), an entitlement program, with Temporary Assistance to Needy Families (TANF), a block grant program with a spending cap, was another signature feature of policy changes in the 1990s. Part of the Personal Responsibility and Work Opportunity Reconciliation Act of 1996, TANF left families with less flexibility than AFDC. The new restrictions included a two-year limit on receiving uninterrupted cash assistance and a five-year lifetime limit on receiving cash assistance. Although TANF was largely successful in getting families off of welfare, research shows that the flexibility allowed under AFDC meant that families who left the program were more prepared to do so and enjoyed greater economic success as a result (Ozawa and Yoon 2005). In addition, the four policies (financial incentives, sanctions, time limits, and diversion) that characterize the shift from AFDC to TANF also work in tandem with the economy to reduce the number of families on welfare (Danielson and Klerman 2008). Despite these restrictions, the renewed focus on a commitment to work was something that garnered widespread support for TANF. Welfare reform under Clinton reinforced the values of work and marriage but had disastrous effects on the programs that homeless families and individuals relied on most (Wagner and Gilman 2012).

The George W. Bush administration focused on ending chronic homelessness. Called "compassionate conservatism," targeting the most difficult to serve segments of the homeless population was geared toward maintaining the sanctity of city streets and saving money spent on shelter and services (Stein 2003; Culhane and Kuhn 1998). During this time, the US Interagency Council on Homelessness (USICH) executive director Phillip Mangano helped to popularize the "Housing First" approach pioneered by Sam Tsemberis, CEO and founder of Pathways to Housing (Tsemberis, Gulcur, and Nakae 2003; Jensen 2005). This innovative strategy focused on permanent housing with supportive services, rather than on submission to program requirements as a prerequisite for shelter. Yet the focus on chronically homeless people came at the expense of other segments of the homeless population, families in particular. In addition, the methodology for counting homeless people changed so that those unwilling to be interviewed or not directly involved in service were not counted. This is arguably one of the primary reasons for the 30 percent drop in chronic homelessness from 2005 to 2007.

Overall, policy changes reflect the gravity of homelessness in the 1980s and a gradual shift in focus from emergency mode to better service coordination and prevention and eventually to ending homelessness. By the time Barack Obama took office in 2009, the Housing First approach had gained nationwide attention as a way of reducing chronic and overall homelessness. Rather than narrowly focusing on immediate emergency needs, the new approach to homeless services that incorporates Housing First is more holistic and is focused on prevention and re-housing, transitional and permanent housing, on the needs of specific populations, and on ending homelessness in ten years. It still depends on an accurate count of the homeless population to estimate the number who are sheltered, the number of available shelter beds, and the number who are unsheltered. The methodology of the PIT count is therefore crucial in providing both quantitative and qualitative data that inform policy decisions.

The 2009 enactment of the Homeless Emergency and Rapid Transition to Housing Act (HEARTH) reauthorizing McKinney Vento homeless assistance programs was part of the larger Helping Families Save Their Homes Act of 2009 (National Alliance to End Homelessness 2011). The HEARTH Act meant new responsibilities for USICH, including the creation of a Federal Strategic Plan to Prevent and End Homelessness. Released in 2010, Opening Doors is the first comprehensive federal to prevent and end homelessness. The four key goals are:

1. to finish the job of ending chronic homelessness in five years

2. to prevent and end homelessness among veterans in five years

3. to prevent and end homelessness for families, youth, and children in ten years

4. to set a path to ending all types of homelessness

(United States Interagency Council on Homelessness 2010)

Despite policy changes and innovative approaches to ending homelessness, the 2000s also brought the nation a natural disaster that would render thousands newly homeless and bring the trailer back into the spotlight as a form of emergency housing.

Disaster Strikes

In August 2005, Hurricane Katrina, a Category 5 hurricane, moved across the Louisiana, Mississippi, and Alabama Gulf Coast. The devastation from Katrina meant that 950,000 families were eligible for assistance under the Individuals and Households Program and over one million homes were damaged (Davis and Bali 2008).[4] Siting for individual trailers and trailer parks was controversial, as NIMBYism and local politics affected the selection and approval of host neighborhoods (Davis and Bali 2008; Aldrich and Crook 2008). The Federal Emergency Management Agency (FEMA) distinguishes three different types of sites: "private sites" on private property (when a homeowner is in the process of repairing an uninhabitable home); "commercial or group sites," which are preexisting commercial trailer parks, including those enlarged specifically for FEMA trailers; and "industry sites," which are greenfield sites converted to host house trailers.

Originally intended for temporary use, in August 2006, one year after Katrina hit, over 100,000 trailers and mobile homes were still occupied. Table 2.2 shows the breakdown of which states used these forms of housing and the type of site most prevalent. Although the majority of trailers and mobile homes were on private sites, the larger "commercial or group" sites received the most attention. Associated with urban blight, it would be years before the trailers were fully purged from host cities (Associated Press 2010). Residents not only endured overcrowding but were exposed to high levels of formaldehyde from the trailers themselves (Brunker 2006).

Table 2.2: Temporary Housing for Hurricane Katrina Victims

Breakdown of 101,174 trailers and mobile homes serving as temporary housing for Hurricane Katrina victims			
	Total	Mobile Home	Travel Trailers
Louisiana	64,150	3,169	60,981
Mississippi	36,127	4,709	31,418
Alabama	897	0	897
Breakdown of households by site			
	Commercial or Group Sites	Private Sites	Industry Sites
Louisiana	9,344	52,594	2,212
Mississippi	5,507	30,620	0
Alabama	149	748	0

Source: Federal Emergency Management Agency 2005.

In this moment of crisis, the federal government scrambled and famously failed to develop an immediate and effective response. Although local officials issued desperate, emotional pleas for assistance, for many people it was too late. Unlike the sympathy and compassion directed toward Dust Bowl migrants, racial stereotyping and overt discrimination characterized the response to the poor black communities affected by Katrina. Decades of economic hardship and a legacy of environmental racism compounded the problem (Waterhouse 2009). Among the most grievous assaults was the "shoot to kill" order given to National Guardsmen in an alleged attempt to restore order in the days following the hurricane (Dyson 2005, 112).

The aftermath of Katrina and the rhetoric associated with trailer park living brought the ugliest stereotypes to the fore. Inhabitants were blamed for needing assistance, accused of taking advantage of it, and characterized as dangerous inhabitants of a squatter-like zone. Yet, Katrina draws attention to the use of trailers as emergency housing and to the convergence of problematic identities with marginal modes of living. In comparison with the other government-authorized use of trailers discussed in this chapter (namely during World War II and the postwar era), victims of Katrina endured pre- and post-tragedy victimization. Not associated with industrial production or with the war effort, those who lost their homes during Katrina would take years to recover, and some never would.

Examining this instance of trailer living highlights the contrast between viewing people who are experiencing homeless as deserving or undeserving. For people who have problematic social identities, in this case due to the stigma associated with race and social class, any form of housing they occupy is suspect and they themselves are blamed for their plight.

Vehicle Living in Paradise

The visible presence of homeless people is surprising in a city known simply as "paradise" (Rosenthal 1994). Santa Barbara's first sizeable homeless population rose to prominence in the 1930s and 1940s with a collection of approximately fifty shacks known collectively as "Jungleville," "Childville," or simply "the hobo village." Jungleville was located on the private property of wealthy widow Lillian Child.[5] As such, it offered a degree of protection that homeless people would not experience again until the late 1990s, when vehicle living rose to prominence. Homelessness in Santa Barbara skyrocketed in the 1980s, along with homelessness nationwide. Factors accounting for Santa Barbara's increase in homelessness include the decline in available affordable housing, demolitions and conversions, abandonment and arson, unstable working conditions, rising unemployment, the absence of low-skilled labor opportunities, deinstitutionalization, and declines in social service programs like supplemental security income (SSI) (Rosenthal 1994). With the corresponding increase in the volume and diversity of people on the street also came community backlash. Popular rhetoric ranged from the mild annoyance expressed by housed citizens:

> Shopping should be fun; if customers have to run the gauntlet, they're going to go somewhere else (*Santa Barbara News Press*, 22 February 1988, B3).

to politically supported calls for elimination:

> Get rid of Street People. Disperse those unable to be rehabilitated. Establish a program to revitalize downtown and eliminate undesirables. Relocate and disperse Street People to a controlled environment for either rehabilitation or processing—encourage transience (people moving on). Warehouse bad people—create

containment area (Santa Barbara Committee on Alcoholism, Vagrancy, Etc. (C.A.V.E.) Report, Summer 1983).

For homeless people sleeping in any of the public locations popular during the 1980s (Rosenthal 1994; Haggstrom 1994), one thing was clear; they were not wanted in public areas. Yet their presence shaped regulation strategies and social movement activities for years to come.

Between 1976 and 1985, Santa Barbara enacted a series of "anti-sleeping" ordinances, which Jane Haggstrom (1994) estimates effectively rendered 1,350 people potential nightly criminals between the hours of 10 p.m. and 6 a.m. This rallied the Santa Barbara homeless community to participate in social movement activities focusing on ending police harassment and gaining increased rights (Rosenthal 1994). Santa Barbara's homeless population also enjoyed national media attention in the 1980s, through an association with homeless activist Mitch Snyder and protest activities, including demonstrations held at former President Ronald Reagan's nearby ranch and at the opening of the city's downtown shopping mall Paseo Nuevo.

Of the three organizations Robert Rosenthal (1994) describes as central to Santa Barbara's social movement activity during this period, the Homeless People's Association (HPA) was the only group founded by and comprised of homeless people. "The HPA served as a daily, visible reminder that the problem of homelessness would not simply fade away, as many politicians hoped" (Rosenthal 1994, 105). Although dependent on the Santa Barbara Legal Defense Center for advocacy, members of the HPA argued for the right to vote. They also won the right to legally sleep/camp on undeveloped city property and organized public demonstrations geared toward raising awareness. In spite of these activities, the jungle was still subject to city "sweeps" designed to remove both people and belongings. In addition, and despite earlier legal gains, Santa Barbara eventually reinstated restrictions on sleeping on the beach, in city parks, or on developed city property (Rosenthal 1994). Nevertheless, homeless people in the 1980s doggedly claimed various downtown areas as their own, notably the Fig Tree and De la Guerra Plaza, where the city's newspaper and city hall are located, and the aforementioned jungle.

In the late 1990s, Santa Barbara began a debate with police, lawmakers, and citizen groups on one side, and vehicle owners and their advocates on the other, in an attempt to solve the city's "RV problem." This debate continues to the present. RV parking in Santa Barbara is prevalent on public streets, and in parks, waterfront parking lots, and, occasionally, on private property. Most RVs cluster in the same area as the jungles of the 1940s and 1980s. Strategies used to regulate "homeless" vehicles rely on the appearance of the vehicle and the association with activities deemed "illegal" or "unreasonable," including sleeping. Vehicle owners resist regulation by fighting citations issued for violating local ordinances. With the assistance of local advocacy groups, vehicle owners attempt to re-characterize unreasonable activities as necessary ones and preserve their vehicles as a home base.

Convergence

Examining the convergence of vehicle living and homelessness shows that public perception is time, place, and resource dependent. It also shows that social stigma affects not only housing choice but also public perception and public policy. Tracking shifts in the nation's understanding of and response to homelessness and vehicle living shows a growing class polarization that defines those in trailers and motor homes as illegitimate users of public space. This results in substandard locations and services, as NIMBYism drives unwanted populations far from wealthy neighborhoods with political clout. It also results in policies that quell immediate needs, ironically replicating the emergency response that homeless people employ in the struggle to survive. Yet, as the following chapter will attest, vehicle living provides unprecedented resources that are transformative for many homeless people, offering a bridge to apartment living that allows them to preserve safety and autonomy.

As the nation develops improved policies for serving homeless people, the unsheltered populations in many cities continue to grow, particularly in California, one of three states with multiple economic and demographic risk factors for increasing homelessness that exceed national averages.[6] Vehicle living is a midway point between shelter and housing as it provides improved conditions but requires ongoing vehicle maintenance and often entails continued dependence on service facilities. Vehicles offer an unintended niche in the housing market that positions owners as socially marginalized yet with greater resources than other homeless people. This examination of vehicle living explores its relationship to unsheltered homelessness and makeshift housing solutions, including emergency shelter. In so doing, it questions the efficacy of vehicle living as a mode of survival, resistance, and transformation.

Notes

[1] As Thornburg (1991, 22) indicates, these new tourists packed provisions including canned meat, vegetables, and fruit, prompting one bystander to summarize, "They drive tin cans and they eat outta tin cans and they leave a trail of tin cans behind 'em. They're tin-can tourists, that's what they are." The Tin Can Tourists association was seen as harkening back to a rural and idyllic past, celebrating adventure and self-sufficiency. Still in existence today, the Tin Can Tourists association focuses membership and activities on owners of vintage trailers and motor coaches (http://www.tincantourists.com/).

[2] Automobiles are a classic example of how hegemony works through cultural and political channels to ensure widespread buy-in. From the authorization of the Interstate Highway System to the cultural fascination with vehicles, the only growing opposition to the automobile industry comes from sustainability advocates. RVs are still portrayed as quaint and comical modes of living and transportation, as seen in recent films such as *Two Weeks Notice* (2002) and *RV* (2006) and as luxury vehicles on television (*Extreme RVs, RVs Exposed, RV Kings*). The idea of RV living as an adventurous vacation but a marginal mode of housing pervades, although some attempt is made to counter the stereotypes of those living in RVs as dirty and uneducated.

[3] The bill was named posthumously after two state representatives. In 1987, President Reagan named the bill after Republican Representative Stewart B. McKinney of Connecticut. In 2002, President Clinton renamed the legislation after Representative Bruce Vento of Minnesota. For additional details on the McKinney-Vento Act, see http://www.nationalhomeless.org/publications/facts/McKinney.pdf.

[4] Although the use of trailers after Hurricane Katrina was highly publicized and highly controversial, emergency trailers are routinely used as housing in cases of natural disaster. FEMA cites the following disaster types as potentially requiring trailer housing: hurricane or tropical storm, earthquake, dam or levee break, fire, flood, mudslide or landslide, terrorism, tsunami, volcano, snow storm, typhoon, chemical or biological event.

[5] Lillian Child owned a large estate on what is now the Santa Barbara Zoo. She allowed the fifty or so shacks that comprised the jungle to locate on her property until her death in 1951. The men who lived there were primarily white male pensioners. In a series of letters from a camp resident called "the Bookman" to a local business owner, he explains why the men chose to live in the jungle over other available alternatives:

> "The philosophy of these men is rather peculiar. They are independent, for one thing. Quite a number could qualify for old-age pensions, yet they prefer this life to one which they claim is a burden on taxpayers. Others, World-War veterans, could enter the various military houses but prefer the freedom of the hobo to that of being in an institution" (Santa Barbara Historical Society, Folder 4, "Child Estate").

[6] California's risk factors include the unemployment rate, the foreclosure rate, housing cost burden, uninsured rate, and number doubled up per 1,000 (Sermons and Witte 2011). Half of the states in the nation have rates worse than

the national average for two of the five indicators, but only California, Florida, and Nevada have rates that exceed the national average on all five indicators.

3

Navigating Vehicle Living

Preserving a vehicle as a home base is a way of resisting the idea that shelters are the proper place for homeless people. Even those with limited resources have some choice of shelter. Local conditions and personal characteristics and circumstances dictate availability and set the terms of entry, but it is up to the individual to make the choice. This chapter examines how vehicle living compares with other housing solutions available to homeless people in Santa Barbara, California, how people go about acquiring and maintaining vehicles to live in, and why they would choose this option over other alternatives. The first half of the chapter presents data on the numbers and locations of vehicles, ethnographic data on those living in them, and compares RV living with other housing solutions. The second half examines the contingencies involved in purchasing a vehicle, keeping it on the road, and managing social ties. Overall, this chapter evaluates vehicle living from the perspective of the vehicle owner and examines it as a form of resistance.

Purchasing and maintaining a vehicle to live in is both expensive and complicated, requiring that RVers negotiate various social and institutional ties and resources (Wakin 2005). Those willing and able to do so preserve a degree of personal safety, autonomy, and control far greater than what they experience in street and shelter settings. RV living may also be the only affordable housing alternative, as low-income and homeless people are often priced out of apartment rentals. RVs fill a gap not only in the housing market but also in service and shelter provision as they offer housing for those in emergency situations and those suffering from physical and mental illness. Of course, there are risks associated with RV living, including social stigma, regulation, and the complications brought on by various social relationships. Situating RV living along a continuum of housing solutions available to homeless people underscores the fluidity of homelessness as a social category. Upcoming chapters will examine the policy implications of this fluidity as in-between categories of homeless people go undocumented and underserved.

Numbers and Logistics

People living in their vehicles cluster in areas close to homeless services and other amenities like public bathrooms and showers. Figure 3.1 shows the primary locations for people living in their vehicles in Santa Barbara. It is an area known as "the golden triangle" of commerce and tourism. The confluence of restaurants, shops, parks, beaches, luxury hotels, apartments, and condominiums on one side, and homeless shelters and services on the other, make this area ripe for anti-homeless regulation. Historically, this is the area referred to as the "jungle," housing the infamous Fig Tree mentioned in the previous chapter. Homeless people therefore feel entitled to occupy this area, as do tourists, business owners, and residents.

Figure 3.1 Primary Locations for People Lliving in Vehicles in Downtown Santa Barbara

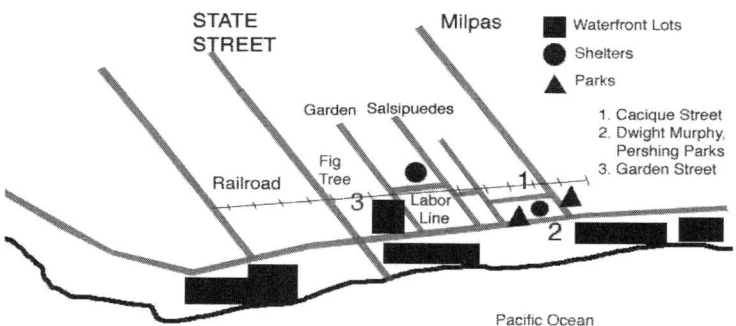

People living in their vehicles in Santa Barbara occupy one of the types of vehicles shown in Figure 3.2. The most problematic types of vehicles are large and regular RVs, followed by trucks and vans. They are problematic because of their size and because of the purported visual blight they cause the city, particularly in the golden triangle. Their size also makes them easier to find and cite for various offenses, including those related to the vehicle (parking) and those related to the individual (sleeping). In order to establish a baseline estimate of the number of vehicles, I conducted nine counts, three annually, in 2002, 2003, and 2004, to track changes in the population over time and estimate the effects of regulation (the focus of Chapter 4).

Figure 3.2 Vehicle Types

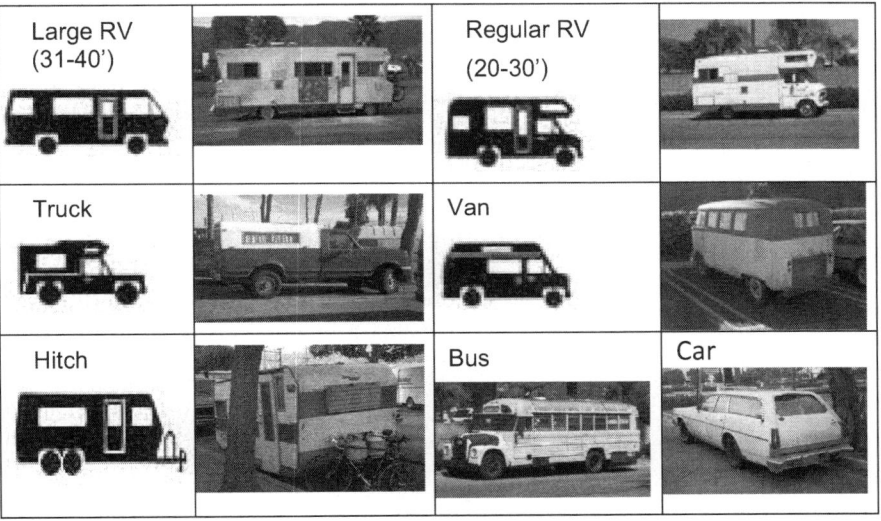

To perform these counts, I employed individuals who were currently living in their vehicles to assist in identifying and enumerating vehicles being used by homeless people as a source of housing. We conducted street-by-street counts of the downtown and waterfront areas and neighboring suburban communities. For each vehicle, we recorded the license plate number and registration information, the make, model, year, and color of the vehicle, its location, and details about its condition including digital photographs. These details provided evidence of the location, general appearance and age of the vehicle, and controlled for multiple counts of the same vehicle in the same year. During the counts, residential or "homeless" vehicles were identified through visual indicators pointed out by informants. These included rust, wear, an unusual or dilapidated paint job, a tarpaulin on the roof, curtains covering the windows, worn tires, storage tanks, generators, and the prevalence of sleeping, cooking, and leisure supplies. Some vehicles also had numerous unpaid citations that were either placed under the windshield wiper or visible on the dashboard. Others had letters posted to police[1] explaining their situation and asking to be spared from citation. Still others were personally known by the author or by informants.

Table 3.1 lists all of the recorded vehicle types, followed by the number of vehicles counted per year, and the overall average for each type. The counts conducted in 2004 occurred after the implementation of city ordinances restricting the length of vehicles parked in the waterfront area. As a result, the number of large RVs plummeted from twenty four to one, and no buses were recorded after 2002. Interestingly, the number of regular RVs rebounded in 2004, perhaps due to the additional space vacated by larger RVs. The number of trucks, vans, and cars also declined significantly after 2002, suggesting either regulation as the cause or that these vehicles were overcounted in 2002.[2] When the 2002 count is excluded, large and regular RVs are the most common vehicle type, followed by vans and trucks.

Table 3.1 Vehicle Count Results, 2002–2004

Vehicle Types	2002	2003	2004	3-year Average
Large RV	29	24	1	18
Regular RV	46	26	45	39
Truck	50	4	15	23
Van	126	7	25	53
Hitch	9	1	7	6
Car	25	0	0	8
Bus	4	0	0	1
Total	289	62	93	148

The counts that occurred in 2003 were conducted just prior to new and restrictive city ordinances. With these counts, we distributed outreach packets to all vehicles including information on legal parking options and ways of contesting citations through legal advocacy. Each packet also contained a four-page survey, to be completed anonymously, with a self-addressed, pre-stamped envelope for its return. The survey contained questions addressing general demographics, housing history, current parking preference, vehicle maintenance, police contact, medical and service history, and source of income. It also included open-ended questions addressing the best and worst aspects of vehicle living. We distributed 150 surveys in Spanish and English and received seventy five responses. In 2003 and 2004, I conducted fifty semi-structured interviews with RV owners, in both Spanish and English, addressing the resources and risks of vehicle living and how it compares with other forms of housing.

Survey data show that RVers are typically between 45 and 50 years old and are on general relief (GR), supplemental security income (SSI), or supplemental security disability income (SSDI),[3] with monthly payments ranging from $500 to $700. Men make up 69 percent of the vehicle population, with women at 31 percent, and the overwhelming majority (83 percent) of both men and women are single. Despite the characterization of RV residents as "transients," survey responses show that 55 percent have lived in Santa Barbara for over ten years, and 35 percent have lived in their RVs in Santa Barbara for three to five years. Surprisingly, and despite the emphasis on transiency that is automatically associated with vehicle living, these findings suggest that this is not a highly mobile or transient population. Many RVs were also not in working order, as ethnographic data would later corroborate, further limiting mobility.

Most RVers reported living on the street immediately prior to living in the vehicle. Over 40 percent of all respondents reported living on the street in the past year, and 50 percent lived on the street within the past five years. This demonstrates the high degree of overlap between street and vehicle living and the degree to which those on the street use vehicles as a form of affordable housing. Related to this, the majority of respondents have not lived in a house (82 percent), apartment (92 percent), or shelter (88 percent) during the past year, calling into question the attractiveness, affordability, and availability of these housing options. During the past five years, more respondents reported living in a house or apartment than in a shelter. Although ethnographic data are used throughout this chapter to substantiate these results, they suggest that those living in vehicles are loath to submit to shelter options and that more permanent housing is preferable. They also suggest that once homeless, RVers are homeless for some time. RVs can therefore be understood as a step up from streets and shelters and a step down from houses or apartments. RVers are familiar with other forms of housing and are therefore able to weigh the benefits and dangers of vehicle living over other alternatives. Detailing the living situation of vehicle owners is a way of examining how viable house and apartment living is versus the vehicle, the shelter, or the street.

Safety, Storage, and the Streets

People who live in their vehicles indicate that maintaining belongings, a private space, and safety and autonomy are the features they prize most about vehicle living (Wakin 2005). In comparison with camping in street locations, vehicles are considered safer because they provide a physical barrier from the elements and from potential attack.

Woody, age 61, lived in the bushes before he bought his RV, which he has lived in for ten years. When I asked him to describe the differences between street living and RV living, he said, "You can lay down and sleep and hear the rain and not get your ass wet. That and you don't have to worry about somebody kicking you in the head." Other RVers concur that various kinds of assault are common in street settings. Sandy, age 52, describes feeling at risk in her camp in comparison with living in her RV.

> You feel safer [in the RV]. You're behind closed doors and you've got your own security and it's like, whenever I was sleeping down there by the tracks, down by the zoo, I didn't feel safe down there. I feel safer in my own home. It's something I got for my own self. It [the jungle] is no place for a woman really... Whenever I had one [a camp] some guy would come into camp and just sit there jacking off right in front of me, *in my own camp*.

For many RVers, living on the street means vulnerability to conditions, including violence and sexual assault, which are beyond the camper's ability to anticipate or prevent. Homeless people in street settings, and women in particular, are often seen as fair game for attack. RVers are not immune to assault, but it is typically the vehicle rather than the individual that bears the brunt of it. As EZ, age 50, relates, "The day we parked on that gravel lot for the first time, somebody shot my window out with a pellet rifle." Other RVers report having bottles broken against their vehicles or having people knock on their doors or bounce the vehicle up and down. This kind of harassment is common in Santa Barbara and elsewhere. In Santa Cruz, California, a man named Mike, who describes himself as a "hard core car inhabitant," showed me two photographs of graffiti tags done by a local street gang. One said "move on van troll." "They call me the van troll," Mike related. "They basically bother me whenever they see me, but I'm pretty safe in this thing [my van]." Personal, physical, relative safety is an important feature of RV living that distinguishes it from street settings.

RV living is also safer in terms of storing belongings. As an RVer named Jim, age 53, explains, "It's a step up from the street, just let me be alone and have some security as to where my stuff is at." A 67 year-old RVer named Nelda concurs: "I value my privacy and I like that I don't have to put up with anybody else. I know where my things are and that they are safe." While people living on the streets store their belongings outdoors, have others watch them, and use public pay-per-use lockers, none of these options offers the same degree of control as having a locked door. Related to the issue of personal safety, having to worry about protecting one's possessions is an added burden that RV living alleviates. Privacy is also something that vehicle owners emphasize as a benefit. Treated in more depth later in this chapter, privacy can be a transformative resource.

Shelter Options

Submitting to unstable or unacceptable conditions is not only part of street living but is also part of emergency shelter living. Casa Esperanza, Santa Barbara's first official emergency homeless shelter, opened in 1999. Prior to this, homeless people slept in the armory in the winter and outside for the rest of the year. In addition to Casa Esperanza, the religious-based Mission is also an official part of the city's emergency shelter stock. It allows ten night stays per month and requires attendance at a Catholic mass as a condition of shelter.[4] The Salvation Army—known as "the Sally"—and Transition House are the other emergency shelters that are available to those who meet the entry requirements of consistent employment or are members of special populations, including adults with children, veterans, or those who have documented mental health or medical needs. Once admitted, they must also follow rules, daily program requirements, and a case management regimen in order to stay. None of these shelters allow couples without children to stay together, and none have facilities to store pets or belongings. In addition, none of them are "wet shelters," meaning that clients must be sober, or sober enough, to gain entry. Table 3.2 details the stay limits and admission requirements for Santa Barbara's four emergency shelters.

Table 3.2 Available Shelters for Homeless People in Santa Barbara, California

Shelters	Bed Availability	Stay Limits	Specific Requirements
Casa Esperanza	200 unrestricted beds 30–70 restricted beds	Unrestricted from 12/1 -- 3/31 Restricted from 4/1 --11/30	From 4/1 --11/30, must be employed
The Mission	103 mats/night 1 emergency unit	10 nights/month	Monthly restrictions, nightly religious services
The Salvation Army "The Sally"	73 program beds	3-month/ variable	Must be employed, must be a veteran, must have mental health or medical needs
Transition House	21 total units 70 beds	2-month initial stay	Must have children, must be employed
Total Homeless Prevention, Shelter, and Transitional Units = 343 beds; 103 mats; 22 units (City of Santa Barbara 2003, Draft Housing Element)			

Adhering to program requirements, rules and regulations, and the stipulation of being a member of a particular target population are all things that confuse homeless people, that they resent, and that keep them out of shelter. In an early conversation with Louie, age 53, he describes going to the Mission for a meal and being asked to stand during the mandatory mass. He told me that one of the staff members "said that me and Judy were being disrespectful to God because she wanted us to stand up when she said stand up... Are you walking all day? Are you on the streets?" This perceived lack of empathy for the everyday struggles homeless people face is one of the things that makes shelter life difficult.

In addition, the sense that homeless people should be submissive and grateful for "bare life" provisions is also viewed as intolerable (Feldman 2004).

During my field work at Transition House, a family shelter with rigid program guidelines, a man arrived at 7 p.m., after working all day, and sat down to have a meal. We were preparing sandwiches for lunch the next day when he stood up and indignantly told one of the staff members, "Do you know I found a hair in my sandwich the other day? I was so disgusted I could not eat, I had to throw it out." She apologized to him, but when he was out of earshot she turned to me and said, "I don't know what he's complaining about, at least it's *free*." In this person's estimation, as long as goods are free, they should be gratefully accepted, regardless of their condition. This sentiment is part of the implicit philosophy of emergency shelter and entry-level service provision. Beggars, the adage goes, cannot be choosers, so providing them with the simplest of provisions will ensure that they do not "get comfortable," that they want to move on, and that they do not take advantage of the system. Although this has many names, *churning* (Piven and Cloward 1993) and *discouragement* (Bennett 1995) are two apt characterizations, emphasizing the problematic nature of emergency shelter provision. As David Wagner (1993) points out, subjecting an already downtrodden population to scrutiny and rigorous entry requirements makes entry-level service a non-option and the alternative a form of resistance.

Despite the obvious lack of resources in street and shelter settings, homeless people are still interested in having autonomy and control and avoid places that take these things away. So, part of how housing choice is evaluated is based on weighing resources and risks. RV living is one of a number of resistance strategies used to combat regulation in the form of shelterization and criminalization. It is important to point out, however, that although emergency shelters are typically viewed as institutions that demean and objectify homeless people, this is not always the case. Louie describes coming into the emergency shelter during the winter months as a negotiated compromise:

> I was sleeping behind the woodpile over there and they (shelter staff) came out and told me they'd give me the corner, you know, cause I wouldn't be in no trouble, get in no fuckin' fist fights, nothin' like that. They just put me where I wouldn't have to deal with the stress, people stealing from me, that shit. I have my medication and stuff so I didn't want people jerking me around. It's either stay out or give me a place I feel comfortable.

For Louie, having some control over the conditions of his stay made the difference between shelter and street sleeping. Although it may be impossible to make everyone in a 200-bed facility comfortable, or to provide autonomy and control, conditions that are dangerous or unsafe not only make shelter less desirable than the streets, they also make rehabilitation unlikely because they keep the focus on immediate survival over long term planning. As a result, many people choose other forms of shelter.

It is worth noting, however, that several innovative housing and shelter solutions, including those designed to serve youth (Ruddick 1996), the mentally ill (Wagner 1993), and programs like PATH (Roberts 2004) and the Housing First initiative, have demonstrated that it is possible to provide user-friendly services and shelter. One of the key features of these programs and approaches is that they are consumer driven and take homeless people's preferences into account as a formative feature of service provision. Although such approaches are gaining momentum nationwide, they require a significant change in the overall philosophy as well as the infrastructure of homeless service provision.

Apartments, SROs, and Transitions

There are two forms of subsidized housing homeless people can apply for in the city of Santa Barbara: Section 8 housing, and public housing units owned and operated by the Santa Barbara Housing Authority. In addition to differences in cost,[5] Section 8 apartments can be "program units," meaning that they are attached to a particular apartment or program within a specialized SRO, or individual vouchers, meaning that they are essentially owned by the person who holds them and can be moved from one eligible apartment to another. Landlords must agree to rent apartments as Section 8 units and receive 30 percent of the rent from the occupant and the remainder from the city housing authority. Rules pertaining to usage, including restrictions on pets and roommates, are specified on the lease, as with other apartment rentals. Both city subsidized housing and Section 8 units require a lengthy waiting period of two to four years, or longer. As long as the applicant meets the eligibility requirements, she is placed on a waiting list. When a voucher or apartment becomes available, a letter is sent to the applicant, who then has a two-week period in which to respond. If the letter is not received or the applicant does not respond within two weeks, she must reapply and endure the waiting period once again.

Even after enduring the wait, many people report being dissatisfied with the conditions of Section 8 housing. As Lyn (age 47) relates,

> I applied for Section 8 and was living in an apartment out in Isla Vista. I had mushrooms growing out of the ceiling in my bathroom and the landlord tried to tell me that I planted them. The water had burst and mold was growing in there. Eventually the whole ceiling started to go... When something happens, they do not help you fix it if you are on Section 8. You can fix it yourself or go through rental mediation.

When I asked Lyn how she ended up leaving that apartment, she replied, "That asshole of a manger decided to put his hand on my thigh and said 'I'll help you fix the bathroom darlin.'" This incident permanently soured Lyn's taste for apartment living.

For many RVers, apartment living is only affordable with a Section 8 voucher. In California, a studio apartment is approximately $500 more per month than someone on SSI or making minimum wage can afford. Both Louie, mentioned previously, and Nancy, age 52, have lived in RVs and apartments. For Louie, RV living was a midway point between street, shelter, and apartment living. The one thing that threatened his apartment stay was having a dog, which violated his lease agreement. Although Louie gave up the dog to keep the apartment, for Nancy, the dog would come first. "If I was that man, I'd get out of my housing in a second before I give up my dog. I lost my Section 8 and you wanna know why ... because of these [dogs]... My dogs are more important to my soul, my mentality, my existence, than your housing is." Nancy has lived in a combination of apartments and vehicles since she was in her mid-thirties. Both Louie and Nancy make housing choices based on personal preference and by weighing resources and risks. Louie chose apartment living over keeping his dog because he views street living and RV living as unacceptable. Nancy, in comparison, sees RV living and keeping her pets as a way of life.

Resources

RV living is not only a matter of preference. As I discuss elsewhere (Wakin 2005) there are essential steps involved in purchasing and maintaining a vehicle that, if they are not followed, mean that the individual may live in the RV temporarily but not in the long-term. Even with adequate financial resources, if the individual lacks the paperwork necessary to secure a license, registration, and insurance, and is unable to perform routine repairs on the vehicle and park it legally, residency is short lived.

Locating a vehicle to live in can be as simple as establishing a relationship with someone who has a vehicle and doubling up with them or finding a vehicle to inhabit on a temporary basis. This does not involve the next step of purchasing the vehicle, merely its location. The purchase requires an initial layout of funds similar to the first month's rent, last month's rent, and security deposit needed to rent an apartment. As Nancy indicates, purchasing a vehicle was the only affordable option for her.

> Well, I ended up living there [with her parents] for a year because every time I'd have some money together, something would happen and I'd have to spend it and so, that didn't work out. Finally, my mom and I started fighting, and I just couldn't live in the same house. We just knew, I mean, I'm 37 years old at this point and you just can't live with your mother. So my mom finally looked at me and said, 'What is it you really want, Nancy?' I said, 'I want to get a pickup camper, mom. I want my own place and it's not looking like I'm going to find one, I just can't come up with the first, last, and deposit. I just can't do it.' I was making $700 [a month] at the time and had some medical bills I was trying to pay off and so they helped me. We searched and searched and I found one. $2,500 for a beautiful truck with a brand-new ten foot camper on top. They put a deposit on it for me and I paid them off $100 a month. For the first time I had a bed for me and a bed for my son and it was unbelievably cool.

Several RVers reported securing informal loans from friends, family, and organizations in order to purchase vehicles to live in. Lyn bought her second RV, a 1988 twenty-five-foot Dodge El Dorado, with a $3,000 loan from the Committee for Social Justice, a local advocacy group, and paid the money back over time. When I asked her about the specifics of this arrangement, she told me that she made monthly payments of $200 to Catholic Charities, who were the administrators of the loan. When I pushed for further information, she said, "I don't think that this is the kind of thing they are going to be arranging for people. I think it was really just me." In fact, the Committee for Social Justice made several loans to RV owners, with various terms for reimbursement. The one uniform stipulation is that the committee holds the vehicle's pink slip until the loan is paid in full.

Still other RV owners purchase vehicles with money they earn from employment or from SSI benefits. Louie purchased his first vehicle, a 1978 Toyota Dolphin with 99,000 miles on it, with SSI income. As was noted in Chapter 1, he initially applied for SSI in March 1999 but did not receive his first payment until approximately two years later. One reason for this is that the process of filing the necessary paperwork to receive these benefits is often complicated enough to take months or years (Bennett 1995). When the case is finally approved, beneficiaries are sent all of the monthly payments they would have received since the time of the application.[6] SSI payouts are often the only way that vehicle purchases are facilitated. In Louie's case, when he was finally approved for SSI benefits, he received a total of $8,421.34 for monthly payments he would have received between August 1999 and February 2001, with additional monthly payments of $726 to follow. His case is then renewed annually, and as long as he remains disabled and unemployed, he continues to receive small annual payment increases.

Rentals

In Santa Barbara, people who do not own their vehicles can sometimes rent space in other people's vehicles. Renting a vehicle is far less common than doubling up in one, or owning one. Rented RVs are typically stationary and are parked outside of an apartment or house. In many cases, the rental price includes the use of an indoor bathroom and sometimes the kitchen. Rental prices range from $10 per day to $75 per month, far below the rental price for a campsite, apartment, or motel. Unless the RV is parked on private property, however, rentals are inevitably short-lived.

Rhonda was 19 and new to Santa Barbara. She was renting an RV that was parked outside the house of a shelter staff member. Before this, she had been staying in a camp beside the railroad tracks with her boyfriend. When he was taken to jail during a sweep, she faced the danger of camping alone. One of the RVers in the neighborhood took her in for the night, and the next morning a shelter staff member offered to rent an RV to her for $75 a month, including the use of the bathroom in the main house. She accepted the offer and lived there for four months until she left Santa Barbara.

Other RVers rent out their vehicles and receive money and services in return. Louie lived in a Section 8 apartment yet still owned his RV. When it stopped running, he left it parked outside of the apartment and rented it to a couple for $10 per day, including the use of his bathroom and kitchen. When they were unable to pay the daily fee, they would cook or clean the apartment for him instead. This arrangement was also short lived as the RV was eventually ticketed and towed.

Although renting an RV is uncommon, doing so solves the problem of accessing bathroom and kitchen facilities, a significant issue for people living in vehicles. Unless the vehicle's facilities are functional and can be maintained, it is necessary to park within easy access to bathrooms and showers or be able to move the vehicle frequently. Occasionally, RVers who own their vehicles pay rent to use kitchen and bathroom facilities. Such is the case with Jacob, a 72 year-old Filipino veteran who bought a vehicle after he was asked to move out of the room he had been doubling up in. He pays $70 per month to use the cooking, bathroom, and laundry facilities in a friend's apartment. Rhonda, Louie, and Jacob were all able to use vehicles as a way of preventing homelessness. They also show that "doubling up" applies not only to sleeping in another person's apartment but also sleeping in someone else's vehicle and accessing kitchen and bathroom facilities. When vehicles remain stationary, or when occupants are beholden to others for additional amenities, their long-term use is jeopardized. The following section examines the contingencies involved in owning and maintaining a vehicle on a long-term basis.

Ownership and Maintenance

People who own their vehicles have two things in common: they have limited incomes with which to maintain their vehicles, and they typically drive older, previously owned vehicles. As is common with any older used vehicle, maintenance is frequent and expensive. Utility systems in large RVs include water, propane, refrigeration, lights, and wiring, each of which requires different parts, service, and maintenance activities. Virtually all maintenance is also contingent on having the money, know-how, and mobility to get the vehicle to a garage. As a result, vehicle owners often prioritize which facilities they maintain. Maintaining one's water system, for example, involves storing the water in portable tanks and using a water pump to provide the needed water pressure to run the shower, toilet, and kitchen sink, which are standard facilities even in older vehicles. Keeping the water system in working order involves maintaining the pump and internal system and getting rid of accumulated waste water from the bathroom, and gray water from the kitchen. It means at minimum "dumping the tanks" regularly at a waste processing facility or risking citation if dumping illegally. Unless the vehicle is parked close to a waste processing facility, being able to dump one's tanks means that the vehicle's engine is in good working order at the time of acquisition and that the owner can pay for gas. Because the water system is the most difficult to maintain and one of the first to stop functioning, inhabitants typically park close to bathroom and shower facilities. Particularly when vehicles are not operating well or when owners lack gas money, more time is spent visiting shelters to use their services and amenities. This means that there is a lot of overlap between street, shelter, and vehicle communities.

Vehicle mobility is dependent on the owner's income and on the functionality of the vehicle. Due to the rigid parking restrictions in Santa Barbara, which regulate against overnight parking and include hourly daytime restrictions, vehicles must be in frequent motion to avoid parking or other citations. Given the high price of gasoline and maintenance costs, vehicle owners frequently find themselves in a bind of wanting to conserve gasoline by remaining immobile, but realizing that they risk citation by doing so, a "can't move must move" dilemma (Carr 1994). Being vigilant about mobility is a key feature of long-term vehicle maintenance. The most common fines for not moving the vehicle include violating the 72-hour limit, which carries a $60 fine, and various parking violations which range from $20 to $35. Interestingly, RVers still struggle with the mobility/permanence distinction that has characterized auto camping since the 1920s. Many RVers move around but not out of town, which accounts for the overlap with homeless people on the streets and in shelters, and is also part of how they are targeted for regulation.

Even without incurring any type of citation, RV living is expensive. When I first met Sandy, described earlier, she was living in a camp beside the railroad tracks. Her boyfriend Jim owned his own vehicle and eventually sold it to move into Sandy's RV, which was in better condition and twice the size. Although Jim has no regular monthly income, Sandy receives monthly SSI payments of $700. She also panhandles regularly on the pier and at the Saturday Farmer's Market and usually makes between $10 and $40 per day, one to two days per week. In one month, Sandy and Jim spent $400 on vehicle repairs to be able to keep their registration current, $65 in registration fees with late penalties, and $100 for emissions and smog. Even if Sandy made $160 panhandling, an optimistic estimate, this would leave them $295 for gas, food, and all other expenses for the month for the two of them and their dog. This points to an additional and perhaps obvious reason for the overlap between people living in vehicles and those living on the streets and in shelters. All three populations converge on the available meal programs, showers and restrooms, and other services associated with emergency shelters and day centers.

Recovery, Emergency, Disability

Although many RV owners lack financial resources, the other resources they have set them apart from the homeless community and position them as potential providers for those in need. Of course, this has to do with personal preference and the availability of space to offer, and it comes with its own set of risks. Despite the harsh conditions they encounter on the streets and in shelters and despite their resource poverty, many RVers allow people to stay with them on a temporary or permanent basis, particularly in cases of emergency and recovery from illness. For Rhonda, mentioned earlier, doubling up in a vehicle was an emergency measure that kept her off of the streets until she could find a more private, permanent situation.

Others use the RV as a temporary recovery space. Because the recovery or "medical" beds in shelters are limited in terms of their availability and length of stay restrictions, and are not private, RVs are sometimes used for this purpose. In one case, a man named Joe was waiting to have surgery on his back. He was in a lot of pain but would not be admitted to a medical bed because of the stipulation that they be used for recovery *after* surgery. Lyn allowed him to stay with her but resented the dearth of services. "He should not have had to go outside of the shelter for help while he was waiting to get assistance… There was no other place for him to lay his head, and he was in so much pain." After Joe had surgery, he received Section 8 housing and moved out of Lyn's vehicle.

In another case, a woman everyone called Moms had to have surgery on her neck. The cartilage between two of her vertebrae had deteriorated and she had to have a plate inserted to keep the bones from rubbing together. She told me matter-of-factly, "I go next Saturday for surgery. They're going to fit me with screws and a titanium plate." "Wow," I replied, trying to be encouraging. "You're going to be one tough woman." She laughed and said, "I'm *already* that, what are *you* talkin' about?" Despite her bravado, it was major surgery and she was incredibly nervous about it. She was admitted to the hospital on a Friday, and when I called on Sunday, I was surprised to find that she had already been discharged. Prior to surgery, Moms was camping beside the railroad tracks. After being discharged from the hospital, she stayed in an RV that belonged to a friend who was living with his mother in Santa Maria. The RV was his mother's vacation vehicle, and he leant it to Moms for the weekend as a recovery space. When the weekend was over, she returned the RV and went back to camp. Within three days Moms collapsed alongside the railroad tracks and was taken away in an ambulance. This time she was admitted to the intensive care unit, where she stayed for a full week. For Moms, the RV was a temporary recovery space, the only one that allowed her to stay with the friends she was used to. She was terrified of being alone and ill-accustomed to the routines of shelter life. Even a temporary RV stay offered her resources that neither shelters nor streets could deliver: control, autonomy, and a safe, clean place in which to recover.

Other RVers suffer from long-term disabilities that make shelter life unbearable. Lyn suffers from cerebral palsy, which limits her movement. Living in the RV facilitates the everyday activities that allow her control over her living environment and her schedule. Louie suffers from chronic pain related to neck and back injuries. When living on the streets and in the shelter, Louie got into frequent violent arguments with other residents. After purchasing his first vehicle, this behavior ceased. When I asked him to account for the change, he replied:

> When you're living in a shelter your state of mind stays a certain way because you're dealing with the same thing every day and it really gets to you. With a motor home you can go somewhere and sleep and relax—if you can find a place you know, and sleep is very, I mean, you can't get that out here and get it good and it's bad for your health.... My attitude was a lot more violent when I didn't have this thing.

Part of what Louie is describing is the luxury of privacy, which many homeless people simply do not have. The physical, mental, and emotional toll taken by a life in public is so substantial that simply managing it is a full-time activity.

Still other RVers suffer from mental health problems, including post-traumatic stress disorder (PTSD), which makes any congregate living situation—even apartment living—impossible. A woman named Hope, in her mid-thirties, told me that she lived in her car despite the fact that she had a Section 8 apartment. "Why don't you live there?" I asked her. "The apartment has a common wall so I can hear everything that happens in the room next door. The people harass me by banging on the walls. They play music all night sometimes and I know they're doing it to bother me." "So how do you manage to eat and shower?" I persisted. "I go in once or twice a week when I know they won't be there and I take a shower and make my food for the week. I have a little cooler and I can make chicken that I keep in Ziploc bags and my vegetables. If it's only a few days at a time, they won't spoil." In other conversations, Hope shared details of her abusive past as the source of her current PTSD.[7] In her estimation, living in her car was the only option that did not terrify her.

Family Ties

RV living offers a solution to the lack of affordable housing and services for both individuals and families. When asked whether she saw many families living in their RVs, 38 year-old Tanya replied:

> There are families out there, but you don't see them. Few of them go to the shelter. People fall through the cracks, man, you know? I mean, these were people who, most of their lives, they were probably told you're a failure if you don't pay rent, you know, keep up with the Joneses and stuff, so for it to happen for the first time in their lives, and to be living in a vehicle, they don't want to come to the shelter because that's more scary for them.

In Tanya's estimation, parents use RVs to protect their children, to provide for them, and to avoid the social stigma of homelessness that the shelters exacerbate. As Sheila Crowley (2003) indicates, submitting to the shelter environment often requires that parents relinquish some amount of authority as they, like their children, must appeal to shelter staff for permission to conduct various activities, to serve or consume meals, and to regulate daily schedules.

Although shelters are seen as a harsh compromise that requires parents to admit defeat, the social stigma associated with vehicle living is also problematic. Nancy describes vehicle living in a positive light, yet she indicates that it was difficult for her son to handle.

> When I got my pickup camper it was my first home and it was wonderful.... But it was rough too because Paul got teased about being in an RV. He got called trailer trash. It was also rough on me, I don't mean to be idealistic. I was a single parent and I felt so guilty about poor Paulie.... Now I know why my son lives on the streets, because this is where he's comfortable, because this is where he was brought up.

Other parents share this sentiment. Lyn confided that her daughter avoided getting a ride to school in the RV because, as she put it, "They'll call me trailer trash." Regardless of how well or how poorly RV owners parent their children, the children still feel the pain of social stigma as their peers remind them that they, like adult homeless people, are seen as "trash."

This takes a toll on children's self-esteem and can affect their physical, cognitive, and social development. Children living in RVs, like other homeless children, are susceptible to illnesses including nutritional deficiencies, growth problems, upper respiratory infections, skin and ear disorders, gastrointestinal problems, lice infestations, and chronic physical disorders (DaCosta Nunez 1994). They also frequently experience developmental delays related to sporadic school attendance or familial trauma. One RV parent confided that her son began seeing a school psychologist in third grade because he stopped cleaning himself after going to the bathroom. Sometimes, she told me, "he would just go right in the middle of class." The psychologist told her that he lacked a sense of self-esteem and saw no reason to take care of himself. He just stopped caring.

There are, of course, contrasting cases of parents who live in vehicles with their children and whose children are successful in school and in negotiating social ties. One such parent is Charlie, who lived in his converted school bus with his sons Andrew and Michael, ages 6 and 8. Charlie's bus was over thirty-five feet long, and he towed a Harley Davidson motorcycle behind it. I visited Charlie and his sons on several occasions and was, at first, concerned that the children were being home schooled and that they would lack social interaction. After finishing out their first year in Santa Barbara, Charlie enrolled the boys in public school. Not only did they maintain good grades, but both boys placed well above their peers on standardized tests. They were also polite and articulate. Unfortunately, Charlie, Andrew, and Michael were anomalous. Although most of the families I encountered were single-parent families, Charlie was one of only a few men I met who was raising his children in a vehicle. Most of the women I met who were doing so struggled with addiction, with the stigma associated with homelessness, or with caring for their children in the shelter environment.

Tanya's initial assessment, that families are more likely to submit to shelter as a last resort, may be the reason that families were difficult to find. The stigma involved with being a homeless parent may also necessitate some degree of hiding. The fear of being seen as negligent, the shame associated with vehicle living and homelessness, and the fear of citation are all factors that make families and individuals avoid attention. Although RV living is often seen as a way of protecting oneself or caring for others, it is still seen as a symbol of social failure.

Personal Stigma

Adults living in their RVs also feel the pain of the stigma associated with homelessness and vehicle living. Although I discuss regulation elsewhere, merely being seen as degraded is something RVers relate that they constantly struggle with. Doug, who has "done the homeless thing my whole life," still feels the pain of stigmatization: "This to me is the lowest form of life you could ever have, living in a vehicle. Nobody should have to live like this ever! It's embarrassing. I feel less fortunate." Rob, age 38, concurs, "It's embarrassing.... I can't stand the way I get looked at around here. I don't think anybody should be judged by what they live in as long as they pay their taxes, do what's normal, status quo, call it what you want. I'm still doing it, I just can't afford to pay to live on the Riviera. That's the only reason why I get looked at like that—it's absolutely ridiculous."

Many people differentiate vehicle living from other forms of homelessness, a classic form of identity work. RV living is seen as a cut above street and shelter living yet is still not fully legitimate or acceptable. In an attempt to answer the question of whether he considers himself homeless, Rob, who lives in his van, says:

> I've only been homeless for a year.... I'm 38 years old, I've never been homeless in my life.... I still don't consider myself, well no, when me and Heather were living on the beach that was pretty much as low as I got.

For Rob, as for many people experiencing homelessness, there is an unwritten continuum of housing solutions, and street living is at the bottom. RV living is seen as more desirable, provided inhabitants have the resources and wherewithal to maintain the vehicle. Part of this has to do with being able to negotiate their own place on the continuum and specifically as potential providers for others in need.

RVers as Providers

> He came out of the woods while I was fixing myself a plate of food. I was in my usual spot by the ball field and he just wandered over with his hair everywhere and mumbling to himself. I didn't know what he was saying but I just noticed that he kept staring at my plate, so I asked him "are you hungry?" and he nodded at me, so I fixed him a plate and he went away. –Margarite, age 50

Although many RVers frequently cross paths with those living in shelters and on the streets, the resources that RV living offers make them unwitting providers for others, and a target for those in need. In addition to temporary emergency and recovery requests, and food requests like the one above, RVers are frequently called upon to provide living space for friends, family, and those they are romantically involved with or interested in. Some RVers simply refuse to permit anyone to stay with them, but most admit guests who are friends, lovers, or family members. It is their own generosity and reluctance to refuse others in need that makes RVers vulnerable to the same entanglements that plague other service providers.

Like servicing the vehicle's engine, regulating what goes on inside is a key aspect of long-term maintenance. Lyn raised four children in various vehicles and maintains friendships and intimate relationships therein. Because Lyn suffers from cerebral palsy and has difficulty driving her RV, a 38 year-old man named Jimbo acted as Lyn's driver and lived in the RV in exchange. As Lyn indicated, "It is beneficial in Bertha [her RV] to have a man around, and he can have his own space, his own room." She also admitted her romantic interest in Jimbo and confided "he's my ideal man." Yet Jimbo did not return her affection and merely used her vehicle as a source of shelter. Although she told me bitterly, "You'd never see a woman staying somewhere for free," she still allowed him to do so.

Lyn kicked Jimbo out of the vehicle when her fourteen-year-old daughter Sally came to live with her for the summer. Three of Lyn's four children live with foster families for the majority of the year. Sally lives with her biological father and spends some summers with her mother. Lyn had not seen Sally in almost a year, and when Sally returned, she had matured both emotionally and physically. "She's built like a brick shit house," Lyn bragged, with some amount of motherly pride. This particular summer, Sally stayed with Lyn for a full three months. When Lyn abruptly kicked Jimbo out of the vehicle, I asked her what happened. She said, "He threw a pass at my daughter and I had no choice but to believe my daughter." Although Jimbo left when she asked him to, Lyn worried that his actions would further sour Sally's distaste for RV living and for spending summers with her mother.

Lyn's experience illustrates one of the paradoxes of RV living: although RVs provide a potentially safe haven for children, guests can turn the vehicle into a hazardous place. Like apartments and houses, RVs can foster various kinds of abuse and domestic violence. RVers who are parents are also under added scrutiny. Although Lyn feels that there is no shame in vehicle living, Child Welfare Services disagrees.

Three of her four children were placed in foster care before age 10, and Sally's visits are always temporary. As is clear from Lyn's experience, inviting guests to stay in the RV risks the social and familial environment therein.

Louie allowed a woman named Maureen (Mo) and her 5 year-old daughter Crystal to move in with him when he bought his first vehicle. Until this point, Mo and Crystal were sneaking into an abandoned RV in the neighborhood or sleeping on the streets. Mo's alcoholism got them "86ed" from most shelters. The first night Mo and Crystal spent in the RV, Louie bought beer for Mo and candy for Crystal. They were all excited, and Crystal ran up and down the length of the RV jumping on the furniture and shouting "mine, mine, mine!" Crystal's excitement only enhanced Louie's happiness, so he hardly minded when she threw up most of her candy all over his new upholstery. Mo was on her fourth beer by this point, so I held the bucket for Crystal while Louie mopped up the mess.

With two new people to take care of, Louie was desperate for money. His wife Tanya, mentioned earlier, had also begun writing to him from a prison in Arizona where she was serving a five-year sentence for trying to pawn a stolen gun. Although they had been estranged for years, her letters were pleading and emotional, and Louie was drawn in. Out of his first SSI check of $741, he sent $300 to Tanya and gave $200 to Mo, leaving $241 for the rest of the month. Rather than helping her get back on her feet, the RV provided Mo with a safe place to drink, and she stopped talking about moving on. She also spent more time in the shelter neighborhood, which had a negative effect on Crystal. Things also started to become tense between Mo and Louie. Initially, Mo cooked meals and cleaned the RV, but as time wore on she did nothing to help, and Louie grew frustrated.

After nearly eight months in the RV, Mo and Crystal finally left. Louie was heartbroken to lose Crystal, who had begun calling him "grandpa." But he was also relieved to see them go. By the time they left, the RV had lost its original upholstery and the shower no longer worked. Louie also let his insurance lapse and had his first accident in the vehicle. With more time to focus on his future, and realizing that the RV would not last forever, Louie decided to try to get his life together and applied for a Section 8 apartment. He also began dating a woman named Jackie, who had a valid license and could assist with driving the vehicle. Louie continued to send money to Tanya, however, and when she was released from prison, she arrived in Santa Barbara and knocked on his door. Traveling to Santa Barbara so soon after her release meant that Tanya violated the terms of her parole, yet it was clear that she had come to stay. Louie put his relationship with Jackie on hold and tried to start over again with Tanya. Like Mo before her, Tanya considered the RV hers. For the first few weeks, she could usually be found sitting quietly in the driver's seat chain smoking. Gradually, the stress of being with Louie again and her recent release from jail were too much for her to handle, and she began using heroin.

In the past, she and Louie did drugs together, so when Tanya started using, it was only a matter of time before Louie joined her. They supported their habit by allowing one of Tanya's dealers to live with them in the vehicle and deal drugs out of it. In return, he paid for a campsite for them in Lompoc, northwest of Santa Barbara. The three of them returned to Santa Barbara and began dealing drugs out of a local park adjacent to the shelter and under heavy police surveillance. One night the police arrived at the door of the RV and pulled Louie and Tanya out at gunpoint. Although they found nothing during the search, Louie realized that if he continued using and dealing, he would lose his vehicle and perhaps his life, so he stopped and began to distance himself from Tanya. Desperate to make a change, Louie slept on the streets and at Jackie's apartment and allowed Tanya to live in the vehicle by herself. Tanya used a combination of prostitution and "borrowing" or stealing to support her habit, and Louie stayed clean. Tanya knew where Jackie lived however, and she visited frequently to ask for money. Eventually she stole Jackie's television set and VCR, and one morning Jackie found her hiding in the closet. That was the last straw; Louie called the police to have Tanya arrested for violating her parole. She was sent back to Arizona, and Louie resumed control of the vehicle and continued to pursue Section 8 housing.

As the cases of Lyn and Louie demonstrate, maintaining long-term ownership brings financial as well as social and emotional challenges. RV owners often find themselves literally and figuratively between the homeless and housed communities, and they must connect with yet somehow remain separate from both. Sustaining relationships and parking in proximity to resources homeless people draw on is part of what gives RVers their in-between status. It is what makes long-term maintenance desirable and, at the same time, what makes it risky. Yet the resources that the RV provides, although limited and difficult to maintain, can lead to permanent housing. The final section of this chapter examines how long-term maintenance can provide RVers with the stability needed to transition to apartment living.

Transformation

Louie is one of the few RVers who made the transition from homeless to housed. Doing so requires, at minimum, a steady income to pay rent and the desire to transition to apartment living. Individuals who can afford RV living do so with the assistance of SSI, SSDI, or full-time employment. Part-time employment and other forms of assistance are typically not enough to afford public or subsidized housing in Santa Barbara and would be subtracted from SSI or SSDI payouts, reducing the overall monthly amount. SSI and SSDI are the most common sources of financing RV living and public or subsidized housing.

Louie financed his RV purchase with the assistance of SSI income. He also applied for Section 8 housing. Approximately two years after he submitted his application, he received a notice that he had been granted a voucher and was told to report to the housing authority. I drove Louie to his appointment and sat with him as his case manager explained the process of searching for an apartment and filling out the necessary paperwork. Louie was given a list of apartments and began his search. He had sixty days to find an apartment from the time he received the voucher or he would return to the bottom of the waiting list.

Without a phone but still driving the motor home, Louie filled out three rental applications within the first ten days of receiving his voucher. He was responsible for following up with landlords and checking on the status of his application. In some cases he called too often and in others not often enough, and the first three apartments slipped through his fingers. He eventually found an apartment in Goleta, about fifteen minutes from downtown Santa Barbara. A short drive from the shelter and from Jackie's apartment, Louie's apartment was a one-bedroom split level bordering a long stretch of oceanfront conservation land. The full rent was $1,100 and Louie was responsible for $330. It took him two months to adjust to apartment living and to get used to mailing the check in on time for it to reach the landlord. Louie parked his motor home outside and, at least initially, drove it to the shelter almost every day for lunch and to see Jackie. Ignoring the rental agreement, he also bought a small Chihuahua named Myla, which he tried to hide from the landlord. After receiving several warnings, Louie decided that his longevity in the apartment was more important than the dog, and he gave her up.

Although pleased with his apartment and feeling the benefits of a place to sleep and cook without interruption, Louie also became isolated, removed from his routine and his friends, and subject to new rules that made him feel nervous and lonely. Previous to apartment living, Louie was almost never alone. He slept in public places or in the emergency shelter and was surrounded by people for the majority of every day. Although he developed friends in Goleta, it was never the same as having a constant din of activity surrounding him. Yet apartment living allowed Louie to take care of his physical disabilities in a more substantial way than he could in the RV, which required constant maintenance to ensure mobility. He took frequent walks on the beach, slept better, and stretched more. After the recurring pain in his knee grew worse, he also had knee replacement surgery. "There's no way I could drive that thing [the RV] with a busted knee," he confided. Owning the RV in addition to renting the apartment allowed him to gradually transition from his former routine to apartment living.

Louie's story is typical in the sense that those who make the transition from RV living to permanent housing do so with the assistance of SSI, SSDI, and housing subsidies. They are also able to negotiate the terms of the subsidy or the rental, abide by the rules, and pay the rent on time. Louie is atypical because he was able to keep his RV and his apartment, something limited finances and the rigid parking restrictions in Santa Barbara usually don't allow. He also had a landlord willing to endure some false starts and misunderstandings without evicting him. Some RVers know they will not be able to negotiate these kinds of contingencies and do not want to risk losing their RVs for a temporary apartment. Other RVers have experienced substandard housing, predatory landlords, noisy neighbors, and other negatives that leave them wary of apartment living. Still others are not interested in being sedentary. Living in an RV affords some degree of house-mobility that apartment living takes away. As mentioned earlier, this can also be related to PTSD from traumatic events not uncommon for the RV community, something I discuss in detail in Chapter 5 (see Kim and Ford 2006).

Perhaps the most important thing about Louie's transformation is that he no longer has to endure the fear of regulation. In his RV, Louie worried about citations, vandalism, and being kicked off of whatever land he was parked on. Once he rented an apartment, Louie was no longer under scrutiny. Aside from adhering to the terms of the rental, he did not have to be as careful or vigilant in his everyday activities because he was no longer seen as a problematic presence. Being a renter gave Louie a degree of privacy and legitimacy that allowed him to transcend his former labels as "homeless bum" or, as he later called himself, "rubber tramp." Because he was isolated from the shelter and jungle neighborhoods, he was also able to avoid having constant visitors and squatters, something he could not avoid in his RV. The RV allowed him to manage relationships but also made his life difficult and chaotic, and allowing guests eventually jeopardized his ownership of the vehicle. Although he endured sporadic visitors from his shelter days in the apartment, he never let them stay for any length of time, knowing that eviction could be a dire consequence. Instead, Louie made friends with other apartment renters in the area with whom squatting was not a serious risk.

Conclusion

Long-term RV living is a commitment to living on the margins. At least in Santa Barbara, where usage and price restrictions make campgrounds and motor home parks prohibitive, RVers must park on the streets.[8] Parking in close proximity to public bathrooms and showers, and accessing available meal programs, means being dependent on the same services other homeless people use. There is therefore a significant amount of overlap between groups. Those with vehicles are seen as having valuable resources, and so they often become providers or targets for people in need. Because of the overlap with those on the streets and in shelters, RVers must constantly be able to judge which people and activities will jeopardize long-term vehicle maintenance.

The status that vehicle living offers otherwise homeless people allows them a sense of pride. The added resources of privacy, autonomy, and the ability to resist shelterization make vehicle living a far more amenable housing solution than shelters or makeshifts. Making the transition to apartment living also means that otherwise homeless RVers essentially disappear off the grid of homeless services and police concern. Vehicles can therefore serve as a counter to the enforcement side of regulation, the focus of the following chapter.

Given the difficulties involved in mere survival as a homeless person with or without a vehicle, it is not surprising that much attention has been devoted to describing these strategies. Vehicle living provides an addition to the list of possible housing options and adds to the complexity of resources and risks associated with each. Yet it is important to note that vehicle living in this discussion is not associated with a particular type of person, lifestyle, or subculture (Southard 1998). Trying to assign personality characteristics to people living in their RVs is as problematic as trying to do so for renters versus owners—and, of course, the latter distinction is rarely an issue. Focusing instead on skills and resources as sets of contingencies to be negotiated allows for a view of the in-between status of vehicle living that calls into question the homeless label.

Notes

[1] One such letter, addressed to the Santa Barbara Police Department, reads:

My name is Adam Johnson. I am working at OneStop Copy and Imaging (114 White Ave.) and this is why my vehicle is parked here. This vehicle belongs to my wife, Samantha, and I. We have recently relocated here from Indiana. I am aware that my registration has expired (I have already received a few "registration violation" tickets—more do not help). I am not flagrantly disregarding the law—I am merely having challenges fulfilling my responsibilities with the limited resources of time and money that are available to me. I have been in the process of registering this vehicle for some time. I am awaiting parts that are necessary to pass "smog," which is necessary to gain California registration. I have receipts and documentation to authenticate my efforts. I have been told by the California DMV that I am not eligible for an extension as the vehicle's registration is out of state. Barring further difficulties I will have current plates and registration within days. Please feel free to speak to me regarding this matter—I have full intentions of complying with the legal requirements; please be patient and understanding.

Other letters were written in support of RVers by neighboring property owners. The following letter was written by a local business owner and posted on the RV, with the property owner's name, address, and contact information:

Ron Shamus has my permission to remain on our premises and for his vehicle to be parked in our lot 24 x7. Ron has been very effective in minimizing the amount of vandalism that has occurred in and around our building. We appreciate the city's concern but assure you we have no problem with Ron remaining at the location.

[2] As is often the case with point-in-time counts, the 2002 counts were suspect for overcounting. Since this was the first year the counts were conducted, both the informants and author wanted to err on the side of overcounting rather than missing potential vehicles. In subsequent years, we were far more careful about ensuring that the vehicles we counted were being used as full-time housing. This included knocking on doors to talk with occupants, if they were not known by the informants or the author. We also recorded signs of permanent usage and checked to see if the vehicle had been counted in the previous year.

[3] The primary difference between supplemental security income (SSI) and social security disability insurance (SSDI) is that the latter benefit is for those who have paid social security taxes. Beneficiaries in both categories must prove that they are blind or disabled, and those seeking SSI must meet additional requirements including having a limited income. The amount of the payment varies; SSDI is based on social security earnings, and SSI is need-based and can vary by state. For additional details on the difference between these benefits,

please see http://ssa-custhelp.ssa.gov/app/answers/detail/a_id/245/~/difference-between-social-security-disability-and-ssi-disability.

[4] Requiring that homeless people participate in religious service as a condition of shelter violates the free exercise clause of the First Amendment. As Chapter 4 details, this is an important issue as homeless people living in their vehicles are expected to submit to shelter to avoid citation. While this expectation is also controversial, combining it with religious prerequisites makes it illegal. When religious shelters are the only lodgings available, people sleeping in their vehicles have legal grounds to protest citations for sleeping and camping.

[5] Section 8 is a federal rent subsidy program in which those with vouchers are required to pay the difference between the actual rent and the amount covered by the subsidy. Those with vouchers typically find their own rental units in the private market, although there are subsidized units that are linked to a given site. HUD-assisted public housing consists of a number of units that are operated by the local housing authority. Tenants typically pay rental amounts calculated according to annual income, less deductions for dependents, elderly family members, qualifying disabilities, etc. Public housing in Santa Barbara is owned by the city housing authority and typically exceeds the price of Section 8 housing.

[6] The issue of SSI payouts is controversial. In 1997, drug addiction and alcoholism were eliminated from the possible "impairment categories" for which people receive assistance (see *Contemporary Drug Problems* 2003 (30)). It is still the case that those with other impairments or who have a history of drug and/or alcohol addiction need to establish a representative payee to help them manage their money.

[7] As was the case with several RVers and unsheltered homeless people I met in the service of this work, Hope asked me to keep the details of her past confidential. Although Hope allowed me to record interviews with her and to have this information publicly disclosed as long as her anonymity was preserved, in the end she decided she did not want me to reveal her story. For Hope and others, keeping confidence became more important than sharing details that, while they would give a fuller profile of individuals experiencing homelessness, were usually not anomalous.

[8] In addition to the approximate cost of $35 per night to park in an RV park or campground, there are size restrictions. Many parks exclude vehicles over thirty-five feet in length, making it that much more difficult to find parking.

4
Negotiating Public Spaces

Homeless people are locked in a cycle of regulation and resistance with police, city officials, and the courts, whereby they must minimize their occupation of public spaces or face NIMBYism, harassment, and citation. This chapter examines regulation as a defining feature of homelessness and one of the primary things people living in vehicles have in common with those who are unsheltered. Forms of regulation stem from a desire to assist homeless people and to control them as they pose a challenge to the normative order in terms of behavior and in terms of their existence in public spaces. The first half of this chapter focuses on routine interactions between police and homeless people, and the second half examines municipal court trials in which RVers are cited for sleeping in their vehicles. Both forms of regulation target appearance and behavior as punishable offenses.

Police interact with homeless people on a daily basis and are, among others, enforcers of the public order. Unlike staff employed by agencies specifically designed to serve homeless people, police view them as merely one category of nuisance that they have to deal with. This is not to say that officers are uninterested in helping homeless people, but the more rehabilitative side of regulation is not the focus of police work. Officers, in fact, are often frustrated in their ability to manage homeless people who simply will not go away and who do not commit crimes serious enough to put them away for long periods of time. Similarly, police interested in assisting homeless people by referring them to services or shelters are also frustrated by the cyclical nature of chronic homelessness and by the dearth of services. Homeless people and police meet in the arena of public space, where police attempt to regulate and homeless people to resist. Examining interactions between police and homeless people underscores the ascribed status of vehicle owners and homeless people as illegitimate and therefore subject to regulation.

Although *sweeps*[1] are one of the most common ways of removing homeless people and possessions from areas considered problematic, this chapter focuses on *routine interactions* with individual homeless people and those living in vehicles. While some mention is made of sweeps in subsequent chapters, they are often conducted when homeless people are not in their camps or makeshift dwellings. They also typically target areas that are less visible or are not primary tourist areas. The issue of homeless people in public spaces is heightened when they occupy what police officers, citizens, and business owners consider prime real estate.

Homeless People: "Indicator Species," Nuisance, or Asshole?

Don Mitchell (2003, 136) describes homeless people as an "indicator species," whose presence demonstrates the "presumed ill health of public space and the need to gain control, to privatize, or to otherwise rationalize public space in urban places." Homeless people occupying public spaces detract from a city's ability to attract capital and from the overall desirability or quality of life of a given area. They are, quite simply, bad for business. Anti-homeless laws regulate homeless people in a bid to make the city a viable destination, if not for tourists, then at least for capital. When homeless people persist in public parks or other public spaces, this particular use value threatens their exchange value, as housed citizens and businesses may think twice about locating there. Regulating homeless people is therefore designed to enhance the exchangeability of the urban landscape.

But regulating homeless people is also about identity, morality, and right and wrong. The "ideology of public space as 'owned' by a normatively enshrined 'we' of home dwelling citizens" (Feldman 2004, 3) reinforces the idea that homeless people should be regulated and that the proper place for them is jail, shelter, or simply out of sight. It also reinforces the legitimacy of those in apartments, houses, and other more acceptable forms of housing. Police work is commonly understood, both by citizens and police themselves, as engaging in a "struggle with those who would disobey, disrupt, do harm, agitate, or otherwise upset the just order of the regime" (Van Maanen 2006, 305). If homeless people are seen as disturbing this order, which they usually are, the officer is in the position of taking action.

In his review of how police understand and characterize the individuals they come into contact with, John Van Maanen (2006, 306) distinguishes between mere "suspicious persons" and potential "assholes." The former are those who have potentially committed a serious offense. Their moral worth is not in question; rather, the concern is simply whether they have engaged in illegal action. "Assholes" by contrast are those who do not accept the police definition of the situation and who challenge or disrespect officers during the interaction. The possible violation or offense is the reason for initiating contact and leads to the determination that the individual is a nuisance or an asshole.

Van Maanen characterizes the process through which officers understand and label the asshole. The first is the *affront,* which represents a challenge to police authority, control, and definition of the situation (Van Maanen 2006, 313). The affront can occur through specific language, behavior, or appearance. It can be overt or covert, but it signals to police that they are not being given the proper respect. The second stage of the process is *clarification.* During this stage, the officer decides whether the affront, and ostensibly the individual, is reasonable. Determining culpability hinges on whether or not the individual is seen as in control of and aware of her actions or simply acting out of a lack of wherewithal or understanding of logical alternatives. How the affront is clarified is the determining feature in labeling someone an asshole and in deciding on a course of action, which is the third stage, the *remedy* or solution.

If the individual is seen as unaware of the affront and incapable of acting differently or determining right from wrong, the only remedy is to isolate, through jail or removal from public places. If the officer believes the subject could have acted differently if made aware of other options, the remedy is to teach, by offering services, shelter, or other assistance. The less benevolent forms of "teaching" include threat, ridicule, and harassment. Those who are seen as aware of their offense and in control of their actions, meaning they could have chosen to act differently, are punished. In rare cases, affronts are ignored when the person in question is seen as momentarily lacking control of her actions or presents an explanation that the officer accepts as logical.

Applying Van Maanen to the Case of Homeless People

As an *a priori* category, homeless people are seen as illogical. Why would someone knowingly become homeless? Why wouldn't they do something, anything, to avoid it? While officers understand that some homeless people suffer from mental illness or other issues that prolong street living, many also view homeless people as too lazy, too stupid, too drunk, or too drug addicted to change their situation. Without a thorough understanding of the causes of homelessness, most homeless individuals are viewed as culpable. They have alternatives but do not exercise them, and the only remedy is to castigate or teach. In this sense, homeless people are part of a permanent category of problematic person, a nuisance. They are therefore the subjects of routine police attention, and it is during these interactions that their character is determined anew (Van Maanen 2006, 312). Because of the frequency with which officers approach homeless people, and sometimes the same homeless people repeatedly, to determine possible violations, the possibility for an affront is also magnified.

In rare cases, interactions between police officers and homeless people proceed through all three of the stages Van Maanen describes and result in the officer ignoring the affront or understanding it from the homeless person's perspective. I collected one example of this in a reported incident in which a police officer approached a homeless man who was dumpster diving, or rummaging through the trash, something this particular officer confided "really pisses me off." The man did not stop what he was doing and appeared annoyed with the officer, constituting an *affront*. Once the contact was initiated, the man explained that he found winter jackets in the dumpster, barely used, and wanted to use them to keep warm. The officer recognized this as a logical reason for the otherwise illegal action of dumpster diving, which *clarified* the man's actions for the officer. The man knowingly dove into the dumpster and could have acted differently under the circumstances, yet he is not castigated because he explains the logic of his actions and the officer accepts the explanation. The *remedy*, then, although it is clear that the man could have chosen to stay out of the dumpster, is to ignore the action. This kind of interaction is not par for the course.

In most confrontations between homeless people and police, contact occurs because of visibility and action, and it occurs repeatedly. Officers routinely encounter the same unsheltered, chronically homeless people in the same places doing the same things, and the problem for the officer is what to do about it. When individuals or groups of homeless people present a constant affront to officers, it results in routine confrontation that rises to the level of a "project," described below. The clarification stage also becomes routine as officers hear the same story from the same person over and over again, until officers skip over this stage and move straight to the remedy. This abbreviated process frequently occurs in confrontations between homeless people as a problematic social category, and the officers who police them. Routine interactions also muddy the stages of this process because officers repeatedly police the same homeless people, who by their presence alone are seen as an affront. Anything that happens during the clarification stage of the interaction typically affirms guilt and warrants a remedy. The remedy stage itself is compromised, as the remedies at the officer's disposal rarely result in a solution to the problem of homeless people in public spaces. At best, they are inadequate, and they typically result in the repetition of this cycle.

Making People a Project

> "Sometimes we get annoyed and we'll make somebody a project because they've pissed us off. If we have to bring the hammer, we will." —Officer, Transient Detail, Santa Barbara Police Department

During all of my ride-alongs with police officers in Sonoma, Santa Cruz, and Santa Barbara counties, officers indicated that they worked with individuals or teams of officers who made homeless people the focus of enforcement by targeting groups, individuals, locations, and behaviors specific to homeless people, for police attention. In some cases, making people a project is born out of animosity toward the target, and in other cases it develops out of frustration about what to do with people who, for one reason or another, have become a problem. Homeless people are seen as interfering with the normative moral and spatial order as well as with police authority (see Spradley 2000; Van Maanen 2006). Most of the police contact described in this chapter is explicitly focused on territory. When homeless people become a "project" they incur repeat police attention and are considered an affront to officers when they occupy public spaces. Any challenge or clarification that happens once contact is initiated affirms the idea that homeless people are unreasonable, illogical, and worthy of citation.

Below I offer examples of making people a project in each of the three counties under study. The first is Santa Barbara County, where an officer initiates contact with a man living in his RV and proceeds to argue with him about enforcement and question his lifestyle. The second is in Sonoma County, where an officer initiates contact with a panhandler because of a bet he made with his sergeant. The third is in Santa Cruz County, where an officer attempts to step up his policing strategy to target a particular panhandler in a local shopping plaza. These examples are intended to show how individual homeless people become a project and what measures police officers have at their disposal to regulate them.

Whereas most cities are divided into "beats" and assigned rotating teams of officers, the city of Santa Barbara has what is officially known as the Tactical Patrol Force or Transient Detail that officers voluntarily apply to be a part of. Also called the "Baker boys," after the officers who originated it, the team is made up of six officers and one sergeant who pursue citywide issues related to homelessness. "We call ourselves the flies. If it stinks, we're on it," one of the officers explained. Although the same officer said he liked homeless people to dictate the tone of the interaction, he also admitted that he did not shy away from conflict: "If they want to confront me, I'll confront them—because I know I'll win." While none of the officers I rode with admitted any personal aggression toward homeless people, all of them indicated that they worked with other officers they described as "real go-getters, lots of contact with homeless people, lots of tickets."

When police repeatedly target the same people, they develop adversarial relationships with them and devote a significant amount of time and energy to pursuing a remedy. The following discussion took place between an officer who is a regular member of the Transient Detail and a man who lives in his RV and is cited repeatedly. The officer was doing his usual street patrol and decided to "check in on some transients" he frequently visits to see if they were in violation of city ordinances. The fact that the officer visits specific individuals to pursue the possibility of an affront demonstrates the degree to which homeless people are seen as a problematic category of person. In this interaction the officer tells an RVer named Jim that he will no longer be working the Transient Detail but will continue to visit him because

Officer:		I know you and I, we got a special relationship.
RVer:		How's that, you harassing me?
Officer:		That's right. It's a symbiotic relationship.
RVer:		No, it's called discrimination.
Officer:		How you figure? We're both white—you can't call it discrimination.
RVer:		Yeah, it is—what gives you the right to come out and only target RVs and people living in their vehicles?
Officer:		That's my job description.
RVer:		No, it's supposed to be the city ordinance; you're supposed to mark utility trucks, anything over three-quarter ton—you don't do these vehicles—just the RVs.

Officer: Right, that's what the car markers do—our job is to deal with people that live in the vehicles.

In this interaction, Jim is referring to a city ordinance that prohibits street parking for over ninety minutes for vehicles over three-quarter ton capacity and accuses the officer of selectively enforcing the law to target RVers. The officer affirms that, in fact, he sees his job *as* policing people living in vehicles rather than others who violate the same ordinance. The adversarial nature of this confrontation underscores how routine the regulation-resistance dynamic is for homeless people and police officers. In this case frequent interaction between this particular RVer and police officer has set the stage for an extended affront in which the RVer accuses the officer of harassment and selective enforcement. This sequence shows that it is the mere existence of people living in their vehicles that is objectionable, and applying the law to target them is seen as an essential although inadequate remedy.

In addition to being targets for regulation, RVers report that officers mark their tires several times daily, forcing them to move frequently to avoid citation. RVers consider this practice a form of harassment because it is expensive to keep the RV in motion and because they do not see the same vigilance being applied to parked cars or other vehicles. This form of "teaching" is also an inadequate remedy because it does not lead to removal from public space, merely relocation. After the interaction above, which the officer viewed as playful, the man in his RV became visibly angry and shaken. The officer proceeded to question him about his income and daily activities to further instruct him, albeit in a confrontational manner, on how employment might be a way to avoid vehicle living.

Officer: Do you get SSI?

RVer: No.

Officer: What do you do for work?

RVer: I'm her [Sandy's] caregiver, caretaker, and stuff.

Officer: Oh really? So you make her go out and work and beg for money all day?

RVer: Yeah, cause I got to sit here and fuckin' deal with you guys. What, am I going to go find a good paying job and come back with five tickets, just because you're on duty?

Officer: (laughs) Oh my god. You are funny.

RVer: No, you're funnier.

Officer: Think about this, if you spent half the energy you spend fighting with us out getting a job and actually working, [yells] you would live in a mansion. You would live in an absolute mansion.

RVer: I've had a fuckin' job. I've worked in this city before. It's called discrimination. You're targeting us because some work and some don't? It's bullshit and you know it.

Officer: If you spent half your time even trying to find a job, you'd live in a mansion.

RVer: Oh, trust me, I've worked in this city, probably longer than you've been on the force.

After this interaction, Jim retreated to his vehicle, infuriated, and the officer continued on with his patrol without issuing a citation. Admittedly he was just visiting because of their "symbiotic" relationship, one regulating and the other resisting. The officer attempts to clarify the situation by asking Jim to explain why he is homeless, which he responds to by claiming that routine police action forces him to remain in his vehicle to resist regulation. Clearly the officer is not satisfied with this explanation and proceeds to instruct Jim in proper time management, suggesting that employment is the way out of homelessness. Jim, in response, struggles for the upper hand, indicating that he does have prior job experience and has worked in the city for longer than this particular officer, a classic form of identity work. He also blames the officer for his inability to work, noting that he must move the vehicle frequently to avoid citation. None of his explanations satisfy this officer, as "transients" themselves present an affront for which there are few long-term remedies and no adequate explanation.

The officer has already determined that "transiency" is avoidable and, in the case of this particular RVer, that the only immediate remedy is instruction or citation. Many officers realize that repeat citations are not a long-term solution and do not issue them. The unfortunate part of making this RVer a project is that it undermines his already damaged sense of self-esteem and fair play. His mere existence is seen as an affront, regardless of whether he is engaging in illegal action. The only attempt at clarification he offers is an attempt to justify why he does not work ("I'm her caregiver, caretaker, and stuff"). This is not his reason for committing an offense but his reason for being unemployed and, ostensibly, his reason for being homeless. The officer rejects this justification and ostensibly the RVer as illogical, unreasonable, and "funny."

This kind of heated exchange was rare for me to witness during a ride-along and is only one way for officers to target individuals. On a ride-along in Sonoma County, an officer, who promised "to find you some bums," described his own individual version of making people a project.

> We had all these shopping carts down by the recycling center and I went in to the officer who's, like, our second in command and he looked stressed out, and he said, "I've got all these issues and there is no fix." And I was joking with him and said your job is so easy I could do it. He says he has all these letters from the city council complaining about homeless people, and I still said I could take care of it. It is the recycling center that draws them. So I told him, "Tomorrow they'll be gone, guaranteed," and he said "I dare you."

> So there is this one guy who has, like, five shopping carts and was causing most of the problems. He was the major complaint, so I went out and talked to him and asked if he ever wanted to live anywhere else, and he said, "I've always wanted to live in Ventura." And so I went and got some money from people at the PD and I bought him a bus ticket and he was gone. He was completely cooperative and saw this as an opportunity. I haven't told anybody this but I saw him just the other day. He's back. Everybody thinks it's funny because I shipped this guy out on a bus, so I'm not going to tell them he's back.

Like the officer in Santa Barbara, this officer has a similar problem; how to get a homeless person, who presents a constant affront, to leave town. It is worth mentioning that there was no behavioral affront in this situation, no explicit challenge to the officer's authority; in fact, he reports that this man was "completely cooperative." This underscores how the mere visibility of homeless people in public is seen as an affront that warrants a remedy. "Bus therapy" is sometimes the only way to get homeless people out of a given area, but, as this officer indicates, it is not a permanent solution as homeless people consider certain areas "home" despite their lack of access to conventional dwellings.

Both the RVer and the panhandler present a problem that the police are confronted with, whether by complaint from the city council, private citizens, or other officers. Homeless people are an affront to the moral sensibilities of cities and signify that the police have lost their "edge" and are not doing their job to keep the city orderly (see Van Maanen 2006). This is a problem for which there is only one remedy, which simply isn't adequate: move them along or move them out, what Joel John Roberts (2004) calls "the leaf blower mentality." This solution isn't adequate because it is not permanent and does not rise to the level of either rehabilitation or long-term punishment. In short, the RVer and the panhandler remain in or return to the areas they consider home and must contend with the problem their presence poses. Being combative versus cooperative is less of an issue than one's mere visibility, although people who are combative will be more likely to "bring the hammer."

In comparison with Santa Barbara and Sonoma, Santa Cruz County is known as a relatively lenient area with respect to alternative lifestyles, yet homeless people are still targeted when they interfere with tourist or resident activities. One officer describes being confronted by business owners who want homeless people to stop hanging out and panhandling in front of their stores. "They kept asking me, 'What do we do?' so I told them to talk to the owner or property manager. We can continue to cite them but it's an infraction, so once they accumulate enough tickets, they go to jail for a few hours. They just get free and come back." To rid this particular shopping plaza of homeless people for good, this officer proposed a program that all of the business owners could participate in. He suggested that they take notes on homeless people and their actions, to document their presence as undesirable. "If they can take out a restraining order on one guy, it is a misdemeanor or violation of a court order. Then if the guy is there he can be cited or go to jail. He would still be released, but now he's got a real court order that he's got to contend with. If you're there you violate your probation by being there. If you do that even once, the rest won't be around there spanging [asking for spare change]."

Unfortunately for this officer, local business owners were uninterested in pursuing this strategy further for fear of developing a bad reputation. Although they felt that panhandlers interfered with their operations, they were not willing to take such a strong stand against them. The same officer described the police as "neutered" in their capacity to cite and arrest homeless people, but he attempted to create a more permanent solution to the problem of panhandling. His theory is that posing a serious legal problem for one homeless person would serve as an example for the rest.

The cases presented here are similar because the homeless person in question is the focus of routine police attention. Their visibility and categorical identity as a "transient," "bum," or "panhandler" presents the initial problem or affront, and there is little room for clarification. Although frustrating, routine confrontation rarely leads to an adequate, long-term remedy, but rather to future affronts. In the first case, the officer in Santa Barbara does not issue a citation, although he visits an RVer and argues with him about his lifestyle and income, and selective enforcement. In the second, the case of the panhandler who was given "bus therapy," the remedy is only temporary as the man eventually returns to town. Although Santa Cruz is seen as a more lenient area, the action considered by the officer in this case would pose a serious legal problem for one homeless person, a remedy the officer hopes would send a message to other panhandlers in the area. Yet in all three cases, officers pursue short-term remedies that simply frustrate them and the homeless people they confront.

What's the Violation?

Officers in all three jurisdictions express frustration with the lack of permanent solutions and merely try to keep homeless people from breaking the law or hanging out in areas where they attract business or citizen complaint. One of the primary struggles officers face is that there is often no illegal activity taking place, just the presence of a person deemed undesirable or problematic in terms of behavior, appearance, and action, and therefore culpable. Without an actual violation, officers do not have the tools to remedy the situation. Even when a homeless person is suspected of an offense, without proof there is little the officer can do.

An officer in a rural area of Santa Cruz County, the only one in fact who literally walked his beat, went into a local music store to see how things were going and got into a conversation with the owners about what to do about a local homeless man who tried to sell equipment they suspected was stolen. They described the man as "a gentle type, he's not dumb" and the officer responded, "He's a good con, he knows how to play that game, that's the first thing you learn in prison. When he hasn't had his meth [methamphetamine], though, then he's dangerous." The owners looked frightened, and one of them admitted, "I didn't know what to do for the guy so I eventually paid him $10 to leave. But what should I do?" The officer replied, "I wouldn't deal with the guy. I wouldn't let him in my store. Sooner or later things will disappear, so you have to make the decision based on your conscience. If he comes back you can call the police for trespassing." Mulling over this solution, the owner responded, "I don't want him to break my windows if he gets mad. Why can't you guys deal with him?" "What's the violation?" the officer replied. "I have to catch him with methamphetamine, or for trespassing; otherwise, there's really nothing I can do. If I give him a ticket, he'll be right back out again." This example shows the frustration that business owners feel and the pressure they put on the police to solve a problem that officers don't have the tools to solve permanently. For this officer, who works in a suburban to rural area with a small shopping district, the homeless man's presence was something he saw as unpleasant but nothing he could really control unless the man was found guilty of a specific violation.

In the city of Santa Rosa, officers also struggle with the problem of visibly homeless people in public places. An officer I rode along with described a homeless man who reportedly suffered from mental illness and was described as "Santa Rosa world famous" for standing in the middle of the street in a busy intersection in a suburban area. The officer approached him and said, "Listen, this is a suburban area—people here, you know, you stand out to them and they call in on you. You need to find somewhere else to go, like downtown." When I asked what happened, the officer replied, "I haven't seen him since—maybe he actually listened to me." Put simply, in this officer's opinion, downtown is the place for homeless people because they stand out in suburban areas and are more likely to be seen as objectionable to residents. Like the officer who used "bus therapy" to get a homeless man away from the local recycling center in Santa Maria, out of town or out of my beat is often the best answer for police attempting to regulate homeless people.

RV Living: Pursuing a Remedy

While individual homeless people become "projects" for officers when they persist in public places, what happens when an entire subset of homeless people is considered a problem and targeted for enforcement? This section examines how police and city officials attempt to find a remedy to the problem posed by RVers as a group. As with other unsheltered homeless people, RVers are targeted for the visible occupation of public spaces and for sleeping and camping in particular. Visibility is typically the reason for contact, and homeless people living in their vehicles present a categorical affront. Part of the confrontation or clarification process involves figuring out whether the person is actually sleeping and whether she has an explanation for why she is doing so and for her status as a homeless person. Deciding on an appropriate remedy for RVers takes the form of repeated and perhaps adversarial contact, as already shown, and in municipal court trials that not only decide the remedy but are a forum in which the affront is clarified. It is, in fact, these extended clarifications that demonstrate the need for advocacy and assistance.

As with other groups of unsheltered homeless people, the first ingredient in making RVers a project is visibility. Although the vehicle allows for individual protection, the larger the vehicle, the more obvious it is and the more easily it becomes a target for regulation. The second ingredient in making RVers a project is complaint. When citizens and business owners complain about unsightly RVs "blocking my view of the ocean," the response is typically swift and immediate. In October 2000, the Santa Barbara City Council began reviewing possible solutions to the problem identified through visibility and complaint. The primary solutions under consideration included increased parking and new tools for regulation. Previous to this, the citations issued to RVers included one targeting parking and another targeting the activities of sleeping and camping. Together, the upshot of these ordinances meant that RVers could not leave their vehicles parked on city streets for longer than two hours, and could not sleep or camp in them within city limits.

Whereas on-street parking can be regulated using the same "chalking" method used for passenger cars, determining whether a person is sleeping or camping in their vehicle is substantially more difficult. Officers typically rely on gaining access to the inside of the vehicle or use visual cues or familiarity with the vehicle to determine how it is being used. To explain the issue of entering a vehicle to determine usage, I examine a case in which a couple was cited for illegal camping for sleeping in their vehicle. The officer in this case uses his familiarity with the vehicle and its inhabitants to determine that they are homeless and therefore merit citation. In the narrative included with the police report, he writes: "On this date I saw three vehicles belonging to subjects I have warned or cited in the past for illegal camping." He goes on to write that he repeatedly attempted to contact the subjects by knocking on the door but got no response. "I then used my body weight to bounce the vehicle up and down as I was standing on the rear bumper. I still did not get a response from inside." This officer goes to great lengths to initiate contact with these vehicle owners to establish whether they were sleeping.

Initially frustrated, the officer moves his patrol car out of the immediate area and surveys the vehicle until one of the occupants leaves. He then approaches the vehicle, and "to prevent being locked out... quickly put [his] foot on the step inside the door and entered the vehicle." Despite the owner's protests, which are also included in the report, the officer gained access to the vehicle and cited both occupants for illegal camping. Although he did not literally catch them in the act of sleeping, his testimony focuses on what he saw when he entered the vehicle, namely visible bedding and food items. His actions in this case surprised me, so I asked a retired public defender, the primary legal defense in these cases, to explain the legality of the officer's actions. He said:

> There's this whole distinction in the law about search and seizure about things that are moveable. Cars—for example, regular passenger cars—are not entitled to the same protection that residents are because one of the theories is that by the time the law enforcement agency got the search warrant, the vehicle would be gone. So you have to balance this idea that this is your home, your castle so to speak, versus the fact that it's a mobile vehicle. The US Supreme Court reversed the California Supreme Court decision and said unless the officer has reason to believe and knows this vehicle is used as a residence and not being moved he's entitled to treat it as a car and enter without a warrant and conduct searches with minimal cause as they might in a regular car.

Struck by the irony of this, I summed up for validation: "So he can conduct the search as if it was a car to prove it's being used as a home," which is in fact the case. The officer's proof procedure, albeit complicated,[2] is also difficult to duplicate, as few officers have the time or inclination to stake out RVs to gain entry.

The Need for Sleep

Despite the difficulty of proving vehicle sleeping, a surprising number of cases appeared in Santa Barbara Municipal Court from 2000 to 2003. The retired public defender quoted above worked for a local advocacy group, the Committee for Social Justice, and voluntarily handled these cases. Of the total 135 cases heard during this time period, approximately 122 resulted in acquittal or dismissal and thirteen cases were lost, meaning that the citation was upheld. The primary defense in these cases is the *necessity* defense (*Eichorn v. Superior Court* [1988] 69 Cal App 4th 382, citing *People v. Pepper* [1996] 41 Cal App 4th

1029, 1035). Necessity is established when the defendant can prove that violating the law occurred to prevent a greater danger, that the defendant had no adequate alternative and believed the offense to be necessary, and that the defendant did not contribute to the circumstances leading to the offense. This formal clarification is an attempt to demonstrate why RVers would knowingly violate the law and sleep in their vehicles.

1. to prevent a significant evil

2. with no adequate alternative

3. without creating a greater danger than the one avoided

4. with a good-faith belief in the necessity

5. with such belief being objectively reasonable

6. under circumstances in which the defendant did not substantially contribute to the emergency

(*Eichorn v Superior Court* [1988] 69 Cal App 4th 382, citing *People v. Pepper* [1996] 41 Cal App 4th 1029, 1035)

Ironically, although the wording of this defense trades on the morality and reasonability of the act of sleeping in a vehicle, proving this is difficult. As an *a priori* unreasonable category of person, unable to order their lives or priorities appropriately, RVers are seen as belonging in shelters or on the streets. Justifying RV living over other housing alternatives, particularly when it is objectionable and in potential violation of city ordinances, is difficult. In addition, police officers, lawyers, and commissioners, most of whom have no direct experience with homelessness, view shelters as the most appropriate form of housing for RVers and for homeless people in general.

Municipal court trials typically focus on the second element of the necessity defense, the adequacy of shelter and housing alternatives. If the defense can prove that there was no other housing deemed appropriate or adequate for the defendant at the time of citation, the citation is dismissed. The first and third elements of the necessity defense are not typically the focus of these trials, as sleeping is a biological necessity that prevents the danger of staying awake, in motion, and behind the wheel. The fourth and fifth elements of the defense rely on the defendant's belief that specific actions are necessary and that this belief is held to be objectively reasonable. This is a bit more difficult to prove, as most prosecutors and commissioners do not find sleeping in a vehicle to be a reasonable activity. The final element of the defense examines whether the defendant is essentially responsible for her own homelessness and for living and sleeping in the vehicle.

To prove the second element of the necessity defense, and ostensibly the need to sleep in the vehicle, RVers must prove that they are in pursuit of an adequate alternative, other than the vehicle, on a regular basis. The only legal alternatives are a homeless shelter or an apartment. If no shelter is available, the necessity defense is easier to prove. Given the limited availability of most shelters (as was discussed in Chapter 3), many cases are won on this basis. Yet if shelter is available, the prosecution typically argues that the RVer should leave the vehicle and its contents and at least attempt to sleep there instead. As one commissioner ruled:

> I think that the shelter is a viable alternative despite the fact that they require you to at least sit through a sermon.... That is a reasonable alternative.... I think that a reasonable person who does not have housing that they consider to be adequate, that would be the first order of business in terms of life, along with food. Those are the two biggies. Because the shelter was available, I don't think the defendant has met the necessity defense, so I do find her guilty of the violation.

This decision underscores the extent to which RVers are expected to submit to conditions, including participation in religious services, to receive shelter. As the defense argued in an appeal of this case, supported by a letter of *amicus curiae* from the American Civil Liberties Union, this suggestion violates the Free Exercise Clause of the First Amendment. This decision also trades on a held-in-common definition of reasonable alternatives and reasonable people, and presumes that even RVers must know their living situation is inadequate and seek shelter.

Other alternatives proposed by the prosecution are equally problematic and, in fact, involve violating the law. One prosecutor suggested that an RV appellant, cited for sleeping in his vehicle after he got off work at 4 a.m., should go to a public park rather than return to his vehicle to sleep with his wife. "The parks are open at that hour [4 a.m.], you just can't habitate on a public street, so there is an alternative, not a great one, but a legal alternative." Despite this suggestion, sleeping in a public park is, in fact, illegal in Santa Barbara, according to Municipal Code Ordinances 15.16.070 and 15.16.085. Aware of these ordinances, the commissioner hearing this case dismissed it.

These cases show that like police officers, municipal courts and local officials are frustrated by the problem of RVs in public spaces and are limited in their ability to handle it. Part of this stems from the fact that it is difficult to explicitly regulate access to public places based on identity. In a particularly candid moment, one commissioner expressed her desire to allow RV vacationing and punish RV living:

> There has to be a distinction between someone who lives in an RV, which in and of itself is not illegal to do, who may legitimately be traveling, and many people do that, and travel from campground to campground, and they stop in various places along the way.... People will get out and go to the beach and then they'll come back and change their clothes perhaps, or they may go to a restaurant or park on any public street and go shopping, and the fact is it is a vehicle and they can use it to drive places and go and do legitimate things.

In this commissioner's opinion, shopping, traveling, and going to restaurants are legitimate activities, directly tied to tourism and consumption. Being unable to afford gas is illegitimate, as is living in one's vehicle rather than vacationing in it. Unlike tourists, homeless people are accorded a degraded social and legal status such that even when they own their own vehicles, they are not entitled to sleep in them without some form of sanction. It is also clear from the above statement that the court's desire is to specify the affront as it applies to person and not action. If the person sleeping in the vehicle is a tourist, the remedy is to ignore or allow the action.

It is worth mentioning that these trials are typically stressful for RVers, cost a significant amount of time and money, and are all waged over $25 citations. Part of what is at stake for RV appellants is arguing for the right to sleep in their vehicles and to have this be seen as a legitimate, reasonable, and legal action and themselves as reasonable people.

In addition to weighing shelter alternatives, RVers are asked about their income to make sure they cannot, in fact, afford an apartment. The director of the Santa Barbara Housing Authority was frequently called upon to identify housing costs and availability. In one trial, he estimated that available housing on the south coast is "at 1 percent vacant or less." He went on to state that Section 8 is available but that "there are approximately 3,000 households waiting for assistance. The wait for a person on the list depends, but the average wait is two to three years. A veteran who has a high preference may get housing sooner." Even with a voucher and income to cover rental costs, landlords must agree to participate in the program. In addition, applicants must be able to receive mail and check it consistently, as they have just two weeks to respond to the initial notification.

Determining whether RV appellants can afford or "belong" in housing depends, in part, on their testimony about income. One case involved a married couple who were both issued citations for sleeping in their RV at 8:30 a.m. Despite the fact that all available shelters require clients to exit by this time, the testimony focused on possible sleeping alternatives. The man testified that he was on his way to work and that he made $8.20 per hour, for an approximate total of $800 per month. His wife was receiving SSI and received approximately $680 per month. Their combined income would place them within range of a two-bedroom rental apartment, though this would leave little to no money for food or additional expenses.

Testifying about her income and her husband's employment was stressful for the RV appellant, who suffers from Attention Deficit Disorder (ADD) and admittedly has difficulty organizing her thoughts. During one particularly heated exchange, the prosecuting attorney repeatedly asked her if her husband was working on the night of the citation. She initially replied that he was and then mistakenly said that he was not, and the attorney laughed. Flustered, she yelled, "I really do have ADD, you know, and if you would like I could bring the records of him [her husband] up here. I do have that. Why do you belittle me? I'm a very intelligent person, don't belittle me!" Feeling belittled is not uncommon for RV appellants who are called upon to demonstrate that living in an RV is socially legitimate. Doing this in a courtroom is particularly stressful as such legitimacy has already been called into question. As a result, RVers are often defensive when asked about their income, eager to dispel the myth that they are indigent. The wife in the above case testified that in addition to her SSI, she plays a keyboard at the farmers market and makes anywhere from $20 to $100 per week. Not only is this a gross overestimate, but she also did not have a keyboard at the time of the citation.

In a similar case, a man who identified himself as a street performer who does "juggling and balloon sculpting" was cited for sleeping in his vehicle with his girlfriend, a woman who is on SSI and is developmentally disabled. When asked about his income, he responded, "At the end of the summer I could make as much as $300 to $400 a week but it drops out right after that." The prosecution used this information to argue that with the man's income at $1,600 a month and his girlfriend's SSI payments at $785, the two could afford an apartment in Santa Barbara—and that this would be a better alternative than RV living. Although the commissioner in this case admitted to finding the man "sympathetic," she upheld the citation because of testimony about their combined income.

These cases show that the consequence of trying to appear legitimate and productive, a classic form of identity work, is that too much legitimacy leads to a remedy of upholding the citation and an apartment as a reasonable alternative. Conversely, having little to no income also leads to a remedy of upholding the citation and a shelter as reasonable alternative. In either case, the RV has already been deemed inadequate, inappropriate, and illegal.

Upping the Regulation Ante

The drive to rid Santa Barbara's tourist areas of unsightly RVs resulted in an ongoing struggle between regulation, through both citation and the creation of programs and services, and resistance to these forms of regulation by advocates and RVers. The latter argue that RV living is an acceptable housing alternative and that RVers should not be subject to anti-homeless ordinances. Adjudicating this struggle in court proved both costly and time consuming, with no apparent solution. As a result, two things happened. The first is that the city considered stepping up its enforcement activities, and the second is that it considered creating an RV park or program to offer structured provisions. I examine these two possibilities in order as they represent the punitive and provisional sides of regulation, designed to curtail the existence of those living in vehicles in public spaces or to remove them entirely.

The success of the necessity defense and the lack of year-round nondenominational shelter meant that to rid tourist areas of unsightly RVs, a new regulation strategy needed to be considered. In a consolidated case decision, detailed below, the city began to re-think its regulation policy. The RV defendants in this case have several things in common: they are all well known in Santa Barbara, they have all received numerous citations related to living in their vehicles, and all of the citations under consideration were issued during the daytime, when the occupants were not inside the vehicle. In ruling on the matters in common in these four cases, the court considered whether citations for sleeping in a vehicle are more appropriately pursued as parking and standing violations governed by the California vehicle code (VC) rather than as criminal matters governed by the Santa Barbara municipal code (SBMC). In the decision reviewed here, the court realized that pursuing these as vehicle code matters would circumvent the defense of necessity by making these cases infractions, and thereby eliminating the provision of a municipal court trial and a public defender. The decision states:

It seems that the purpose for which the parking occurs as judged by the People is the determining factor for when the matter should be charged as parking violations and when it is to be charged criminally.

In all of these cases, the defendants are charged with illegally inhabiting vehicles that are parked. If they were not in the vehicle, the illegal use of the parked or standing vehicles could not be alleged. There were numerous other allegations that could have been filed under the circumstances… to which VC section 40200 by its terms could not possibly apply. These may have all had some proof problems that are different or brought the defendants charged within some legally recognized defense [i.e., the necessity defense] …. All these defendants are charged with the use of a parked or standing vehicle, therefore VC section 40200 applies (Memorandum of Decision, *People of the State of California v. Haralson, Cooper, Carver, and Burrows*, 2002).

The most significant implication of the above ruling for RVers is that citations are filed as violations of the vehicle code rather than the municipal code. This means that challenging a citation involves submitting a fee with a written appeal, rather than being assigned a public defender and holding a trial to determine guilt or innocence. In essence, this cuts out the stage of clarification and proceeds straight to remedy. Ignoring the citation leads to an eventual arrest warrant and potential towing of the vehicle.

Six months after this change in strategy, the city adopted a new amendment regulating overnight parking throughout the city and several ordinances specifically regulating parking on the waterfront. Overnight parking, previously illegal throughout the city from 3 a.m. to 5 a.m., was extended from 2 a.m. to 6 a.m. On the waterfront, all personal property was banned from parking spaces and all vehicles over thirty-five feet in length were prohibited, with the exception of twenty-three oversized vehicle spaces distributed across the five waterfront lots. The combined impact of these new ordinances is that all vehicles within the city, particularly those in the downtown area, are at increased risk of citation based on appearance and accoutrements, size, and location. Prior to the implementation of these ordinances, city police launched an information campaign to alert RVers of the ordinance changes. Flyers marked "WARNING: New RV Parking Restrictions" were distributed to all RVs in the waterfront area. Most RVers viewed this as a request to leave the city. Vehicle counts, discussed earlier, show that the number of large RVs (over thirty-five feet) declined from thirty in 2002 to one vehicle in subsequent years. The number of regular-sized RVs (twenty to thirty feet) plummeted in 2003 but rebounded to approximately forty-five vehicles in 2004, roughly the same number found in 2002. Since many RVers could not comply with the new regulations, more than fifty vehicles were ticketed and towed. Those living in smaller vehicles also declined from 2002–2004. Yet, smaller vehicles as well as regular-sized RVs can "slip into the neighborhoods" or scatter to outlying areas where the restrictions do not apply or where they will be less visible.[3]

If We Build It, Will They Come?

Because of the increase in RV activity and the subsequent legal backlash, the Committee for Social Justice urged the Santa Barbara City Council and County Board of Supervisors to provide legal parking spaces for residential vehicles. Based on a program operating successfully in Eugene, Oregon, the committee suggested that a similar program be adopted locally, allowing up to three vehicles per site to park from 7 p.m. to 7 a.m. in designated areas. Examining the feasibility of such a program in Santa Barbara meant evaluating the similarity of the two communities. The city appointed a Task Force on Vehicle Dwelling and sent representatives from the Planning Division and the Police Department to Eugene to collect information and make recommendations. Although the two communities are similar in terms of population size and square mileage, the most significant difference is in quality of life. Santa Barbara, the report states, may not be able to accept the same "quality of life compromises" that Eugene has managed to.

After months of deliberation, the task force made three primary recommendations: (1) provide an RV park or parks and develop alternative forms of affordable housing, including single-rent occupancy (SRO) units; (2) provide linkage to social services; and (3) develop no new enforcement until adequate provisions have been made. These recommendations were meant to be considered as part of an "RV package" to be adopted in tandem. Instead, they were considered separately. The city council flatly refused to approve the third recommendation; a halt in enforcement. As was shown in the previous section, enforcement procedures were swiftly implemented, resulting in a decrease in the number of larger vehicles, particularly in the waterfront area. The police were also given new tools for enforcement that regulate the location and duration of RV parking.

Deliberations on the development of an RV park were lengthy and inconclusive. Eleven locations were identified as possible sites, with a list of thirty-seven possible rules and regulations. Among the issues to be decided were how many vehicles a site would hold, whether there should be multiple sites, and whether sites are intended for 24-hour use or restricted to nighttime parking. In addition, it was not clear how much of a "program" would be needed on-site. As stated, the working goal was to provide stability for RV owners so that they could "make positive changes in their lives." Although RVers were a part of the task force, they were not included in making either program decisions or site restrictions. In fact, these decisions were largely decided by county staff who admittedly had little to no knowledge of the daily requirements of this population. Despite the failed negotiations for an RV park, a local nonprofit organization received permission to pursue a parking program that would operate out of church and nonprofit parking lots. The creation of this program is the focus of the following chapter.

In addition to the creation of a program to serve RVers, the Committee for Social Justice filed suit against the city, arguing that any new citations affecting citywide parking would need to be posted. This presented an obstacle for the city, as appropriate signage needed to be created and posted at all city entrances and exits. Even then, the enforcement problems continued as RVers returned to the waterfront lots. Making RVers a project resulted in much more serious legal problems than RVers previously had to contend with. Although on the face of it, an infraction is not as serious as a misdemeanor, the new classification eliminates the legal support RVers received through the Committee for Social Justice and makes paying the fine the first step in resolving the conflict.

Conclusion

This chapter views regulation, at least in part, from the perspective of police officers, who have the task of regulating homeless people. Without the tools necessary to pursue long-term solutions, officers who make individuals or groups of people a "project" do so by selectively enforcing existing laws, by repeatedly issuing minor citations, by harassing homeless people, or by finding creative ways to move them out of an area. These kinds of regulation are common for homeless people to endure, regardless of where they sleep. People living in their vehicles have an in-between status as they are thought of as on the margins of homelessness. They overlap with homeless people in the sense that where they sleep is seen as inappropriate, illegitimate, and perhaps illegal. Yet, they also overlap with those in apartments as the explicit suggestion is that they should pursue shelters or apartments as an alternative to the vehicle. It is important to note that in many jurisdictions, including Sonoma and Santa Cruz counties, people living in their vehicles do not rise to the level of a project and are able to avoid regulation.

Regulating homeless people shows the extent to which their mere presence in public space can create a problem both for the officers charged with eliminating their presence and for homeless people unwilling or unable to brave the shelter or the street. Although vehicles offer a private place to conduct otherwise public activities, the visibility of the vehicle (like the accoutrements that unsheltered homeless people carry with them—a bed roll, a shopping cart, a wagon) still presents a problem. Vehicles themselves are also subject to regulation, presenting additional opportunities for officers to remove homeless people from public view. Making people who live in their vehicles a project means further marginalization, as well as long-term legal consequences that make transitioning out of homelessness even more difficult. The risks of becoming a project include not only stress, but the possibility of losing the vehicle and facing life in the shelters or on the streets.

Using Van Maanen's stages of affront-clarification-remedy shows how little opportunity there is for homeless people to avoid citation and, more broadly, to challenge the idea that they are responsible for their own homelessness. Being visible in public is itself an affront whose remedy is removal. When RVers are confrontational, it underscores the idea that they are unreasonable, illogical, and culpable. Although this chapter details some of the more punitive aspects of regulation, as the "RV problem" became a citywide project, the chapter that follows examines the programmatic aspects of regulating RVers and homeless people.

Notes

[1] During my ride-alongs with police officers in Sonoma, Santa Cruz, and Santa Barbara counties, I encountered several instances of enforcement involving violations of the open container law. These involved both individuals and "drinking camps." But only once did I witness the destruction of property during routine policing of homeless camps, known as "jungles," in Santa Barbara. To be fair, even this does not amount to a sweep because it involves only one camp, but it demonstrates how aggressive policing and selective enforcement apply to homeless people. The following example is taken from my field notes.

> We pulled off the road in our SUV and there were two cop cars on the opposite side of the esplanade. There was nothing visible from the street except a small break in the bushes. We climbed over a small chain link fence and Officer X held out his hand to help me climb over. We had to duck to about half-height to go down a short and

winding tunnel of brush to get to the camp. There was a woman, who X referred to as a "hooker" sitting on top of a cooler in handcuffs. It smelled as if she just wet herself or as if the toilet was close to the camp. She twitched and jittered her legs up and down as if she could not keep still.

There were two cops—one short and one tall—going through their stuff—a large tent and various belongings. I guess there were three people at the campsite—two men and this woman. She said six or seven people were sleeping there but gave no names. The officers had already questioned her and reported to Officer X that she said she had diarrhea and her period. He said that was too much information. The short cop told Officer X that one of the guys just drank a cap full of heroin when they walked up. They also found a bunch of needles and some heroin in the tent.

They continued to go through everything in the tent and the stench was horrible. The woman was quiet for a minute although it was clearly hard for her. Officer X tossed a knife to the tall officer so that he could tear the tent open with it. I asked what the procedure was, if they pour bleach on the stuff or what. The officers proceeded to do so and said it was a welcome relief from the smell.

[2] In Herbert's (1997) discussion of territoriality, policing, and the Los Angeles Police Department, he notes that spaces are defined in situ, on the basis of interpreting the public/private boundary and the officer's rights in transgressing it. Policing on the basis of the activities of sleeping and camping relies on gaining access to the private space of the vehicle. To cite residential vehicles for these offenses, local police rely on what Herbert (1997, 52–53) calls "pooping and snooping," or the creative use of probable cause to transcend the boundaries between public and private space.

[3] Many RVers and people living in cars and vans wish to remain hidden. This is easier to do in smaller vehicles, but I did encounter a number of people who indicated that they were able to "pass" as tourist vehicles and avoid regulation. In one particular case, a woman and her husband, both of whom were employed in the waterfront area, said that they moved their vehicle regularly, kept their windows open, and kept possessions out of sight. They had been living in Santa Barbara for four months when I interviewed them and had not received any tickets for sleeping and camping.

5

Service Provision and Programming

Emergency shelters are billed as the first step toward recovery, rehabilitation, and the possible transition to permanent housing. Yet they are often ineffective in helping homeless people make this transition. Leonard Feldman (2004) characterizes emergency shelters as providing "bare life" provisions; William DiFazio (2006) describes them as offering food and cold storage. Emergency shelters often do not take into account the disparate relationship between behavioral compliance and housing safety; between what shelters require of clients and what they provide. Shelters offer protection from the elements and from regulation but require adherence to rules and regulations as prerequisites for entry. When the reward for compliance is as meager as a cot in a warehouse, many decide that the price is too high.

The linear residential treatment (LRT) model of service provision espoused by the continuum of care (CoC) offers emergency shelter as the first stage in the recovery/rehabilitation process. This model has undergone significant critique through the Housing First initiative. Housing First suggests that the stepwise transition from emergency shelter to permanent supportive housing is ineffective in the sense that many homeless people do not want or need to go through this progression and that it, in fact, perpetuates the cyclical, episodic nature of homelessness (Pearson, Montgomery, and Locke 2009). Housing First also emphasizes safety over scrutiny and behavioral compliance as the appropriate first step in moving homeless people toward rehabilitation, access to needed services, and the transition to permanent housing.

Some municipalities have moved to a "triage" approach in which more time and resources are spent at the "front door," assessing need to determine which housing solution is most appropriate and sustainable.[1]

Both triage and Housing First approaches understand that housing and supportive services need to be tailored to the needs of individuals and families as consumers and delivered together as a service delivery package. Although the idea of the CoC is that all homeless people make a stepwise transition to permanent housing, where they enter the continuum must also be flexible. The LRT model is a "one size fits all" solution that subjects an already struggling population to additional stress, which exacerbates rather than alleviates existing problems. Combine this with squalid provisions and societal marginalization and you have a recipe for disaster. Inverting this model so that housing is provided as a first step has proven successful in inspiring rehabilitation and a transition to housing stability.

In her comparison of street living with emergency and private shelters, Gwendolyn Dordick (1997) demonstrates that there is community—albeit potentially violent, misogynistic, and prone to addiction—that exists on the street. Private shelters, by contrast, replace feelings of community with a fear of shelter staff and a desire to at least appear as if one is following the rules and being loyal to the institution. Emergency shelters are somewhere in between as they too require adherence to rules and regulations but also allow for the culture of the street and various forms of street justice to hold sway. For many homeless people, shelters represent a loss of control and community, and resisting shelter by surviving on the street means consciously objecting to the idea that there is a proper place for homeless people that involves scrutiny, regulation, and compliance (Wagner 1993). Other forms of resistance focus on occupying public spaces (Wright 1997) and on changing regulation practices so that homeless people are not targets for enforcement.

Whether homeless people need programs and what those programs consist of is still contested, as is what type of housing is most appropriate. This chapter examines the process through which a new program to serve people living in their vehicles was designed and implemented. It examines the NIMBY sentiments raised when municipalities consider where to locate a particular service or program. It also looks at the political process through which a parking program for RVers was vetted and approved, and offers an in-depth qualitative look at the service situation as an organizing moment that identifies homeless clients and affects the service they receive.

As I argued in the previous chapter, homeless people are an *a priori* social category that brings to mind stereotypical images of the "bag lady" carrying her possessions in a shopping cart, the "wino" with the scraggly beard drinking out of a paper bag, or the unkempt person panhandling for change. Based on isolated rather than representative experiences with or understandings of homeless people, these images not only evoke fear and loathing but also shape service provision in terms of where social services are located and how service seekers are expected to behave in order to receive service. Deference and repentance are expected modes of behavior for homeless people who want access to services including shelter. The proper place for homeless people is therefore literal and figurative and involves where homeless people should be as well as how they should act.

The previous chapter examined some of the problems involved in regulating homeless people in public places. This chapter follows that discussion by examining how shelters and programmatic services for homeless people are considered the most appropriate solution. It tracks the formation of the Safe Parking Program to offer nightly parking to people living in their vehicles. Like the more punitive side of regulation, the service side seeks to provide for homeless people as a way of controlling their behavior and putting or keeping them "in their place." This chapter explores the decision making process through which the Safe Parking Program was founded and examines how the program rules and guidelines were established. It also provides a firsthand look at service provision from my perspective as a staff member for ten months of this project. The methodological insights I gained from running this program form the basis of a reflexive, interactional critique that informs the second half of this chapter.

Creating the Safe Parking Program

The original proposal to allow RV parking in the city of Santa Barbara was brought to the city council and later to the County Board of Supervisors by the Committee for Social Justice, a local advocacy group, beginning in October 2000. Based on a successful parking program operating in Eugene, Oregon, the proposal argued for an amendment of the city's municipal code to permit recreational vehicle (RV) parking for overnight sleeping, in the following locations:

   1. Parking lots of religious and charitable institutions

   2. Business property

   3. Land controlled by public entities, including the city and county

To pursue the possibility of offering such a program in Santa Barbara, the city council sent one representative from the Planning Division and one from the Santa Barbara Police Department on a visit to Eugene in January 2001. The considerations emphasized by these officials focused on the restrictions and conditions a possible program might impose, including: prohibiting vehicle camping at the airport, at city parks, and at residential-only use properties (e.g. backyard or driveway camping); limiting the number of vehicles per site; limiting parking lot sizes; and developing a screening procedure for potential clients. City officials also cautioned that "there are differences in the political, environmental and cultural backdrop of the two regions. Where Eugene managed to accept many issues, Santa Barbara may not resign itself to the same degree."

In addition to pursuing the Safe Parking Program at the city level, advocates brought their proposal to the County Board of Supervisors in February 2001. Six months later, after a successful review by the Human Relations Commission, the recommendation included adopting an ordinance to allow for overnight RV parking in church and nonprofit parking lots. County staff were also ordered to return to the board within sixty days with a draft of the new ordinance and a program description or progress report. On October 23, 2001, the County Board of Supervisors received the official Status Report on Recreational Vehicle Overnight Parking and Sleeping, which suggested adopting a resolution to allow overnight sleeping in vehicles on privately owned sites or religious, charitable, and philanthropic institutions, and also suggested pursuing other legal overnight sleeping alternatives. The resolution passed, although the county also stipulated that parallel actions be taken by the City of Santa Barbara in order to make the resolutions effective as adopted. To implement this resolution and allow parking on religious and charitable or philanthropic lots in the county, the following recommended restrictions were submitted:

*No more than three occupied vehicles be allowed on any given night.

*The religious or charitable and philanthropic institution has sole control and use of a parking lot on its premises to be used for this purpose.

*The vehicle occupants have the consent of the institution that owns and operates the property.

*A set back of at least fifty feet is provided between the vehicles and neighboring residential uses.

*Sanitary facilities approved by the Health Officer of the County are available.

*No rent or other consideration is charged to or provided by the vehicle occupants.

*The vehicles are registered, motorized, and operative.

*The use of any given site would also require consistency with any applicable conditional use permit (CUP) for the site.

Discussion at the city level continued to focus on provisions and enforcement as central to any solution for RV dwellers. In January 2002, the city established the Task Force on Vehicle Dwelling to "consider the issues and problems of all parties affected by vehicle dwelling in the city and to identify mutually beneficial solutions in order to maintain and improve the quality of life for all residents." This would eventually mean offering ways of enforcing existing ordinances, implementing changes directed toward reducing or restricting the numbers and types of RVs, and offering provisions for those left on the street. Task force members included local police, advocates, homeless service providers, and two women living in their vehicles. After meeting six times from April to June 2002, the task force submitted the following recommendations to the city council:

A. Legal Overnight Parking Recommendations

    Create an RV park(s)

    Allow for dispersal siting

    Develop alternative forms of housing

B. Providing Social Services Recommendation

    Develop links with social service agencies and housing opportunities

C. Enforcement Recommendations

    No new rnforcement without adequate solutions

    90-day grace period before implementation of ordinance changes

In November 2002 the city council adopted two new ordinances and two resolutions related to RV parking. Together, the ordinances restrict RV parking during the hours of 2 a.m.—6 a.m., restrict waterfront parking to vehicles under thirty-five feet in length, and restrict the number of vehicles up to twenty feet in length, parked in designated spaces, distributed over the five waterfront parking lots. The new resolutions also allowed for the creation of the Safe Parking Program to provide parking in dispersed sites in church and nonprofit parking lots. Although a faith-based service organization agreed to administer the program, no specific links to or provisions for housing or other services were developed, and no alternative housing in the form of additional Section 8 vouchers, SRO housing, or an RV park, ever materialized.

The city council waited ninety days before the ordinance changes took effect and the Safe Parking Program was up and running. They also established a one-year sunset clause, after which the Safe Parking Program would undergo a mandatory review. A public hearing was held on November 12, 2002, to introduce and adopt, by reading of title only, the redrafted ordinances and resolutions. In preparation for this meeting, citizen groups wrote to the city council expressing their frustration with RV owners parked close to exclusive properties and presumably diminishing their value. One of the general partners of a downtown apartment complex, "worthy of Santa Barbara beautiful awards," suggested that vehicle living "will inhibit future development in the neighborhood, reduce rental and property values, and may become life threatening to the people who work in the area." With over fifty letters and e-mail messages similarly condemning RV living as dangerous and detrimental to housed citizens, enforcement rather than provision became the primary focus.

Letters like the one cited above make it clear that, in the public imagination, RVers are similar to the general homeless population in the sense that they are not only considered dangerous but should be banned from the waterfront area in all but small and highly mobile quantities, and restricted from parking on city streets. The Safe Parking Program was the only one of four possible provisions offered to those living in their vehicles. Originally administered by a Catholic nonprofit organization, this program allowed up to three vehicles to park in church and nonprofit parking lots on an overnight basis only, with some restrictions. Maintaining this program involved not only screening clients but also establishing new parking sites, and presenting various aspects of the program to local government and nonprofit groups for program funding as well as specification and review.

Early Implementation

The political decision making process outlined above resulted in the development of the Safe Parking Program, operable in specified city and county lots. Creating this program from scratch, and without any oversight or suggestions from people living in their vehicles beyond task force participation,[2] meant that several false starts preceded the development of a working program. The first problem in putting the idea of the Safe Parking Program into practice was that neither the staff nor the program itself were tailored to meet or identify client needs. Specific programmatic elements were agreed to yet impossible to enforce, jeopardizing the program in the long term. Finally, as discussed throughout this chapter, staffing this program was done in an ad hoc fashion in the sense that the position of program coordinator was ill devised and neither offered nor required training or prior experience.

The organization that initially agreed to oversee the development of the program split responsibilities between an administrative lead, responsible for negotiating the design and operation of the program with city and county authorities, and a part-time staff person responsible for the day-to-day operation of the program. Poor communication between administration and staff resulted in the initial and ongoing violation of several program guidelines. The first of these was the requirement, stipulated in the ordinance, that RVs participating in the program be equipped with working sanitary facilities, or that such facilities be provided by the host site and approved by the Health Officer of the county. While administrators agreed to this condition, staff members were not instructed to have vehicles inspected or to ensure that bathrooms were provided on site. Instead of either changing the ordinance to fit the program or attempting to provide or ensure bathroom facilities for all clients, this became one of several rules that was routinely violated in practice.

Presenting a "good face" in public meetings helped push the program through local government, but it did not take into account the needs of the client population, or the difficulty of convincing churches or nonprofit organizations to provide bathroom access. In addition, the staff position was ill-designed to serve a nightly RV population. Working 9 a.m. to 5 p.m., for example, does not offer much oversight for clients who arrive after 7 p.m. and leave at 7 a.m. In addition, there was some confusion about the overall purpose of the program and need for case management. The program coordinator was initially in charge of managing the actual lots and parking permits. Other aspects of the program were vague: should clients be directed toward permanent housing, treatment for addiction or mental illness, or merely offered safe parking? These questions would remain long after the program was established and would often be decided by the person running the program, creating inconsistencies over time and a subjective, idiosyncratic approach to service.

In April 2004, because of funding problems, a nonprofit counseling center took over the administration of the Safe Parking Program. Yet, because clients had never been required to complete an intake form or sign a release of information, counseling staff were initially unable to obtain the paperwork necessary to determine the names of the clients currently in the program. Because of my interest in this population and because there was no one else willing to act in this capacity, I became the "Homeless Outreach Coordinator" for the Safe Parking Program in June 2004, without training or access to client files. Although the counseling center officially ran the program, my office was located off-site in the Salvation Army offices and was equipped with a computer, but no telephone or Internet access. I typically held open office hours and saw clients by appointment. I was also given a cell phone, which I was expected to answer at all times. In short, I inherited a great responsibility and made many mistakes. Aside from the original list of twelve rules and regulations, there were no program guidelines to follow to interview new clients and determine program eligibility. I also, as indicated above, had no information on any of the clients participating in the program.

Over the course of the ten months during which I ran the program, I typically saw from eighty to 100 clients per month, excluding repeat clients. The program was comprised of ten parking sites distributed across city and county lots, with a total of forty spaces. For new clients, I issued a one-week parking pass and required that they report back for an incrementally longer renewal, initially doubled to two weeks. I interviewed them on the condition of the site, whether or not they were actually parking there, and any potential problems that arose while parking. Presuming no problems had arisen, I issued a new pass and welcomed clients who had specific needs related to accessing services or vehicle repairs to drop in during my office hours or make an appointment. Of course, the resources at my disposal to assist clients did not begin to meet the diverse needs they presented. In addition, many clients did not want to access permanent housing or other services of any kind.

I began this program with the understanding that homeless people often refuse services or are uninterested in pursuing them because of the stringent requirements and the stigma that goes with seeking service. I also began with no mental health training of any kind, no job assistance training or ability to offer employment services, and no connection to the city housing authority or other housing program. My primary goal was to offer safe parking with low threshold entry requirements and to treat people living in their vehicles with respect. Using the requirements necessary to establish legal ownership and operation of the vehicle, I required all clients to produce a current license, registration, and insurance as minimum credentials required for entry. These credentials were photocopied and kept on file, and clients were required to sign a waiver allowing for the receipt and disclosure of personal information. They then received a list of twelve rules and regulations, which they were required to sign, indicating their compliance. Their signed form was then kept on file. Clients were given a map and directions to the parking site, a permit listing the dates they could park there legally, and the specific site hours. Since the program only offered nightly parking, clients were required to move their vehicles daily.[3]

Becoming a Gatekeeper

Overseeing the Safe Parking Program offered insight into the world of staff members in homeless service occupations and the service situation itself as a routine feature of life for homeless people. Becoming a staff member placed me in a different relationship with homeless people than I had encountered prior to this appointment, when I was conducting field work. Instead of merely spending my days with homeless people, I was now a gatekeeper, in charge of meting out services or denying them. There was, in other words, a transaction happening that I had to manage. Being in this new role allowed for a comparison between the population of RVers who parked along the waterfront and in the shelter neighborhood versus those who I had never met before but who wanted access to the Safe Parking Program. In the section that follows I describe the basic stages of the service situation to examine the behavioral expectations placed upon homeless people entering a program. Although these stages are described with respect to the Safe Parking Program, they are also broadly applicable to homeless service situations. I examine the interactional components of the service situation and offer ethnographic examples of how such interactions played out in the field.

The Service Situation

> I call upon all men to bear witness that he is not as he appears but is otherwise and in essence of a lower species (Garfinkel 1956, 421).

Homeless people seeking service are expected to behave in ways that are sanctioned by authority. This can mean filling out an intake form, passing a breathalyzer test, following or promising to follow the rules, or appearing docile or deferent. Meeting these requirements means that, barring other categorical restrictions that specify membership in a specific population, such as women in the case of a women's shelter, those who adhere to program guidelines are admitted. Those who are not part of the population served, who do not conform to the rules, or who do not appear docile or deferent are at greater risk of being refused service or being monitored once admitted. Yet entry into a program is also determined by intangibles like personal preference, which can shape long-term participation and, possibly, the transition to permanent housing.

Like the stages of affront, clarification, and remedy through which police classify potential perpetrators (Van Maanen 2006), putting people into programs also involves a process of determining what type of person they are and whether or not they should be admitted into service. The first stage of this process is the *presentation,* which can involve an intake interview or merely showing up for service at a service agency. This initial presentation is a key feature of whether the individual will be admitted to or deemed worthy or in need of service. The second stage of being put into a program is *assessment.* This involves determining whether the person fits the program criteria and judging whether she can adhere to behavioral guidelines, both explicit and implicit. The third stage is the *placement or trial period,* during which the individual is admitted to the program but monitored to be sure she continues to conform to program guidelines and to see that she moves through the program in a timely fashion.

While each of these stages reaffirms the status hierarchy between staff member and homeless person, they also involve behavioral expectations that inform service interactions and service provision. The stages are also interdependent such that the initial presentation informs assessment and placement. It is also worth mentioning that, on the part of the homeless person seeking service, proceeding through these stages requires a great deal of sensitivity, self-awareness, knowledge of the program requirements, and some amount of guesswork. Because service providers are idiosyncratic in terms of what they prefer or expect, there is no one correct way for homeless people to present themselves (see Marcus 2008). Some providers want people who look as if they are in need of service whereas other providers want people who look clean and presentable. Similarly, how much to divulge on an intake interview is tricky, as disclosing alcohol or drug use can lead to immediate rejection from service or shelter, or a more intensely scrutinized trial period. Yet for programs that specialize in rehabilitating people addicted to drugs and/or alcohol, disclosure and repentance are par for the course. Negotiating all of the possible pitfalls of the presentation and assessment is particularly difficult for homeless people, who already feel the pain of stigmatization and who are often both marginalized and under duress. Once admitted to the program, the homeless individual is, in a sense, controlled by program and staff expectations. It is not always enough, for example, to follow the rules. One must also constantly monitor relationships with staff. The threat of getting "86'ed" from the program can become a way of ensuring behavioral compliance.

Presentation and Assessment

For the Safe Parking Program, the presentation and assessment stages proceed in tandem. To enter into service, potential clients simply show up and explain their needs. Because my official title was Homeless Outreach Coordinator, people came to see me for many reasons besides parking. Some merely presented themselves and asked questions about the Safe Parking Program but were unsure about their own participation. Most people came to see me to gain entry into the program, and I assessed whether they were ready and eligible to do so. The initial discussion typically focused on the rules of the program, the required credentials, and the location of the parking sites to determine if the program was a good fit. Although many of the sites were initially empty, the downtown sites filled up quickly and people seeking these locations were often out of luck, thus ending the presentation-assessment stage. Other clients did not want to submit to regular check-ins or adhere to the rules of the particular site or program and decided not to participate as a result. Although several clients had mental health or drug and alcohol issues, they were all coherent enough to manage the initial presentation. Because the program did not require a high degree of behavioral scrutiny, suspecting that a client used drugs or alcohol or had mental health problems was not enough for me to deny entry. Of course, this approach to service depended on who was running the program. During a follow-up visit to Santa Barbara, I met with the new Homeless Outreach Coordinator, who had a completely different approach to running the program. His approach, as I describe at the end of this chapter, would dramatically alter and in fact decouple the presentation from the assessment stage.

Without a valid license and current registration and insurance, applicants were denied entry to the program. Even for those admitted to the program, failure to maintain current paperwork or keep the vehicle in good working order could mean dismissal. Initially, there was no structured way to assist clients in securing or maintaining the minimum requirements for program entry. Thus, many went unserved. The program requirements in this case can be likened to requiring a valid picture ID to enter an emergency shelter. Without it, the person is denied entry, but if there is no way to assist potential clients in retrieving or obtaining it, there is no way for them to access emergency services. Eventually, a local philanthropist interested in assisting homeless people established a revolving loan fund to cover the cost of maintaining a current license, registration, and insurance, performing vehicle repairs, and assisting with the cost of moving into permanent housing. In a given month, as much as $1,500 was leant to homeless clients to perform vehicle repairs, including smog inspection and certificate fees. An additional $1,500 went toward establishing insurance, paying for new equipment like a generator, and renewal license fees.

Prior to the establishment of the loan program, approximately 10 percent of all applicants did not present the requisite paperwork and were turned away. One of the most difficult of these cases was a woman named Louella. She was 66 years-old and had been living in the back of a small pickup truck for eight months. When she arrived to ask about the program, she was fearful and deferent. She had wild, frightened eyes and spoke to me through her few remaining teeth. Louella explained that she wanted to participate in the program for safety reasons: "They (men) come knocking on my door almost every night where I'm parked and I'm afraid they're going to get in. I'm an old woman but that doesn't seem to bother them." When I asked her for her license, she explained, "Well, it's not my truck, I'm just borrowing it from a friend to sleep in. I don't drive." Without the ability to move the vehicle, it would present a liability in any of the program lots. It could be ticketed and towed or jeopardize the lot for others in the program. Knowing that, in addition to the fact that she was unable to produce the requisite paperwork, I turned her away. I explained the situation and told her that if she was able to secure a license and prove that the vehicle was registered and insured, I would let her in. She left and thanked me but returned several weeks later, with the same story, and I turned her away a second time. I found this difficult both because her story was haunting and because she was "deserving" in the sense that I did not really consider her a threat to the program and did not see her as someone who, once admitted, would cause trouble or violate the rules.

In another case, a potential client was someone I met while conducting field work at the local emergency shelter. Everyone called him "Indian Lee." He lived in a small RV with his 10 year-old son. When he found out that I was in charge of the Safe Parking Program, he called to get more information and see what sites were available. Knowing that he would be a bad fit for the program because of his drug use and because he was patently against the rules and regulations associated with shelter use, I was nonetheless obligated to explain how it worked and what sites had empty spaces. The only downtown lot available was a religious nonprofit lot that required occupants to check out a key so that they could lock the gate in the evening and unlock it again to leave in the morning. "Aw, darlin,' I've had enough of the lock up," he said when I explained the rules of the site. Like Lee, several potential clients elected not to participate in the program after hearing the requisite rules and available sites.

Distinguishing between Louella and Lee helps elucidate the unspoken rules of the service situation. Program rules are written to be applied wholesale, such that someone can be a "good fit" for the program, like Louella, but lack the requisite paperwork and be turned away. Lee, in comparison, had the requisite paperwork and yet was someone I considered a "bad fit."

Although rules are intended to cut across personal preference and bias in determining need, their "one size fits all" nature does not capture the complexity of the service situation or service needs. Even so, staff members who enforce the rules have a great deal of flexibility. One case manager I spoke with who ran a transitional shelter for families explained it this way: "There is the letter of the law and the spirit of the law. If you know a client, have seen her every night, know she's out working and comes in at seven, but one night she doesn't have her pass, what are you gonna do?" When confronted with Louella and Lee, adhering to the spirit of the law would have meant bending the program rules for Louella and patently denying Lee, despite the official program guidelines.

The following case illustrates the implicit bias that taints the nature of service provision and is a feature of the service situation that homeless people attempt to manage and that they often resent.

One day, a man named Paul arrived at the Sally and asked to speak with me. I went to the waiting area to greet him and looked at him through the glass window, sizing him up. He was clean and well groomed, almost slick compared with most of my clients. This put me off. I greeted him, shook his hand, and made small talk with him as we walked back to my office. When we sat down, I expected him to tell me why he was there, to launch into his official story about why he needed parking and why he was living in his vehicle. He did none of these things, and instead began asking me about the details of the program; which churches were involved, how we identified sites, and so forth. I prompted him to give me his story by asking, "So, what can I do for you?" Rather than discuss homelessness, he just talked about how he came to live in Santa Barbara. When he mentioned the local city college, it finally dawned on me that he was not a client but a professor who had called previously, was interested in homelessness, and had come in to talk.

This experience was eye opening for me because it showed me that I expected potential clients to do all of the emotional work of being deferent while also being forthcoming. When Paul failed to take the lead in describing his current situation and need for parking, I was annoyed and confused. I also realized that I had come to treat clients in a different way than I would treat anyone else, including homeless people I had met while conducting field work. With potential clients, there was an agenda. They wanted something from me, and I put them through the stages of presentation and assessment in order to get it. For men like Paul who I saw as potential clients, not adhering to behavioral expectations was not only frustrating but could affect placement in terms of both location and duration of the trial period.

Placement or Trial Period

The placement or trial period means conditional acceptance into the program. Depending on how well I knew clients or how well they adhered to behavioral expectations during the presentation and assessment stages, they were given a parking pass that ranged in duration from one week to one month. When the pass expired, they were required to make an appointment or drop in during office hours to renew. This stage allows for an examination of both short-term and long-term placements and for a comparison of new clients with regulars. Because of my previous field work conducted with RVers in the immediate shelter neighborhood, it also allowed me to assess the differences between those who were willing and able to adhere to program guidelines and those who were not.

In the initial placement stage, clients were required to report in on a regular basis to assess their experience in the program and address their questions, concerns, or needs. One of the first placements I arranged was for a man named Brian and his mother, Nelda. Brian described himself as "second-generation homeless" and told stories about growing up in vehicles all over the Southwest and "ghost towning" to find and sell antique artifacts from abandoned desert towns. Nelda had been retired for years and had been up and down the California coast, currently staying in Santa Barbara to be close to Brian. She panhandled in the shopping areas to make extra money and took care of two mixed-breed dogs that lived in her car with her. Brian had a thirty-five foot RV that they used to sleep in at night.

I originally issued Brian a one-week permit to park in a religious lot in the downtown area. The site was large enough to house his RV and Nelda's car without creating a nuisance or blocking the entrance or exit. At the week's end Brian reported in, and I asked him, "How's it going, do you like it over there?" "You wouldn't believe what's going on down there," he replied. "They leave the doors open all the time, anyone can just walk in." "Really?" I responded. "But how do you know, did you patrol the area?" "Well, yeah," he said. "I like to make sure it's safe and secure over there after dark. I just basically do security patrols." "But does the church know you're doing that, I mean, do they *want* you to?" I asked. "Carol [the site manager], she knows," he replied. "I ran into her the other morning when we were leaving and told her." Before I could verify this, I received a frantic call at 1 a.m. because of a break-in at the church. Apparently, Brian discovered an open door and broken glass and called 911. The police arrived and made sure the church was secure before departing.

Although technically Brian had been protecting the church, the site manager was annoyed by his patrols: "That's not really what he's there for, is it? I mean, I think it's nice what he's trying to do but he's creating more work for us and I don't know that I want him back there." After hearing this, I called Brian in for a meeting and asked that he cease conducting sweeps of the property and focus on other things like employment and taking care of his vehicle, pets, and Nelda, all things he identified as his top priorities. He promised that he would, and the next few weeks passed without incident. Then one night, while checking to see which sites were full, I noticed that Brian had run an extension cord from an exterior wall of the church to his vehicle. When I asked him what it was for, he said it was to power his television. I told him that he was violating the rules of the program, and he removed the cord.

The next time I spoke with the site manager, she indicated that several neighbors had complained about the noise from the radio and television that was coming from the RV. As a result, the church considered withdrawing from the program unless we could come up with a workable solution that would appease the neighbors. The first step was ensuring that Brian and Nelda would not return. I subsequently dismissed them from this particular site and suspended them from the program temporarily, until a more appropriate site could be found. I also negotiated with the church to change the rules of admission to allow women only to park at this site. Altogether, Brian and Nelda participated in the program for three months before getting dismissed; after this incident, they did not seek service again.

Occasionally, because of the relationship we had developed, Brian would drop in during office hours to ask me about a citation he had received or to discuss his current parking situation. During one of these meetings, he told me that he had been thinking about the police constantly, almost obsessively. "I think about what it would feel like to stand up to the police, you know, like go up to Officer X and blow his head off. I can't get it out of my mind." Not knowing what to say to him, I asked, "Well, Brian, do you want to talk to somebody about this? I mean, I don't want you to feel out of control." "Yeah, but I do feel that way right now," he responded. "Well, do you want me to call the PHF unit?" I asked. The Psychiatric Health Facility, known as the PHF or "Puff Unit," admits clients who pose a threat to themselves or to others. "Puffing" someone was a last resort because of the expense and the seriousness of the situation. In Brian's case, being held for seventy-two hours helped him get his aggression under control and prompted him to seek regular psychiatric care.

Other clients had mood disorders that were so severe that they were unable to work, and the symptomatic manifestation of their disorder eventually jeopardized their parking placement. One client named Joe had been in the program for several months when I became the coordinator. He lived in an old station wagon that he had stacked with possessions, filling the entire back seat and cargo area and strapped to the roof of the car. Every night when he arrived to park in one of the largest sites on the border of the downtown area, he would meticulously take all of his possessions out of the car, lay them on the ground, and repack everything. He had a stack of plastic containers that he used for this purpose. Every once in a while, Joe called with an "emergency situation," which was typically a repair for the vehicle or a question about accessing additional services. He called at all hours of the day and evening and often sounded scared and confused. Sorting out what the issue was and how I could be of assistance proved difficult and stressful. Joe continued to participate in the program for several months.

The only other client that parked in the lot with Joe was nicknamed "Hannibal" because he had gotten into a fight with Louie and bit him in the stomach. His real name was Ed, and although I had met him during field work, he was not a regular fixture in the shelter or the neighborhood. Ed had already confided that was a Viet Nam veteran and still suffered the effects of a subdural hematoma.[4] Yet, until I ran the Safe Parking Program, I did not realize that he was also bipolar, which meant that much of the time he was calm and pleasant and would talk to me about his Catholic faith or about the blue jays he fed. Occasionally, though, Ed would arrive at my office ready to yell at me about whatever was frustrating him on that particular day. During these episodes, he was red-faced and frantic, his movements and speech were erratic, and any attempt to calm him down resulted in further escalation. As would be expected, whenever Ed was in a situation that increased his stress level, his manic episodes would gain intensity and frequency.

Ed and Joe parked in the same parking site close to downtown and coexisted for months without incident. Then one day Ed needed to jump-start his RV and he approached Joe's station wagon to ask him for help. Joe, who had been sleeping at the time, was frightened and confused and did not offer to assist. Ed left him alone but became increasingly angry with him and began to approach him whenever the two were parked in the site. One night, he knocked on the window of Joe's vehicle several times and, as Joe described, "It seemed like he was looking for a fight because I wasn't doing anything, I was just sitting there and he charged up on me." Soon, both men began to complain to me about each other. Ed described Joe as unkempt and said that he was making a mess of the lot. Ed also said that he had contacted the site manager about this, which would have long-term implications for their participation in the program. Joe was convinced that Ed was out to get him and told me that he tried to stay away from him to avoid confrontation, but that it was nearly impossible because Ed sought him out constantly.

Sensing that this was a situation about to boil over, I contacted both of them and issued an official "no contact warning," which stated that neither man could initiate contact with the other. If either one violated this rule, they would be removed from the program. Within two weeks, I received complaints indicating that both men had violated the warning. In addition, the site manager indicated that because of this conflict, the church officials were no longer willing to participate in the program. Unlike the previous case, where I was successful in arguing for restricted usage, the manager of this site was adamant that the site should be closed for a probationary period of six months, after which we could negotiate the terms of reopening. Without any open parking sites in the downtown area, Ed and Joe were both instructed not to use their former lot and were offered parking in scattered site lots, all of which were within fifteen minutes of the downtown area. Neither one sought to continue in the program, but both continued living in their vehicles and parking on the street.

The cases of Brian and Nelda and Ed and Joe are similar, not only because mental illness plays such a prominent role but also because they underscore the need for comprehensive services and more intensive case management prior to and after site placement. Negotiating relationships with one another as well as with the site provider and surrounding neighbors proved too difficult for these clients to manage on their own. Both dyads lasted for between three to six months in their sites. Other clients lasted days and either did not use the site, did not return to renew their permits, or had vehicles that became inoperable. Other reasons for termination included the inability to adhere to the site guidelines involving parking location or entry/exit times, and failure to renew the permit.

Stasis or Transition

Clients who pass the initial placement and become long-term users are those who hold steady jobs or receive a monthly check. They also have either a housing voucher or are on the list to receive one, a gym membership, or use shelters or public shower facilities. They are able to perform some maintenance on the vehicle and can afford to access some amenities but do not earn enough to afford permanent housing. In addition, many suffer from depression, addiction, PTSD, medical and/or developmental problems, and a host of other issues. Several clients fell into this category and remained in the program for eight months to several years.

A woman named Elaine came in for an interview during my first month of employment and, because she met the minimum program requirements, was issued a permit. She eventually explained that she kept her gym membership current so that she had a place to shower and stay fit. She had a part-time job working at a T-shirt/souvenir shop on the pier. "They have no idea I'm doing this," she told me, referring to her employers. "If they did, I know I would get fired." When I asked her how difficult it was to maintain her cover, she said, "Well, I go to the gym so I look clean, but I get real paranoid. There's actually this guy at the gym who has been following me around." Many of our conversations focused on how to avoid attention or how to tell if undue attention was being paid. Yet, I was ill-equipped to make an official diagnosis of paranoia or other mood disorder, or to assist Elaine in developing any kind of treatment plan. I offered her access to treatment facilities, including counseling, but she consistently refused because she did not have an existing relationship with any of the staff and was generally skeptical about pursuing shelter and service opportunities. In addition, the stigma associated with mental illness made it difficult to suggest services in a nonjudgmental or nonthreatening way. Despite her reported paranoia, Elaine was able to manage long-term placement without any clashes with neighboring vehicles, or other incidents.

It was, however, difficult to tell whether Elaine was clinically paranoid, suffering from trauma-induced PTSD, or if someone was, in fact, following her. There was virtually always someone who she came into regular contact with during the course of her week that she thought posed a threat. In one particular case, she mailed a copy of the local police blotter, with a letter, to my office. The newspaper reported that a "suspicious man" parked in an area close to Elaine's parking site had been found in possession of a glass narcotic pipe. In her letter, Elaine wrote, "This confirms what I suspected of that creep in the burgundy van who was parking on the dirt lot." "It's so important to keep up on the safety aspect of the parking program," she continued. And then, in a moment of candor, she wrote, "I've appreciated your helping me and talking to me more than you can imagine." I thought a lot about safety after Elaine's gentle admonition, yet the only safety measures in place to monitor sites were conducting nightly patrols and alerting local police to the program.[5] Elaine remained in the program until I left the area and never talked about transitioning out of it. Whenever I raised the subject, she told me that she just wasn't ready to live with people again.

Other clients traveled in and out of the area, usually drawn by employment or family ties, and contacted me for a parking permit when they were in town. Like Elaine, they were grateful to be treated with decency and respect. Such is the case with a man named Mike, who called himself a "shutterbug" and then explained that he actually made the small picture boxes to sell at county fairs, events, and parties. "I make a living," he said. "I don't live high on the hog, but I have my van and something I'm good at." Mike also told me that he suffered from sleep apnea and needed a generator to run his breathing equipment at night. Three months after meeting him, Mike's generator failed, and I issued a $300 loan to cover the cost of a replacement. Mike signed a loan agreement, indicating that he would pay $20 per month, without interest, until the loan was repaid.

Although he was not always up to date in his payments, Mike would send me a letter from wherever he was, with at least $20 enclosed. With one of these letters, he sent $40 and confided, "I finally made some money and restored confidence in myself." In addition to employment, Mike also traveled for health reasons, as he had a chronic heart condition and occasionally traveled to obtain quality treatment. Wondering how he could afford this, I asked, "Are you independently wealthy?" to which he replied with a smile, "I get along alright, you see, I haven't always been a homeless guy. I've got a little income from when I worked and I guess you could say I spend it wisely." Mike eventually repaid his loan and continued to drift in and out of the program until I left the area.

Other clients who can be described as "in stasis" are those who simply live in their vehicles and participate in the program but, for various reasons, do not seek to transition to apartment living. Neither Mike nor Elaine, for reasons including financial, medical, and psychiatric, could manage apartment living. They were also both unsure about pursuing it in the long term. As was also indicated by Brian and Nelda and Ed and Joe, Mike and Elaine make it clear that far more is needed in the way of services than mere parking provides. Should clients be encouraged to transition to permanent housing, or should they be allowed to live "in stasis" as long as they are safe and adhere to the rules of the program? How is this similar to the descriptions of the lethargy that goes along with shelter living that started this chapter?

Two men in particular illustrate the complex distinction between stasis and transition. Long-haired, tall, and tan, Joe and John were inseparable. They parked their RVs in the waterfront area and were known as "the Jesus twins." Both men were in their early fifties and had been diagnosed with Hepatitis C.[6] Both ended up pursuing permanent housing but followed very different paths to do so. Joe had been on the Section 8 waiting list for two years and was eventually awarded a voucher. I accompanied him to the housing office and assisted him with filling out the requisite paperwork and attending subsequent interviews. Once granted his apartment, aside from sending me a thank-you card and generous gift,[7] Joe disappeared. He was no longer parking on the waterfront, no longer spending time with John, and no longer living life in public.

John continued to live in his pickup camper and park along the waterfront until an electrical fire destroyed the camper shell. John was not hurt, but all of his possessions were destroyed. I assisted John in his pursuit of an emergency housing voucher, but he was reticent. "I love my truck, man, I don't think I can give it up yet, I mean, maybe it's not for me." I continued to encourage him to seek permanent housing, and just when I thought he was convinced, someone donated a camper shell that fit onto John's truck. He continued to participate in the Safe Parking Program and no longer talked about pursuing permanent housing. During one of my last visits with him, I asked how he felt about continuing to live in his vehicle versus apartment living. "I don't know, it's like, I don't really think about the apartment thing right now. The new shell fits on, it's comfortable, so I'm good."

Comparing "the Jesus twins" raises one big question: why did Joe transition and leave John in stasis? Perhaps Joe was better prepared for the transition, as evidenced by his pursuit of Section 8 housing. By contrast, John's transition would have been made under emergency circumstances, making it a forced choice. Although John acknowledged the relative comfort that apartment living would offer him, he was also incredibly nervous about changing his lifestyle. A primary reason for this is that he was able to maintain complete control over his vehicle and his surroundings and he saw apartment living as a potential threat. The Safe Parking Program protected him from nightly regulation and left him free to spend his days as he saw fit. Once he regained the comfort of his vehicle, he was reluctant to risk it for the unknowns of apartment living.

Transition Assistance

Whether or not clients transition to permanent housing depends, in part, on their interest in doing so and ability to produce the proper paperwork. Sustaining permanent housing depends on the client's ability to negotiate the terms of the rental, including relationships with the landlord and other renters. Another feature involved in making the transition is the support of program staff. Personal preferences and the overall approach to the administration of the Safe Parking Program had a direct effect on the likelihood of transition. This section examines several cases in which clients transitioned into permanent housing. It illustrates some of the differences between clients in terms of overall readiness to live in permanent housing and some of the differences between staff members' willingness and ability to assist clients.

Transitioning into permanent housing became a key goal of the Safe Parking Program, although there were no formal supports in place to assist clients in achieving this goal. Clients who transitioned typically did so on their own steam or with minimal help from program staff. They applied for Section 8 or city subsidized housing, found a shared apartment, saved their money and moved out of Santa Barbara, or found gainful employment and moved on. In a given month, I assisted two to four clients in applying for Section 8 or subsidized housing and pursuing housing when the voucher was granted. The number of people placed into permanent housing ranged from zero to four in a given month.

Margarite was a client who made the transition. I met Margarite within two months of becoming the program coordinator. She was 53 years-old and lived in her 1990 Ford Tempo. She had been doing so for eighteen months and had applied for subsidized housing prior to entering the Safe Parking Program. Margarite was granted a permit to park by the county food bank, which was halfway between the downtown parking sites and the more remote sites in Goleta and Isla Vista. She was one of the few clients who was almost always parked in the designated spot at the designated time, so I visited her frequently. Margarite kept her food in a cooler and would park early so that she could prepare dinner and relax before going to sleep. During one of our visits, Margarite told me that she was on the waiting list for city subsidized housing.

Before living in her vehicle, Margarite had lived in a house on the outskirts of Santa Barbara with her husband. Two years into their marriage he began an affair with a coworker. "I never thought I would be one of those women who just put up with it but I did for a while," she said. Eventually, her husband took his things and left her with the house and mortgage, which she could not maintain. So Margarite put her belongings into storage and moved into her car until she qualified for subsidized housing. When the letter arrived telling her that she was granted housing and had two weeks to sign a rental agreement, Margarite was beside herself with excitement. She came to my office half laughing and half crying, and showed me the letter.

Moving Margarite into her new apartment was another matter. To assist her with the move, I issued her a $1,065 loan that covered the cost of the security deposit for her apartment, rented a truck to retrieve her stored possessions, and hired two day laborers to help with the move. The total loan amount was a staggering debt for her. Because of her meager income and new expenses, the terms of the loan agreement were that she would pay it back at a rate of $20 per month, with no interest or other charges. Retrieving Margarite's possessions showed how established her life had been prior to living in her vehicle and participating in the Safe Parking Program. She had so much furniture, in fact, that it hardly fit into her new apartment. Yet once she was settled, like Joe, her program needs vanished. Although she still brought or sent in her $20 per month, there was nothing she needed from the program.

Margarite was successful in negotiating with her landlords and maintaining her apartment.

Other clients faced similar barriers to transition, either because of the ongoing cost of storing possessions or because they had become accustomed to life in the vehicle and needed additional assistance. The program coordinator who succeeded me was successful in placing some of the most difficult clients into housing. One long-term client named Jenny had been parking in one of the program lots since its inception. An articulate woman in her late fifties, Jenny was both lonely and verbose. During one of our many long conversations, she explained that she had lived in Washington state for years and still had a storage unit she maintained there. We frequently discussed the possibility of moving her into permanent housing, yet she insisted that retrieving her possessions was a prerequisite. Jenny had worked all her life and retired early. She received a monthly check of $865, which was enough to cover the storage fee, maintain her vehicle, pay for food and access to public showers, and take care of her cat. Although her storage unit presented what I viewed as an insurmountable roadblock, when I returned to Santa Barbara I was surprised to find that Jenny had moved into permanent housing. The new program coordinator explained that moving Jenny into housing meant loaning her $2,364 to drive a U-Haul to Washington and back, negotiating the rental agreement with her, assisting her with moving her possessions, and continuing to negotiate with the management company on her behalf. Despite all of the complications involved in assisting Jenny with this transition, she ended up paying $298 per month, with utilities included.

The final client I will describe illustrates the mixed feelings many clients have about moving into permanent housing. Mitchell is in his early sixties and had been living in his van in a downtown parking lot that required a key to enter. He was comfortable there and enjoyed life in his van. Eventually, the city built a new housing complex in the downtown area and the new Homeless Outreach Coordinator lobbied for particular clients to move in with Section 8 rental agreements. His dogged persistence resulted in several clients being placed into Section 8 units, including Mitchell. I visited with him after he had been in his new apartment for about one year and asked him how he liked it. Although he said he was comfortable, he also said he missed his van. "I can't get around," he said. "I used to drive everywhere, to Carpinteria, and just everywhere." "But this is pretty nice," I said. "Yeah, too nice for a homeless bum," he laughed. "But look at this," and he showed me his computer, which he used to listen to the news. "This keeps me busy."

The cases of Margarite, Jenny, and Mitchell demonstrate differing degrees of client readiness to transition into permanent housing. They also show that personal preference on the part of staff members figures largely into the administration of services. Because I viewed the obstacles involved in pursuing housing for Jenny as insurmountable, I did not assist her to the degree necessary to achieve permanent housing. In addition, the ongoing supportive services necessary to maintain permanent housing for clients ill-equipped to manage it was not, in my view, part of the Safe Parking Program. This limited view of the program did not take into account the need for both a flexible approach and a client-centered view of services that focused on individual needs rather than program guidelines.

My successor was not only persistent in his pursuit of client assistance, he was also more rigid in his interpretation of the program requirements. He required clients to produce two out of three credentials: a license, registration, or insurance. Yet he was far stricter about client behavior. Clients who were suspected of alcohol or drug use were not issued parking permits. This approach decoupled the stages of presentation and assessment, as many clients were turned away before they could produce the requisite paperwork. This is also controversial, as raising the bar at the initial point of seeking service means, perhaps, that those most in need are turned away.

Conclusion

This chapter illustrates the complicated nature of service provision. It shows the danger of creating a program that does not centralize client concerns, does not appropriately train staff members, and does not explicitly offer linkages to services outside of the program. Offering a reflexive look at what service provision entails demonstrates the training needed to offer appropriate services and the temperament needed to manage even the most difficult clients. Yet the Safe Parking Program also raises issues of behavioral compliance. To what degree should staff attempt to manage client behavior and urge the transition to permanent housing?

Imposing rules and regulations, although par for the course for most homeless service delivery, is a barrier for clients who are unwilling to submit. Yet, the problem with setting the bar too low is that clients will not be encouraged to make the transition to permanent housing or seek other services. Merely listening to clients, perhaps my one strength as a service provider, led to the discussion of goals and needs without imposing program restrictions. This approach was clearly limited, as several clients made the transition to permanent housing with a case manager who tirelessly offered assistance and was willing to create new features of the program. Although imposing program restrictions presents a barrier for homeless people seeking service, without them, the program lacks coherence and clients potentially remain in stasis.

The most significant gains made by the Safe Parking Program were that it legitimized vehicle living and offered protection from regulation for program participants. There were many potential clients who decided, after hearing the rules and regulations, that they were better off parking on city streets or attempting to "blend into the neighborhoods." For these clients, as well as those who participated in the program but were in stasis, maintaining autonomy and control over their living situation was more important than nightly protection or the comfort of an apartment. This is a central feature of vehicle living that, when combined with legal ownership, allows a degree of safety and stability unprecedented for those living on the street.

Becoming a staff member allowed me to track the similarities and differences between those who were willing to participate in the program and those who were not. Prior to this experience, when conducting field work among the homeless population, I did not have access to people living in their vehicles who chose to remain separate from those in shelters or on the streets. Rather than differences in personality type, this choice was born out of a desire to avoid the shelter neighborhood and the stigma associated with homelessness as a social category. Those who remained separate also had to negotiate access to resources including food and shower facilities, which the shelter provided.

Maintaining the ability to choose one's living situation is also a rejection of the idea that the proper place for homeless people is in a program. The punitive and protective sides of regulation have in common an approach to homeless people that treats them as subjects in need of assistance or correction. As a result, approaches to service that focus on understanding the lived experiences of homeless people and offering rather than requiring service are more likely to be effective. Providing this reflexive examination of how the Safe Parking Program was created underscores the opposition that communities face when attempting to offer services for homeless people. It also demonstrates the tension between wanting to preserve client autonomy while still encouraging transition.

Notes

[1] In 2008, the Special Commission Relative to Ending Homelessness in the Commonwealth of Massachusetts charged the Massachusetts Interagency Council on Housing and Homelessness with implementing the Regional Networks to End Homelessness Pilot. Ten regional networks were awarded funding to better coordinate services across regions and to expand best practices and test innovative approaches. The "triage" approach was tested in two of the ten pilot regions; South Shore and Worcester County. It is intended to offer rapid assessment and a customized treatment plan for all those entering shelter or service.

Prior to the pilot, families entering the shelter system in the South Shore region reported to the Department of Transitional Assistance (DTA), a state entity. Once shelter became available, families were required to move to whatever part of the state had empty beds. This meant a lengthy waiting process, extended motel stays, and being uprooted from friends, family, and schools. The pilot program changed this policy by offering families regional placements, provided that domestic violence did not force relocation. This change meant an overall reduction in cost, with families receiving rental assistance and continued services for the duration of the pilot. Individuals were also triaged upon entering shelter such that a rapid exit, rather than a stay-based treatment plan, was the first priority.

Funding for the pilot program lasted eighteen months. During the first eight months of the pilot, 360 families were assessed and kept local. An additional 319 families were moved into housing. A total of 385 homeless individuals successfully exited shelter and moved into housing, substance abuse treatment facilities, or other systems of care. See http://www.ppffound.org/documents/ichh_final_report.pdf.

[2] It is not unusual in Santa Barbara for the same handful of people to step forward and represent the homeless community. The two women invited to participate in the Task Force on Vehicle Dwelling are the "usual suspects" when it comes to hearing the voices of the homeless. Ironically, neither of them did, or ever would, use a program like the Safe Parking Program. Their participation in the task force was therefore more symbolic than truly collaborative.

[3] With the establishment of the Safe Parking Program, several nonprofits and religious organizations volunteered to participate. Others were contacted through cold calling. During these calls, I typically explained the purpose and functioning of the program and offered to meet with officials from the organization to give them additional information. During the ten months I served as Homeless Outreach Coordinator, I added two parking lots to the program, for a total of eleven parking lots with thirty-five spaces.

[4] Caused by a head injury, a subdural hematoma is a collection of blood on the brain. Symptoms can include confusion, headaches, lethargy, slurred speech, distorted vision, and weakness. Although these symptoms typically dissipate after treatment, seizures caused by a serious head injury can continue years after the initial trauma. Continued symptoms are also a sign that treatment may not have been effective and that the person is experiencing complications. See http://www.ncbi.nlm.nih.gov/pubmedhealth/PMH0001732/ and http://www.nlm.nih.gov/medlineplus/ency/article/000713.htm.

⁵ Alerting the Santa Barbara Police Department to the existence of the Safe Parking Program was risky. During the first training I conducted with officers on the Tactical Patrol Force, one of them quipped, "I guess we'll know where the problems are." For fear of regulation, I was reticent to provide them with a map of the program lots and instead described the purpose of the program and showed them the parking permits that we issued so that they could verify participation. Visits from the police were rare in program lots. Clients were instructed to cooperate with officers, display their permits prominently, and answer all questions. They were also given my cell phone number and told to call for verification as needed. For the duration of the program, I was never called because of police interaction with clients in any of the lots.

⁶ Hepatitis C is a viral disease that leads to inflammation of the liver. It is a blood-borne virus, not uncommon among homeless people. Modes of transmission include intravenous drug use, mother-to-infant transmission, unsafe medical practices, high-risk sexual behavior, and blood transfusion. The disease frequently leads to permanent scarring (cirrhosis) of the liver. Symptoms can include abdominal pain or swelling, fever, itching, jaundice, loss of appetite, nausea, and vomiting. The list of things people with Hepatitis C should stay away from is lengthy, as is the list of things they should do to manage the disease. Needless to say, it is difficult for homeless people to be careful about what they consume and go for weekly medical treatments. See http://www.ncbi.nlm.nih.gov/pubmedhealth/PMH0001329/.

Both Louie, discussed throughout this book, and Joe, one of the "Jesus twins," suffer from Hepatitis C. After reading about the disease and researching possible treatments, Joe began making his own form of medication brewed from herbal supplements and antioxidants. One day, after visiting him, he gave me a bottle of this medicine. "It's organic," he assured me, "with plants and herbs to help liver functioning. It won't hurt you." Knowing that he used it to manage Hepatitis C and knowing that Louie had the same disease, I took the bottle, with some trepidation, and offered it to Louie. Louie reported feeling markedly better after drinking it. He said it tasted terrible but helped manage his symptoms.

⁷ The number of gifts I received from clients in the Safe Parking Program, as well as from homeless people in the shelters and on the streets, is staggering. The list includes the Santa Barbara Surf Club sweatshirt Joe sent, handmade scarves, necklaces, clothing (used and new), and numerous cards. One of the cards came with a bar of chocolate. It read:

> Once again a huge "thank you!" for all you've done for so many of us "vagabundos." I wanted you to try my favorite Ecuadorian chocolate—you'll be a fan too. Every night I cuddle up under the beautiful comforter you gave me for Christmas. Gifts are so powerful as we remember the generosity of the people behind them.

6

Vehicle Living vs. Unsheltered Homelessness

The previous chapter examined service provision as a regulatory mechanism offering safety and legitimacy but requiring adherence to program rules. This chapter also examines the provisional side of regulation by looking at federal and local policies for identifying and serving unsheltered homeless people. It presents comparative data on the unsheltered populations in Sonoma, Santa Cruz, and Santa Barbara counties including an overview of the PIT count and CoC planning process. It also offers a qualitative profile of service provision to examine how well policy goals measure up to the lived experience of unsheltered homeless people and service providers.

Although this chapter focuses on emergency and outreach services, many homeless people would be better served through prevention and rapid re-housing, bypassing emergency shelter altogether. Nevertheless, and in lieu of adequate housing and services to implement a Housing First approach, outreach services and emergency shelter still serve a primary "front lines" function for unsheltered homeless people.

People living in their vehicles, as well as those on the streets, in abandoned buildings, and in other makeshift locations, are included in the "unsheltered" homeless category as defined by HUD. They represent a segment of the overall homeless population that typically seeks service and shelter at the emergency or entry level of the CoC. Unsheltered homeless people are particularly difficult to gather information on as they sleep in makeshift locations and often want to stay hidden for fear of regulation. These characteristics present a challenge for local and regional policy makers and service providers interested in assessing population demographics, service needs, and housing readiness. Yet data gathering is crucial, as it not only drives funding but is a way of planning for and delivering services that meet specific needs.

Concern with those at the entry level of the continuum is driven by two primary issues. One is the large number of unsheltered homeless people in California,[1] and the other is that emergency shelters are becoming more exclusive, "gate keeping" mechanisms that permit a select few entry and eventual transition (Wolch and Dear 1993; Padgett, Gulcur, and Tsemberis 2006). In order to move unsheltered homeless people through the CoC and on to self-sufficiency, they must be able to access entry-level services and shelter with minimum or no entry requirements. When emergency and transitional shelters favor certain populations over others or impose stringent entry requirements, segments of the population risk being shut out of the continuum. Using Kay McChesney's (1990) analogy of housing for homeless people as a game of musical chairs, Marybeth Shinn and Colleen Gillespie show that offering targeted housing for special populations simply determines "who, not how many, are left homeless when the music stops" (1994, 1).

Even if homeless people are able to adhere to behavioral norms and shelter rules, transitional shelters are often similar to emergency facilities. Research shows that emergency shelter programs offer erratic length-of-stay policies and restrictive admissions policies that exclude the following populations: mentally ill, physically disabled, alcohol or drug addicted, and those with medical needs (See Weinreb and Rossi 1995; Wong, Park, and Nemon 2006). Many transitional housing programs offer little if any difference in terms of the quality and quantity of services offered and impose restrictive admissions policies along the same lines imposed in emergency shelter programs. This blurring of emergency and transitional programs is confusing for both providers and clients. Even if all the rules are followed, a step-wise transition may not be possible. The upshot of restrictive policies, as previously discussed, is that homeless people frequently opt out of shelter in a bid to maintain control, autonomy, and perhaps, personality (Wagner 1993; Wasserman and Claire 2010).

Contextualizing the Point-in-Time Count

In order to receive McKinney-Vento homeless assistance funding, cities and counties nationwide conduct annual PIT counts that provide an inventory of shelter and housing options and estimate the number of sheltered and unsheltered homeless people in each region. These data assist communities in developing a continuum of care (CoC) that ideally moves homeless people from entry-level emergency services to transitional and eventually permanent housing. Without an accurate point-in-time count or a clear pathway through the service network, the

CoC cannot directly address gaps in service or transition homeless people into permanent housing. As a result, a growing number of homeless people remain unsheltered and without services of any kind, and CoC regions lack a set of coherent, up-to-date planning documents that chart the way forward.

Beginning in 1995, HUD required communities to submit a single application for McKinney-Vento homeless assistance grants, both to streamline the application process and to encourage the CoC planning process. Despite this encouragement, there is no federal oversight of the CoC or mandates for a written plan or action steps. Ideally, all elements of the CoC are coordinated with the major state and local planning documents, including the ten-year plan, Housing Element, and Consolidated Plan. At minimum, however, the CoC is a fund-driven assessment in the form of an annual or bi-annual count that occurs during the last seven days of January and offers a snapshot enumeration of the number of homeless people who are unsheltered or in one of three basic housing programs: emergency shelter, transitional shelter, or permanent supportive housing. Ideally, the PIT count allows communities to more accurately assess and address service and housing needs. Without oversight of the count or the CoC planning process, the danger is that gaps in the continuum will go unfilled and segments of the population will be excluded or underserved.

The variation in methodology across PIT counts statewide (and nationwide) is of grave concern, as a biased data set leads to inefficient policy and planning efforts (Quigley, Raphael, and Smolensky 2001). The unsheltered portion of the count is particularly challenging for reasons including location, geographical coverage, funding, weather, timing, and changing methodologies and definitions. Unsheltered homeless people are also difficult to find because of their desire to remain hidden. Police "sweeps" are common in makeshift locations, and when these occur just prior to the PIT count, they reduce the overall population and engender distrust for those who remain. The remoteness and presumed or actual danger associated with locations like abandoned buildings, vehicles, or outdoor campsites can also mean over- or undercounting and that many locations are not surveyed at all. Even when communities attempt to do street-by-street counts, it is often difficult to do a visual enumeration of observable characteristics, like gender and age. This is particularly true in January when many people living on the street bundle up for warmth.

In addition to informing policy, the PIT count is also used as a way of focusing community attention on the issue of homelessness and examining population demographics as well as potential solutions. At best, PIT counts are events that bring communities together. At worst, they are head counts that reify homeless people. The PIT count is an inaccurate reflection of the lived experience of unsheltered homeless people and those living in shelter, in part because homeless people are often not the ones characterizing their own needs or demographics. The Housing First approach emphasizes the need for homeless voices in determining housing solutions. The same principle needs to be applied to data gathering. Difficult as it is to find and engage unsheltered homeless people, without doing so, their demographics and needs will neither be accurately identified nor adequately served. This chapter includes a qualitative profile of each of the three counties under study. This is done to examine how well PIT findings reflect the lived experience of homeless people, service providers, and advocates. Measuring how well policy incorporates community voices and experience is often a key indicator of effectiveness. It is also a crucial step in research that focuses on social change.

Housing Market

The high numbers of unsheltered homeless people must also be understood in the context of the California housing market (Quigley, Raphael, and Smolensky 2001). The best way to reduce the need for homeless shelters is by providing affordable housing. Easier said than done, providing affordable housing can be inhibited by environmental constraints, antigrowth policies and regulations, NIMBYism, and a lack of resources to contribute to the planning process (Lewis 2003). As a result, those working for minimum wage or depending on SSI are priced out of the housing market, even at the entry level. Using the measure of affordability as a unit that costs no more than 30 percent of a renter's total income, Figure 6.1 shows the average monthly rental prices for apartments in each of the three counties as well as statewide. It also includes, on average, the amount that individuals making minimum wage or receiving SSI can afford.

According to the National Low Income Housing Coalition (2012), in order to afford a two-bedroom apartment in California, a household must earn $3,962 monthly, or a housing wage of $22.86 per hour. For individuals making minimum wage, this translates to a 135-hour work week, 52 weeks per year, or the full income of more than three full-time minimum-wage workers. Although housing in California is not affordable for individuals on SSI or making minimum wage, rental prices for studio and one-bedroom apartments in Sonoma County are slightly lower than the state average. Even so, the price of housing as

Figure 6.1. Housing Affordability for SSI and Minimum Wage Earners

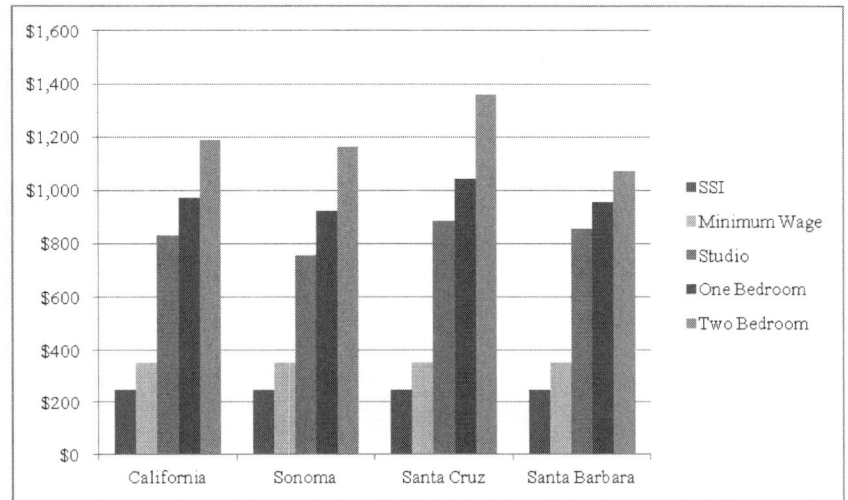

Source: National Low Income Housing Coalition 2012.

well as the age and quality of the existing housing stock, discussed below, show how challenging it is to provide adequate affordable housing.

The majority of homeless people and services in each county cluster in the cities designated as county seats: Santa Rosa, Santa Cruz, and Santa Barbara. Examining the housing stock in each of these cities allows for a comparison of the housing market that homeless people and services attempt to fit into. The housing stock in Santa Rosa is relatively new, with the majority of units built after 1970. Comparatively, the housing stock in Santa Cruz and Santa Barbara is older, with a majority of units built before 1970. An older housing stock means that more of the overall housing budget is spent on structural repairs. To provide affordable housing, cities must rehabilitate existing units, develop new units, offer rental assistance, and pursue "special needs" housing projects.

The State of California identifies "special needs" groups who may have difficulty finding affordable housing because of particular needs or circumstances. These groups include the elderly, disabled, large households, female-headed single parent households, homeless people, farm workers, military personnel, and college and university students. Out of these groups and in accordance with population needs, each city identifies its own list of "special needs" groups and develops a plan to provide them with affordable housing. All three counties have the following groups in common: disabled persons, female-headed households, large households, senior citizens, and homeless people. Santa Rosa and Santa Barbara also include farm workers and Santa Cruz includes college students. Figure 6.2 shows that disabled persons, large families, and senior citizens comprise the largest percentage of special needs groups in all three cities. Homeless people and farm workers comprise the smallest percentage, weighing in at fewer than 10 percent, and both groups are prioritized in Santa Rosa more so than in Santa Cruz or Santa Barbara.

Figure 6.2 Three-City Comparison of Prioritized Special Needs Groups

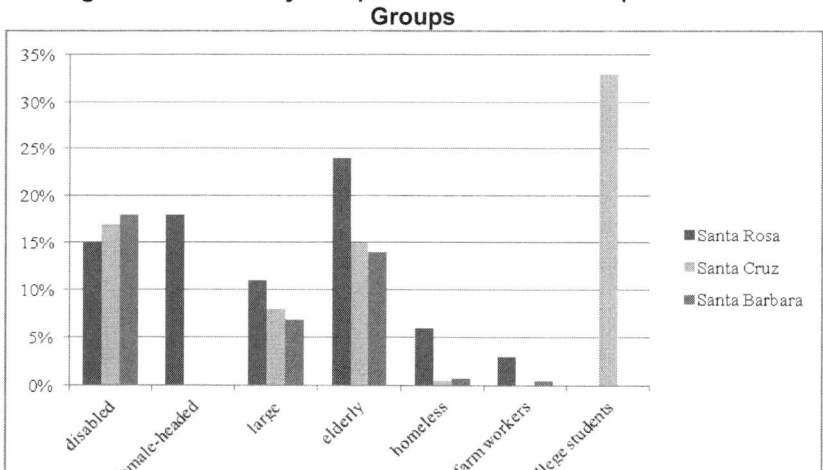

Source: *City of Santa Cruz Housing Element Update 2002–2007; City of Santa Rosa General Plan 2000–2006 (Ch. 4, Housing); City of Santa Barbara General Plan 2004 (Housing Element).*

Each of the three cities also face housing density issues that drive up rental prices and make it difficult to afford housing. The density charts in Figure 6.3 illustrate how dense the three cities are in relationship to each county, underscoring urban spaces as the arena in which the regulation resistance dynamic plays out. Both the city and county of Santa Cruz show the highest population density, making adequate, affordable housing that much more of a challenge. Although the population density in Santa Barbara County is lower than either of the other two counties, the city of Santa Barbara faces density issues comparable to those in Santa Cruz, making both cities ripe for anti-homeless regulation. Sonoma County shows a greater density level than Santa Barbara, but the city of Santa Rosa is far less dense than either Santa Barbara or Santa Cruz. In terms of offering affordable housing, Sonoma County is the most promising region because of its lower population density, newer housing stock, and prioritization of homeless people.

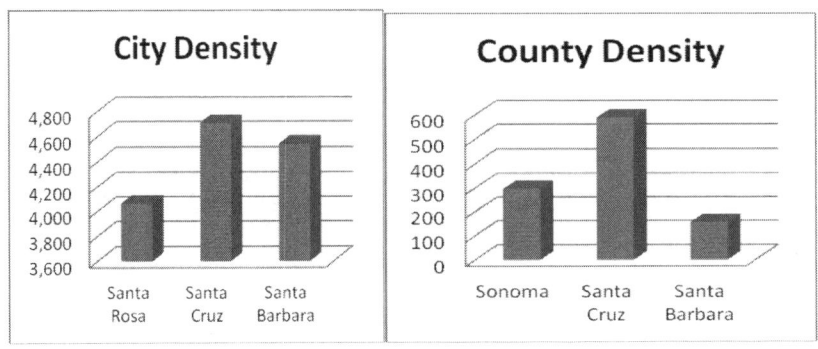

Figure 6.3 City and County Housing Density

Source: United States Census Bureau, Population Division (2010).

Examining housing for homeless people in a housing market that is barely affordable for working individuals and families and has several special needs populations puts the PIT count and the CoC planning process into perspective. Without an accurate measure of the number of homeless people, it is impossible to examine their service and housing needs or apply for funding to meet those needs. Without a clear pathway through the service network, many homeless people are left unsheltered. A lot is therefore riding on the breadth and depth of the PIT count.

Counting the Unsheltered

Representing the northern, central, and southern parts of the state of California, Sonoma, Santa Cruz, and Santa Barbara are similar in terms of the following characteristics: a total population of more than 250,000 but less than 500,000, the absence of a large metropolitan city, suburban to rural environment, and a reputation for scenic beauty and

132 Otherwise Homeless

environmental focus (Santa Barbara County 2006). Eight of California's fifty-eight counties fit this profile, six of which are coastal or Bay Area counties. All three counties under consideration here are prime tourist destinations, and all boast alluring beaches, farmers markets, and seasonal festivals. As Figure 6.4 shows, each of these counties also has a substantial percentage of unsheltered homeless people. Given these staggering percentages, there are two pressing questions: what accounts for the discrepancy between counties, and what new and existing policies are being considered to house and otherwise serve the unsheltered homeless population?

Figure 6.4 Sheltered/Unsheltered Breakdown by County

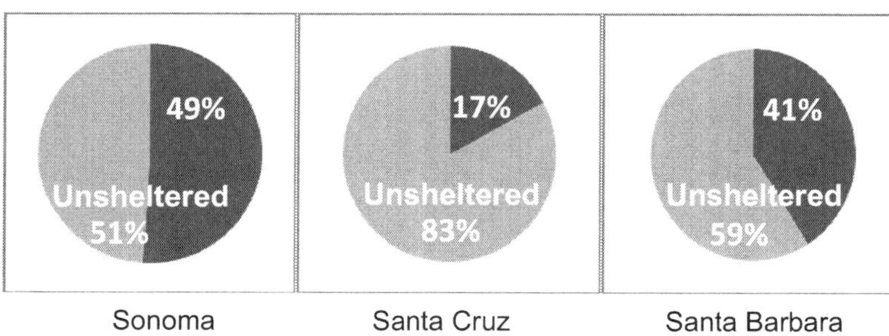

Sonoma	Santa Cruz	Santa Barbara
49% Unsheltered / 51%	17% Unsheltered / 83%	41% Unsheltered / 59%

Source: 2007 PIT count data.

Sonoma County

Sonoma is wine country, with spas and golf courses interspersed between its redwood forests and pristine coastline. Of its nine incorporated cities, five are located along the Interstate 101 corridor, and Santa Rosa and Petaluma are the largest. The geographic diversity of Sonoma County makes its PIT count particularly challenging. Despite this, Sonoma has the most extensive PIT count of the three counties in terms of resources spent, geographical coverage, and information gathered. Sonoma County conducted block-by-block street counts and established twelve central polling stations throughout the county where homeless people could check in, be interviewed, and receive incentive gifts and services, including legal advice, medical check-ups, haircuts, and veteran's services. Six weeks prior to the count, outreach workers began to locate and establish contact with homeless people. In addition to counting those people seen in person on the day of the count who were "staying in a shelter, transitional housing, or a place not meant for human habitation," Sonoma expanded the count to a full week and attempted to interview all those counted. This approach is not only thorough but implements many of the suggestions published in the *HUD Guide to Counting Unsheltered Homeless People* (2004; 2008).

With the assistance of over 400 volunteers, a total of 1,974 homeless people were counted and surveyed. These data form the basis of the summary that follows. Of this total, only 1,314 were eligible for inclusion in the official HUD figures for the Continuum of Care Action Plan. Sonoma County went beyond HUD requirements by using a broader definition of homelessness, which included people without a home under their legal control. This includes active clients of alcohol and drug, mental health, or child welfare agencies, and those who are doubled up with friends or relatives. Although Sonoma County cannot include these figures in applications for federal funding, they are useful in examining the overall homeless population and in planning for adequate housing, shelter, and services.

As Figure 6.4 indicates, the sheltered and unsheltered populations in Sonoma County are roughly equivalent, showing the least disparity of the three counties. The gap between men and women is most dramatic among the unsheltered population, with men comprising three-quarters of the total. Coupled with ethnographic evidence, this suggests that unsheltered living is particularly dangerous for women and that they are more likely to be found in more private locations. This does not mean that women are then safe from domestic violence or other forms of abuse, merely that indoor options are more readily available to them.

Unsheltered homeless people were found in a variety of locations throughout Sonoma County, including vehicles. Although counting unsheltered homeless people is always a challenge, Sonoma identified street locations as well as more private ones. In addition to those listed in Figure 6.5, 2 percent or fewer were found in locations including public places (emergency rooms, churches, etc.) and agricultural or industrial buildings. Individuals were also counted in jails, hospitals, and treatment facilities if they were due to be released within one week. Although HUD does not accept these data, Sonoma County includes them in its count to address discharge planning in its assessment of the needs of homeless people.

In terms of the seven subpopulations of interest to HUD, Sonoma County has the highest number of people reporting chronic substance abuse (see Figure 6.6). Severe mental illness and domestic violence are other prevalent reasons for being homeless in the county, and many people were affected by chronic homelessness. There were few people

Figure 6.5 Locations of Unsheltered Homeless People in the 2007 PIT Count in Sonoma County

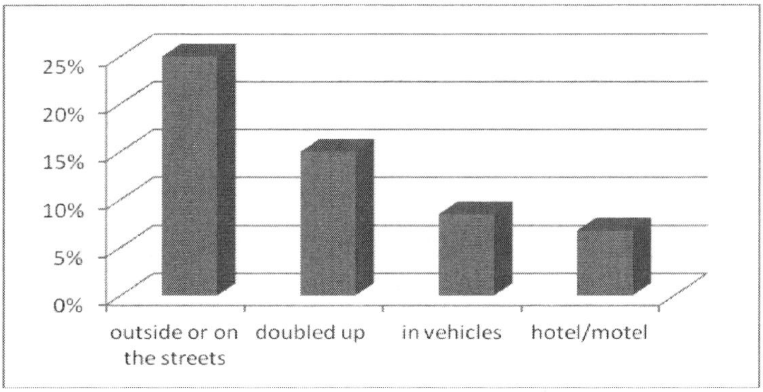

Source: Sonoma County 2007 PIT count.

with HIV/AIDS and few unaccompanied youth identified in the PIT count These findings suggest that the greatest overall service needs include treatment for alcohol and drug abuse, mental illness, outreach for veterans and the unsheltered, and shelters and services for those experiencing domestic violence.

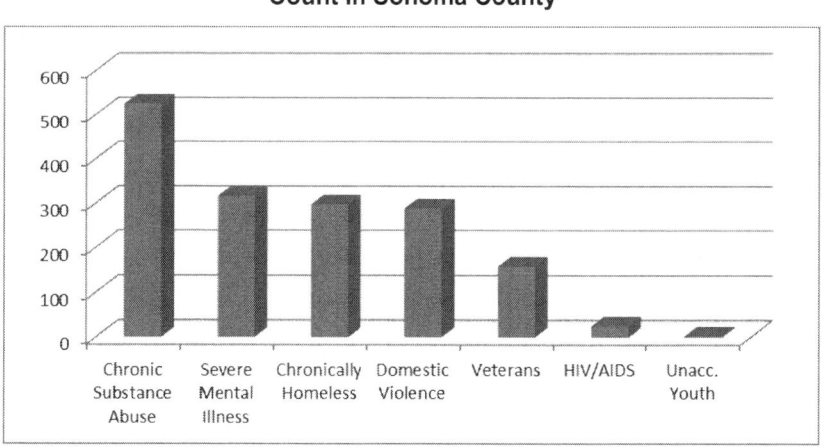

Figure 6.6 The Seven Subpopulations Required by HUD in the 2007 PIT Count in Sonoma County

Source: Sonoma County 2007 PIT count.

Despite the common misconception that homeless people move to areas with better services, the vast majority of those surveyed in Sonoma County report living there prior to becoming homeless. The most prevalent locations were in a house or apartment, or with friends, relatives, or coworkers. Homeless people also identified several barriers that prevent them from returning to housing and stability, including a lack of funding, or mental health or substance abuse issues. Those surveyed also cited divorce, bad credit, illness and disability, domestic violence, and eviction as factors that contributed to their current homeless status and that continue to be barriers to moving on (see Figure 6.7). These barriers are often overlapping and combine with a lack of preparedness for entering or reentering the workforce.

Figure 6.7 Barriers to Securing Permanent Housing in the Survey Component of the 2007 PIT Count in Sonoma County

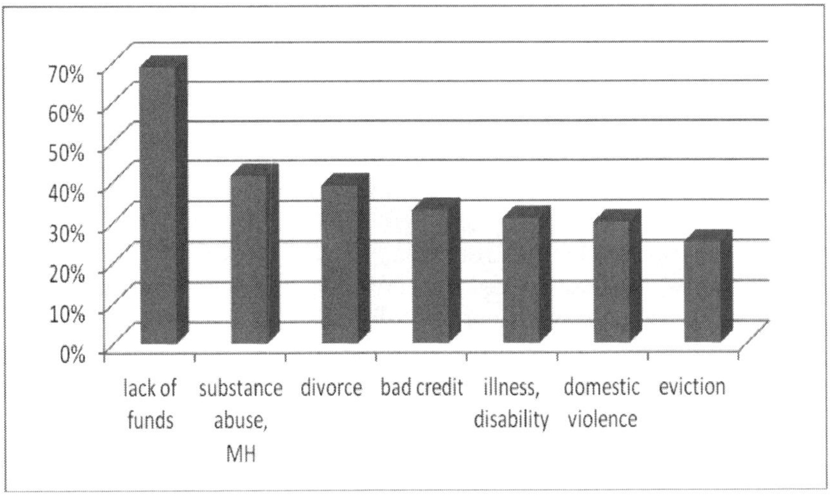

Source: Survey component of the Sonoma County 2007 PIT count.

Related to this, approximately half of all respondents reported that the highest level of educational attainment they have achieved is a high school diploma or a GED. Perhaps even more surprising, one-quarter of all respondents have only completed elementary school. This lack of education is clearly a barrier to gainful employment. Of those who are employed, about one-quarter of all respondents report that the money they earn is not enough to afford an apartment.

Many of Sonoma County's homeless people receive disability income through SSI, SSDI, State Disability Insurance (SDI), or public aid through TANF/GA/Unemployment/Food Stamps. Yet, not everyone who is eligible takes advantage of these options; in fact, less than one-quarter of all homeless people are receiving either category of assistance. This lack of assistance is surprising, as one-third of all respondents reported that they were experiencing either mental illness or physical or medical disabilities. This underscores the need for services that assist homeless people in determining their eligibility for assistance. Mental illness and drug and alcohol addiction are also common among the homeless population, demonstrating an additional service need. One-third to one-fourth of those experiencing one of these conditions are receiving treatment. The majority of respondents were not enrolled in Medi-Cal, greatly limiting their health care options.[2]

Despite efforts to survey the entire homeless population, "sweeps" were conducted just prior to the 2007 PIT count to remove homeless people from outdoor encampments. The California Highway Patrol and the Santa Rosa Public Works and Parks Departments removed more than twenty-five encampments in the two weeks prior to the count. Not only did these sweeps force people to relocate, they also created distrust among the remaining campers. In addition, anti-RV ordinances were passed in the week prior to the count, meaning that many RVers scattered to more rural or hidden locations. Both of these events resulted in a dramatic undercount of unsheltered homeless people.

Sonoma County mobilizes significant human and capital resources to conduct its PIT count. The 2005 and 2007 counts are similar enough to allow the county to track changes in the homeless population in terms of location, demographics, and service needs. In 2009, however, the Sonoma County Community Development Commission and the Sonoma County Continuum of Care Planning Group worked with the nonprofit firm Applied Survey Research (ASR) to conduct the homeless census and survey. Using the methodology outlined in HUD's 2008 *Guide to Counting Unsheltered Homeless People,* the count included the number of people sheltered and the number unsheltered and in jails, hospitals, or detox facilities. The count also included a survey component, administered to 600 homeless people in the weeks following the one-day enumeration of street and shelter populations.

This change in methodology produced surprisingly different results from the 2005 and 2007 counts. The overall numbers rose by 1,273, with a 32 percent increase in the number of unsheltered homeless people and a decrease of 16 percent in the number of homeless people in shelters. Researchers attribute the increase in unsheltered homeless people to greater efforts to reach homeless youth. Numbers again rose significantly in 2011, with an overall increase of 1,292, most of which is attributed to becoming comfortable with the new way of conducting the count. Unlike the 2005 and 2007 counts, no effort was made to count those "doubled up" with friends or family.

These results show that counting unsheltered homeless people is extremely difficult because of changes in methodology and the desire, among homeless people, to remain hidden. Attempting to recalibrate the county's methodological approach yielded greater numbers, yet, the in-depth data from the surveys conducted in 2009 and 2011 were less conclusive because this information represented only a fraction of the population. Uneven results and changing methodology make it difficult to utilize the PIT to inform planning.

Yet PIT count data are used to inform the Continuum of Care Planning Group, which authored the ten-year plan to end homelessness by 2017. The initial draft of the plan was based on the 2005 PIT count. But it also includes an annual report that examines progress toward the initial goals, which include: (1) homeless prevention, (2) new resources for chronically homeless people and families, (3) affordable housing, and (4) strengthening political will and building organizational structure. The first annual progress report shows impressive follow-through on attempts to serve the chronic homeless population, many of whom are unsheltered. Among the most impressive accomplishments is the establishment of a street outreach team that contacted 170 people and successfully encouraged fifty of them to engage in shelter and services. This team also addresses community and business concerns, emphasizing the rehabilitative rather than punitive approach characteristic of Sonoma County's response to homelessness. The report also shows notable progress in reaching the mentally ill homeless population, those with substance abuse issues, those being released from jail, veterans, and those in need of adequate health care.

Progress toward serving the unsheltered homeless population, coupled with attention to homeless prevention, affordable housing, and a community-driven planning process, shows the coordinated approach to ending homelessness that Sonoma County is developing. Although qualitative data will show that homeless people have far-ranging issues, the planning process holds the community accountable for providing adequate housing and services. While changes in the methodology of the PIT count yield markedly different results from year to year, the county consistently attempts to refine its methodology and overall service approach. Yet how well does data from the PIT count reflect the lived experience of homeless people and service providers?

A Qualitative Profile

Service providers, shelter directors, and policy specialists agree that Sonoma County's primary goals are to provide year-round shelter, "wet" shelter (that admits clients who are actively using drugs/alcohol), detox facilities, and discharge services; to encourage self-sufficiency; and to provide transitional and affordable housing. Because all of the county's shelters require sobriety before entering, the most pressing needs are for a wet shelter and medical detox. In many cases, clients are pressured to commit to sobriety to gain access to a bed for the night. As one provider said to a client seeking admission to shelter, "I don't care what you did yesterday—but what about a commitment to not use anymore?—I care about tomorrow." Without already being sober or establishing an immediate commitment to sobriety, the county's homeless people go without shelter.

Another pressing need in Sonoma County is discharge planning from jail or mental health facilities. I asked a nurse in Sebastopol, in the rural area referred to as the west county or Russian River Valley, about the problems associated with discharging homeless patients. "Let me give you an example of a woman that was being released from a mental health holding facility and was scared to death to be on the streets—so she wouldn't leave and the police were called. When the officer arrived, he said, 'I'm sorry ma'am but you'll have to leave,' and she said, 'what would happen if I hit you?' and he replied, 'I'm sorry but I'd have to take you to jail,' so she charged him with fists flailing." At the time of our interview, the nurse had discharged several people to buses because they had no place to go: "One woman got 86'ed from the shelter because she overdosed on prescription medication. She had no clothes and no place to go. We could not give her a taxi voucher without [an address] so we dressed her in what we could find and gave her a bus pass. I feel weird about that and I hate doing it." Jail and mental health facilities are also located in Santa Rosa and Petaluma, meaning that those discharged typically end up in these cities, adding to the local homeless population.

In order to be placed in one of the Santa Rosa's eighty available emergency shelter beds, homeless people must report to the Homeless Service Center, which serves as an intake service for all shelters in the area. One of the primary things this intake service does is find out if the person already has some form of shelter and how long they can stay there. Emergency shelter is treated as the last possible option, demonstrating its increasing exclusivity as a form of assistance. Staff ask about drug and alcohol use and require sobriety or a promise to become sober. If clients are using, they are turned away. When clients ask for other services, like money for a bus ticket, they are asked about their current employment and other income, in an attempt to maximize their self-sufficiency. During my visit to the Homeless Service Center in Santa Rosa, several clients arrived seeking shelter, and it was up to the director to determine alcohol and drug use and assess shelter-readiness. The center offers a look at the entry level service needs, service provision, and the culture of unsheltered homelessness in Santa Rosa.

A man named Homer, in his late forties, arrived at the Homeless Service Center looking dirty and disheveled. Nick, the director, sized him up and then warned, "You have to commit to sobriety, you know," to which Homer replied, "I have no problem with that." Pressing the issue, Nick said, "You just used recently though, today or yesterday," and Homer confessed, "I'm on methadone." Nick's response: "Okay, but if we catch you nodding, you're gone, if you're up all night cleaning the bathroom, you'll be gone too." Homer agreed to these conditions and was placed in shelter.

Within minutes, a man named Russell arrived. He was in his mid-thirties, and he asked for a bus ticket to Klamath Falls, OR. "I have no money until the fifteenth and I want to get up there because the fish are running." He said he had been waiting two days to talk to someone. Nick asked, "Can you go to Labor Ready to make the money?" Russell replied that he lacked an ID and Nick informed him that he would need an ID to ride the bus anyway. After telling his story for several minutes, Russell shrugged and said, "Yeah, that's okay, I can stay here." Russell came in with a woman named Sherry, also in her mid-thirties, who said she needed transportation to New York. "Are you on SSI?" Nick asked. "No. It's just that both my parents are dead and I have no place to go." "Well, how did you get to Santa Rosa?" he asked. "I've just been traveling. I was raised in Phoenix but I'm not sure how I got here." Nick asked where she stayed last night and she said, "near the freeway, with Russ." He asked if she felt safe there and she said, "I felt safe but I'm kind of ticked off because Russell kind of crawled on me and said 'well, you're going to cringe a little bit.' He tried to take off my clothes but I'm wearing this bathing suit so I felt pretty safe." Nick asked Sherry if she wanted to file a complaint with a female officer. She replied, "I've tried talking to them, but there's nothing they can do for me. I'm fine. I don't want to bother Russ. He's a good boy, I'm the bad one." "You're not bad," Nick replied, "you're a woman traveling alone who should be able to sleep somewhere without having to take off her clothes." Sherry responded without making sense. She talked about wanting to go where the snow was and that her father used to be rich. Nick asked her, "Do you know what 5150 means?[3] Do you remember the last time it happened to you, if it ever has?" This brought her to immediate attention, and she said, "I'm just gonna go" and left with Russell before the police arrived.

In addition to the Homeless Service Center, Santa Rosa offers several transitional housing programs, yet providers worry that they are "cherry picking" the most acceptable/easy to serve clients. The intake interviews recounted in the previous paragraphs demonstrate the barriers posed by addiction and the difficulty of addressing mental illness and abuse. They also show how being homeless can lead to additional problems, including loss of identification. When I asked Nick about available shelter beds, he indicated that all of them require sobriety but not drug testing. Clients have thirty days to save their income and have to put 70 percent of it in a private bank account. Nick agreed that a wet shelter and medical detox are the most needed services. He also said that homeless people need life skills training that employment can provide. The problem with homeless services, he says, is that people enable people to be homeless but it is not an acceptable lifestyle. "People still have the victim mentality," he said, pointing to a sign on his door with a picture of a man weeping while playing the violin and the caption, "Please go on with your story." Sometimes, he says, "I feel like a garbage collector: sweep it up, make it look good for the people out there." Nick feels that homeless people should be involved in running all homeless shelters. "My philosophy," he says, is "give people a stake in it—if you get burned sometimes—so what."

In comparison with this approach, the Committee on the Shelterless (COTS) program offers a more rigid philosophy. I met with the director of the Petaluma facility, who began the interview by saying, "I will not answer any questions you can find on the website." The four basic agreements that structure COTS programs are commitment, hope, intention, and integrity, which are communicated to staff, clients, and the community. These are intended to be linear or programmatic, but, as the director indicated, the COTS philosophy is that "we try to fan the flames of hope. You don't want trauma and treatment wards." Other programs, he said, teach people how to be homeless. At COTS, by contrast, "we examine who we are, how we define ourselves, what do we permit to happen here, how far do we let people fall." Many clients become staff members and are models for others, a key feature of the program. They also do random drug testing and indicate that few people have ever been in violation. "There is something about accepting people where they are and having low expectations for them that I think keeps them homeless." He says their rules are strict and are meant for clients to follow city-wide. "Our perspective is that we have a responsibility to the community and we tell people that they are the ambassadors of the program." "Transformative not charitable" is the COTS model. "I'm not giving these years of my life, fourteen years of my professional prime, to run flop houses for ingrates, that's a waste of my time."

In addition to the services outlined previously, Sonoma County has made significant headway in reaching out to homeless veterans. In an interview with the head of the street outreach team, named Ted, the approach to services was described as "consumer run, for consumers. That's the only way to do it. The initial contact is always VET to VET because they feel much more comfortable. You don't have to explain a whole bunch of stuff like you do with civilians like us." The focus of the street outreach team is to provide an initial contact for homeless veterans and assist them in accessing governmental benefits, shelter, and services. "It's one-stop shopping," Ted explained. "We leverage local support based on what the guys say they need. Then we train them in street outreach." When I asked Ted to estimate the percentage of homeless veterans who were camping, he said "probably half. Because of what they've gone through, they don't want to deal with shelters. They feel more comfortable a lot of times being out by themselves."

Veterans are clearly not the only ones who feel more comfortable on the streets versus in shelter. I met a 57 year-old man named Sammy just outside of Santa Rosa. He was walking down the street wearing a yellow jacket that was so dirty it looked like it had been rubbed with charcoal. He said he had been camping in Santa Rosa for over ten years. When I asked him how he survived, he said, "I get social security [SSDI] for schizophrenia but I don't get enough money for rent." Sammy described his fruitless search for employment: "I had a job but I quit because I got really paranoid. So I just worked on the county work project one day a week for food." Rather than live in shelters, he built a hut in Santa Rosa. He got arrested for doing so and spent time in Atascadero, a mental hospital. He was there for eleven months and was placed on SSDI upon discharge and lived in a board-and-care facility. "I got tired of living with all men in that place so I decided to move back out on the street. In other words, I felt I would be happier living outside." When I asked Sammy whether he ever sought shelter, he said, "I stayed at the Mission one winter, a whole winter. It's pretty bad, I didn't like it. You have to go to a church service every night." Sammy also described staying at a shelter that imposed a sixty-day limit. "Do you prefer the streets?" I asked him. "No, it's not that," he replied. "If I had enough money I would rent an apartment. I'd prefer that. If I don't have enough money then I prefer the streets."

Other interviewees reported aging out of foster care as a reason for being homeless. One of them was a 24 year-old man named Woody, who was camping with his pregnant girlfriend and four other people in the woods near a tennis court. I asked him how long he had been on the street and he said, "Off and on since I was 12 years old. I was in group homes, but I couldn't do that now if I wanted to. I'm too old." Sympathizing with him, I said, "Once you age out of the foster care system," and he finished my thought, "There's nothing. They didn't transition me for a job experience, anything like this, they didn't give me nothing on how's this going to work.... 'Here's a reference for this or here's a reference for that,' they just booted me straight to the street and me not knowing anything, I went straight to jail. No transition there either, so I don't have much of a resume." I asked him if he wanted to live inside and he said he did, because his girlfriend was having a baby. "I don't want to do a shelter though. Shelters won't let me have my dog and I have to have a dog. Dogs keep me, uh, a little bit mellow and under control." While camping, he reported having his possessions stolen several times through county "sweeps." Although he acknowledged that his belongings may not have looked like much, he also mourned the loss. "I lost the only picture I had of my biological father. I never met him, so that's all I had."

The other members of the camp were two women, ages 18 and 22, and two men, ages 25 and 33. When I asked them about going to shelter, the younger woman was the only one who responded affirmatively: "I just recently turned 18 and my mom actually didn't want to go to a shelter so she had me out in the streets but now that I'm capable of doing that I definitely want to. I need to get a job and I need to get off the streets, and you can't really do that if you're camping out."

In an interview with a 48 year-old man named Tommy, who was sitting in one of the city's public parks, he explained how he began living in his vehicle: "I was working construction a few years back until my knee started bothering me. I never knew how to do anything else and it's not like I'm 22." When I asked him if he ever lived in the shelter or on the street, he told me, "When my money started to run out, I panicked. I actually drove over to the shelter to check it out and decided to beg, borrow, or steal to buy a camper shell. Living with 100 other sick people is just not where it's at for me." Tommy eventually applied for SSI and used it to support himself and maintain his truck. He described being relatively happy living in his vehicle: "I feel like I'm lucky, to tell you the truth. I see people who are really out there and I feel sorry for them. All I have to do is leave town every once in a while so I don't get tickets." He described policing efforts as sporadic and targeted. Other

RVers typically shared the news about sweeps so that others would know to leave town and avoid ticketing. Once the sweeps were over, Tommy said, most RVers returned to their former parking places.

Overall, qualitative data for Sonoma County reflect an understanding of the need for services that address alcohol and drug addiction, including wet shelters, and those that address mental illness. They do not address domestic violence, although it is reflected in both PIT counts and qualitative data. Outreach to specific populations, including youth and veterans, is in evidence, although it does not appear to be part of a coordinated outreach strategy. Qualitative data also show a concern with prevention, as reflected in the need for discharge planning so that those released from prison, and other institutions, do not become homeless. Despite efforts to manage effective discharge planning, there are no procedures in place to identify those at risk of becoming homeless. Yet, assessing vulnerability is a key feature of ensuring an effective strategy for limiting the growth of the homeless population. Finally, qualitative data indicate that homeless people are split in terms of how they view homeless shelters. Some view them as a last resort because of the restrictions they impose, and others see them as a possibility for transition.

While unsheltered locations like camps or vehicles allow safety and autonomy, the risk is that people living in them are cut off from potentially rehabilitative services. Once they do enter into service, those in the business of service provision show an understanding of the importance of having homeless people participate in establishing the rules, what services are offered, and how they are administered. This approach was espoused by all service providers interviewed, regardless of the type of program or population served. Although it remains challenging to connect unsheltered homeless people with services, once they are so connected, they can serve as role models for others.

Comparing the qualitative data for Sonoma County with findings from the PIT count serves a corroborative function in the sense that they both demonstrate an approach to homelessness that emphasizes raising community awareness as well as focusing on the individual needs of homeless people. The approach is not always low barrier, as homeless people are expected to commit to sobriety and follow program rules. But the county is also making progress toward developing a comprehensive plan to offer expanded outreach services.

Santa Cruz County

Santa Cruz County has four incorporated cities and Santa Cruz is the largest. Located along the protected Monterey Bay, the city has a downtown boardwalk area with rides, games, and attractions. The campus of the University of California–Santa Cruz is located in the northeastern part of the city, on a large tract of land adjacent to a sprawling open space preserve. Of the three additional incorporated cities, Watsonville is the largest, located south of Santa Cruz, along the Pacific Coast Highway. The third most populous city is Scotts Valley, measuring in at only four-and-a-half square miles. Like Sonoma County, Santa Cruz is geographically diverse, with urban, rural, and coastal areas, yet its population density is much higher. Homeless people tend to cluster in the "greenbelt overlay area," which includes over 1,000 acres of protected land surrounding the city. The city of Santa Cruz is home to the largest and most visible population of homeless people within the county, and it hosts the county's only emergency shelter and largest configuration of homeless services.

For homeless people living in the unincorporated "green belt" areas, the railroad tracks, rivers, and roadways serve as pathways into and out of the city. Homeless shelters are located in Santa Cruz and Watsonville, but few if any services are located in more rural areas. There are more unsheltered homeless people in the unincorporated areas of the county, with significant percentages clustered in the San Lorenzo Valley and Santa Cruz Mountains. This is likely due to the seasonal draw of construction and agricultural jobs as well as the cover that remote areas provide, allowing unsheltered homeless people to remain hidden from law enforcement and from housed citizens.

To conduct its PIT count, Santa Cruz County uses a combination of block-by-block street counts and peer interviewing. A total of 2,789 people were counted during the 2007 PIT count, and 429 were interviewed in the weeks following the count. Approximately 700 homeless interviewers were trained to assist in conducting the street count and were paid $20 for completing a training session prior to the count and $10 per hour on the day of the count. They recorded observable characteristics including gender, age, and location. Various kinds of vehicles and encampments were included in the count, yet enumerators were instructed not to approach or enter these sites. Instead, they applied a multiplier of 1.00 for cars, 1.87 for vans and RVs, and 2.46 for encampments to determine the number of individuals.

Unlike the Sonoma County PIT count, in which everyone who was counted participated in some form of survey or interview, Santa Cruz

County performed an enumeration of the sheltered and unsheltered populations to collect basic information required by HUD. A separate survey instrument was administered to a subset of the homeless population. A total of 429 homeless people completed the survey and were offered $5 prepaid phone cards to incentivize participation. Homeless survey workers were also compensated $5 per completed survey. The survey included information on the seven subpopulations of interest to HUD—the daily condition of homeless people, educational attainment, employment, financial income/assistance, family status, disability status, and domestic violence. It provides a more in-depth survey than the one administered in Sonoma, but it addresses only a small fraction of the overall homeless population.

Findings from the overall count show that the vast majority (83 percent) were unsheltered, with the remainder in emergency or transitional shelter. The two primary locations for unsheltered homeless people were vehicles and encampments, as shown in Figure 6.8. Overall, it was estimated that 774 people or 33 percent of the unsheltered homeless population in Santa Cruz County live in cars, vans, or RVs.

Figure 6.8 Locations of Unsheltered Homeless People in the Overall PIT Count and the Survey Component of the 2007 PIT Count in Santa Cruz County

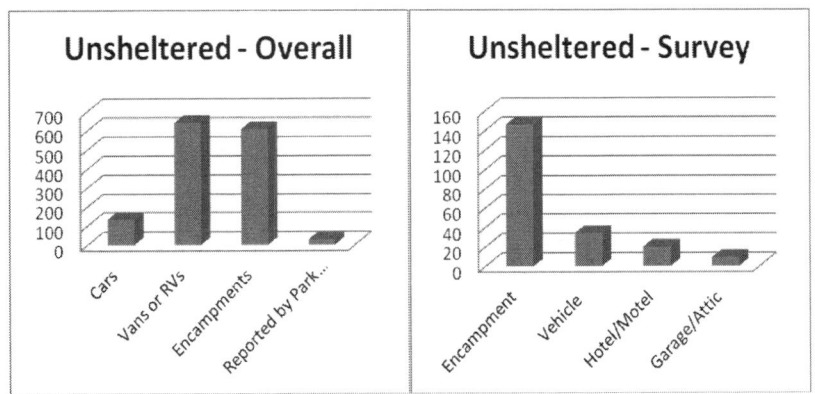

Source: Santa Cruz County 2007 PIT count.

Survey data show a more detailed view of unsheltered homelessness, yet they do not mirror the percentages recorded in the overall PIT count. Although less than half of the survey population identified as unsheltered, they reported more diverse locations than the PIT count captured. Approximately 43 percent of all valid surveys were completed by unsheltered homeless people, including those living in vehicles. In addition to camps and vehicles, people reported living in unconverted garages, attics, basements, or other places in a house not typically used for sleeping, and hotels or motels. In comparison with the overall count, survey data include hidden locations that are more difficult to access in the street count. Because of their visibility, vehicles were more prevalent in the overall count and were separated according to vehicle type. People living in vehicles were less common among survey respondents, suggesting that people living in vehicles may be less likely to access shelter or service locations, where interviews were conducted, or less likely to disclose personal information.

In terms of the subpopulations of interest to HUD, the overall count shows that Santa Cruz has the largest number of chronically homeless people (1,161), and those with severe mental illness (1,062), followed by victims of domestic violence (427), and veterans (424). The other categories have relatively low numbers of people, with 161 reporting problems with chronic substance abuse, eighty-three with HIV/AIDS, and ten unaccompanied youth. As already indicated, most homeless people in Santa Cruz are unsheltered, meaning that those on the street are typically either severely mentally ill or chronically homeless (see Figure 6.9).

Figure 6.9 The Seven Subpopulations Required by HUD in the 2007 PIT Count in Santa Cruz County

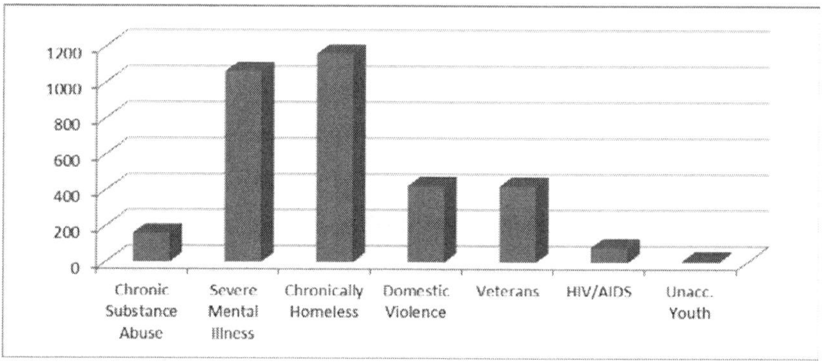

Source: Santa Cruz County 2007 PIT count.

Despite the large number of unsheltered homeless people in both the overall count and among those surveyed, approximately 21 percent of survey respondents reported that they tried to access shelter or transitional housing and were turned away. The two primary reasons for this were the lack of available beds, and alcohol or drug use. This indicates a need for additional shelter and housing services and for alcohol and drug treatment facilities and a wet shelter.

As was the case in Sonoma County, the overwhelming majority of homeless people surveyed report living in Santa Cruz County or in California at the time they became homeless. Homeless people were also asked to report the primary event or condition that led to their current experience with homelessness and to report circumstances preventing them from living in permanent housing (see Figure 6.10). While the reasons for becoming homeless are varied, most respondents cited financial reasons as the primary barrier to achieving housing stability. Virtually no one responded that alcohol or drug use would prevent them from living in permanent housing, despite the fact that several respondents cited this as a reason for becoming homeless. Considered together, these findings suggest that respondents need a stable income through employment or government assistance. They also suggest that,

Figure 6.10 Reasons for Becoming Homeless and Barriers to Permanent Housing as Reported in the Survey Component of the 2007 PIT Count in Santa Cruz County

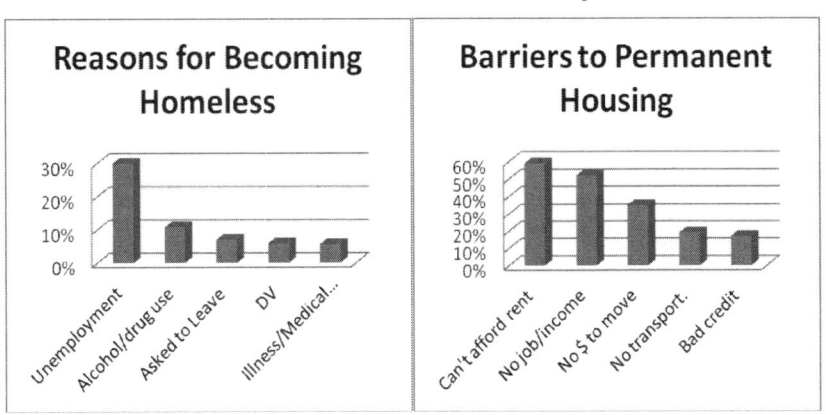

Source: Santa Cruz County 2007 PIT count.

although homeless people do not see things that precipitated their homelessness as barriers to housing, wrap-around services are likely needed to ensure housing stability.

Related to this, although 17.4 percent of respondents reported some military service, there is no direct link in the survey to the current experience of homelessness. Yet numerous studies show that domestic violence and military service can lead to PTSD and/or addiction, which are only exacerbated by a life on the street. Alcohol and drug addiction are also contributing factors to homelessness. The survey separates alcohol from drug use, showing that alcohol use is more common, as one-fourth of the survey population reported active usage. Despite these findings, less than 10 percent reported that they were currently receiving alcohol or drug counseling, meaning that for most people, these problems go untreated. Similarly, over one-quarter of all female respondents reported that they were currently experiencing domestic/partner violence or abuse.

Even if finances are the primary barrier to securing permanent housing, very few of the homeless people surveyed reported that they were employed, and a significant percentage were not eligible for employment. The primary barriers that were identified as preventing respondents from securing full- or part-time work were lack of transportation, no permanent address, physical and developmental disability, chronic health problems, and no phone. Related to this, although education was not included as a barrier to employment, few people surveyed reported that they were educated beyond a high school diploma or GED. This reflects the lack of education among the homeless population found in Sonoma County data as well. Interestingly, none of the planning documents in either Sonoma or Santa Cruz counties focus on education as a pathway to gainful employment.

Some of the barriers to achieving gainful employment, cited earlier, can also qualify homeless people for government assistance. Over half of all survey respondents reported receiving some form of government assistance. The most common form was food stamps, followed by Medicare, SSI/SSDI, General Assistance (GA), or Cash Aid/CalWORKS. The top reasons cited for not receiving government assistance show that a significant number of homeless people did not think they were eligible, did not have identification, never applied, lack a permanent address, or did not have legal immigration status. These findings suggest that homeless people may need assistance accessing forms of government aid, and that housing subsidies are often needed in order to afford permanent housing.

To supplement government assistance or to stand in for employment, panhandling was cited as a form of income. Of those surveyed, almost one-third indicated that they panhandle regularly. The typical monthly income from panhandling is estimated to be between $50 and $200. Given the restrictions in place to prevent soliciting money in Santa Cruz, the prevalence of panhandling as a means of income foreshadows problems with law enforcement that the qualitative data will explore. Related to this, although more than half of the people surveyed reported that they had not spent a night in jail or prison in the twelve months prior to the survey, 17.2 percent reported spending between one and ten nights, 6 percent between eleven and twenty nights, 3 percent between twenty-one and fifty nights, and 10 percent more than fifty nights in jail or prison. This suggests that there are a limited number of homeless people who cycle in and out of jail, draining resources and exacerbating homelessness.

When homeless people need medical care, they typically access the community clinic, the emergency room, or the county clinic. Despite the common depiction of homeless people using emergency rooms frequently for medical care, 42.4 percent reported that they had not used the emergency room for treatment in the past year. Fewer respondents reported using the emergency room once (20 percent) or twice (16 percent) in the past year, and the percentage of respondents using the emergency room three, four, five, or more times is between 2 and 6 percent. A significant number of respondents also reported needing health care and being unable to receive it since becoming homeless. These responses show the poignant need for medical care as a way of treating conditions that become worse with time on the street, and offering rehabilitative services for those able to return to or transition to stable employment and housing.

In addition to the general limitations listed earlier that are endemic to PIT counts, Santa Cruz County notes that some of its particular challenges include an undercount of those en route to employment; the inability to survey all potential vehicles, buildings, and structures; the difficulty of counting street youth, who tend to remain separate from the adult homeless population and/or blend in with the general youth population; and homeless families, who are more likely to stay on private property. Despite these limitations, no police action was noted prior to the count.

Like Sonoma County, Santa Cruz County struggles with the question of what methodology to use when conducting the PIT count. In 2005 the county conducted a street count in ten of the fifty-two census tracts most likely to contain high concentrations of homeless people.

Staff then randomly sampled eleven of the remaining forty-two tracts, counted them block by block, and applied a correlation analysis to the remaining tracts to estimate the unsheltered homeless population. This change in methodology yielded a decrease of 2,057 people. Following the 2007 count, reported here, in 2009 the county contracted with Applied Survey Research (ASR), the same firm that assisted Sonoma County. The firm conducts street-by-street counts from deployment locations throughout the county, conducts a shelter and institution count, and administers a survey component in the weeks following the one-day enumeration.

This change in methodology resulted in an overall increase in the number of homeless people by 950 in 2009, and by 506 in 2011, using consistent counting methods. The initial increase, from 2007 to 2009, was attributed to a 50 percent increase in the sheltered population. Although the county also saw a 33 percent decrease in the unsheltered population, the higher shelter numbers meant an increase overall. Interestingly, using HUD methodology as administered through ASR, the PIT counts conducted in 2009 in Santa Cruz and Sonoma counties show the exact same breakdown between the unsheltered homeless population, estimated at 68 percent, and the sheltered homeless population, estimated at 32 percent.

The PIT count data gathered in 2007 in Santa Cruz County are difficult to analyze because the majority of people counted are unsheltered and the survey instrument was used on only a small fraction of the total. The majority of data collected on the unsheltered population is therefore based on observable or reported characteristics. The PIT count data are used to inform the county's ten-year plan, which is based on 2005 data and is not updated annually. The six primary themes identified in the plan include:

1) Providing housing

2) Homeless prevention

3) Local and regional engagement and collaboration

4) Accessible safety net services for improved care and financial stability

5) Integration of services

6) Outcomes-based accountability

To address these themes, the county identifies a prioritized list of outcome objectives and a potential range of action steps. If the goal is to reduce the percentage of households that will lose their housing and become homeless by 50 percent, then each year marks incremental progress toward this goal. Yet with such specific targets in mind, the range of action steps is vague. Expanding funding for city and county pre-eviction programs, for example, is a good first step in moving toward a prevention model, but without accurate numerical data it is doubtful that specific targets will be met. Plan implementation also calls for additional staff and resources, but funding sources are not identified.

Although Santa Cruz County has made progress in offering transitional housing and emergency services for sheltered and unsheltered homeless people, it has hardly begun to address the issue of how to reach the unsheltered population and offer services and housing. Given the housing challenges in Santa Cruz in terms of population density and the age of the housing stock, combined with the overwhelming number of people who remain unsheltered, the lack of coordinated planning is daunting. This is compounded by the changing methodology of the count.

A Qualitative Profile

A qualitative profile of homelessness in Santa Cruz County shows that there is a culture of the streets that is shared, for the most part, by homeless people, citizens, and law enforcement. Part of this culture involves an understanding of social justice that upholds a homeless person's right to choose street living, as long as she is not a burden to others. A vibrant protest movement also exists among homeless people in Santa Cruz, which is used to resist anti-homeless ordinances and other forms of regulation. I describe this movement in some detail as it sets the tone for how the county approaches homelessness in general and homeless services in particular.

A group called Homeless United for Friendship and Freedom (HUFF) is the oldest and most persistent grassroots homeless organization in Santa Cruz. The group's founder, Robert Norse, hosts a radio show and website that documents the group's activities (http://www.huffsantacruz.org/). Self-described as "a noted annoyer of city council members," Norse and HUFF call attention to local ordinances that they feel impinge on homeless people's ability to occupy public spaces and engage in activities associated with homelessness. During my first meeting with HUFF members, they explained that the city council was trying to pass an ordinance limiting the amount of time people were allowed to loiter in public parking garages to fifteen minutes. Although the ordinance would apply to all citizens, whether or not they were parked in the garage, it would clearly have the most negative effect on homeless people, who cluster in these lots to seek shelter. To protest this ordinance, HUFF designed and distributed flyers that announced: "This is a parking alert. There will be a $124 fine if you don't leave your vehicles in 15 minutes." Activities like these are only one way that HUFF members protest actions seen as anti-homeless. Among the primary issues they pursue are preserving downtown spaces for all citizens, ending police repression, ending the sleeping/camping ban, and providing safe and legal campsites for homeless people.

In addition to organized protest activities, HUFF convenes a weekly meeting to share information about the experiences of homeless people on the street and seeking shelter. During the three two-hour HUFF meetings I attended, the discussion included equal access to veterans services; protection for homosexual clients in emergency shelters; the right to play music during the farmers market; the right to protest anti-homeless ordinances; additional services needed for homeless people, including showers and storage facilities; and targeting members of the police force and city council who are seen as being against homeless people. Although many forms of protest were suggested, without a legal advocate, HUFF simply calls attention to problematic issues. In so doing, its members are seen by police and the city council as agitators interested in stirring up trouble.

Although there is a homeless court in Santa Cruz, organized to offer legal assistance for homeless people facing citation, as one HUFF member described it, "Our understanding is, the Homeless Court is a way of saying: confess you're wrong, we'll give you work to do and send you out to get more tickets." The Human Rights Organization is a group related to HUFF and with overlapping membership. More specific in focus, this group examines the impact of downtown ordinances on people who are poor or homeless (https://scruzwiki.org/Human_Rights_Organization). Like HUFF, its members also discuss issues related to human rights, social justice, and equal access to public spaces. Also similar to HUFF, the group lacks legal advocacy.

Homeless people on the streets in Santa Cruz are highly visible, particularly in the downtown shopping area and main street—Pacific Avenue—and along the waterfront. On a typical day in Santa Cruz, you can see groups of homeless youth playing music, hanging out or panhandling, protest activities by HUFF and other groups, and individual homeless people asking for assistance. On my first evening in Santa Cruz, I was walking on Pacific Avenue and was approached by a man carrying a Bob Marley T-shirt he had draped over his arm. He smiled at me and I smiled back, and then he held up the T-shirt and said, "This is a nice shirt." "Yes, it is," I replied, not sure where this was going. "It's a *very* nice shirt," he repeated with emphasis, and I agreed with him again, picking up my pace. Later on, I realized that this was a form of benevolent panhandling. Although homeless people are prevented from "aggressive solicitation" by a city ordinance that makes it illegal to make a "verbal request, or any non-verbal request made with a sign, by a person seeking an immediate donation of money, food, cigarettes or items of value," they are not in violation when they "passively display a sign or place a collection container on the sidewalk" or receive a donation for artwork or a performance (Santa Cruz Municipal Code Chapter 9.10.010). In light of this law, homeless people either find themselves in frequent contact with law enforcement or find creative, nonthreatening ways of soliciting money and donations.

Regulation is an issue not only for those who panhandle but also for all unsheltered homeless people, including those who live in their vehicles. As a result, people living in their vehicles in Santa Cruz County typically cluster in the more industrial or rural areas, where they will not have frequent contact with law enforcement. As one officer described, "We do tow a lot, but it's something we don't like to do because it's a pain in the ass." He explained that towing the vehicle would mean heavy fines that would either be paid, meaning that the same vehicle would return to the streets, or be prohibitive, meaning that the individual would then be on the street without the vehicle. Not surprisingly, the area considered most problematic for individuals and vehicles is downtown Santa Cruz. As another officer described, "There's a Suburban that has been here since '03. I told the guy to get the vehicle out of the city. I don't want to tow it but people are complaining." The consensus among those living in their vehicles is that unless officers receive citizen complaints or are explicitly against vehicle living or particular individuals, they can slip by undetected.

To test the image of Santa Cruz as more tolerant of homeless people, I interviewed a man named Mike who was living in his van. He described aggressive activities by local residents. "They blew out my back window with a belt of firecrackers," he reported, showing me the damage, and adding, "the police won't investigate." When I asked him whether he had received tickets for sleeping, camping, or illegal parking, he said, "I've gotten so many, I lose count. I try to deal with them but occasionally I forget one and they give me failure to appeal. If this happens, they arrest me and impound the car." He showed me his checkbook, in which he recorded the $20 monthly payments he makes for tickets he has received. "Stupid tickets for something stupid. I never did no harm to no man." Mike also showed me a folder full of documents related to enforcement. One of them was written by a citizen in the neighborhood saying that Mike was harassed by the cops, and one officer in particular. The letter quotes the officer as saying, "I am harassing you because I can," and is not only signed but offers contact information including the person's work and home phone numbers. There were five similar letters in the folder. "I have ingratiated myself with the community," Mike boasted, noting that this was his only protection against police who, in his estimation, "want to run me out." Although Mike said he had only been towed once in the past five years, he also confessed, "I didn't make my last payment and I'm two weeks late."

To compare Mike's experience parking in Santa Cruz with parking in other areas of the county, I interviewed a woman named Elizabeth, who was living in her vehicle in Sebastopol, a rural part of Santa Cruz County. "Sebastopol has the most respectful officers," she told me, and said she had not been given a ticket in the eight years she has been living in her truck. She bought a day pass that allowed her to use the local park and had sometimes used the shower facilities at the Sebastopol Christian Church. "The hospital will let me shower there if I really need to," she explained. "They would rather have you stay clean." She told me that she was receiving SSI, which allowed her to pay for the day pass and to feed the nine cats she keeps as pets. "Would you prefer to live in an apartment if you could afford one?" I asked her. "No. They wouldn't let me have my cats," she responded. "They only allow you to have one, and I have too many." When I asked her if she considered herself homeless, she said "no. I take my home with me wherever I go." This comparatively positive experience of vehicle living is emblematic of the difference between areas, populations, and individuals considered problematic, and those that are seen as benevolent, anomalous, or simply less visible.

During my second visit to Santa Cruz County, I was determined to see the camping areas in the greenbelts and local parks like the Poganip, locations notorious for housing homeless campers. Unlike officers in the city of Santa Cruz, the park rangers did not return my calls requesting a ride-along, so I decided to make contact through the local homeless population. I arrived at the emergency shelter and was introduced to Jenna and Dave, a couple in their mid-forties who were, as they described, "your basic hard core campers." They had seen me in the shelter previously and knew something about my research. Still, they were skeptical: "We'll take you as far as we can," they indicated, "as long as it's safe for you."

After the evening meal, they collected their belongings and headed toward the railroad tracks. The tracks were the path into and out of the city. We walked along the tracks, making small talk, for about twenty minutes when we began to hear voices. Dave turned off the tracks onto a small path leading into the Poganip, saying, "We'll have to bypass this section [of the tracks] here. They're doing things you don't want to get involved in." Jenna explained that there were a group of men who positioned themselves along the tracks as gatekeepers to the camps that lay beyond. They dealt drugs there and kept lookout for law enforcement and others, like me, who clearly didn't belong. "This isn't just for you. We could get in trouble too if they think we're bringing an outsider," Dave reasoned.

We hiked uphill through the Poganip for another ten minutes or so, until we came to the cabins used by the park rangers. Dave and Jenna stopped and conferred about how far to take me. After about another mile, they turned and said, "This is going to have to be the end of the line, but you can see it from here." They motioned to a cluster of tents, barely visible in the distance. Unwilling to risk their safety or mine, I thanked them, offered them $5, and retreated nervously back through the park and into town, feeling safer but somewhat disappointed. In addition to more remote camping areas like those in the Poganip and beyond, many campers slept under the bridges and levees that border the railroad tracks and Route 9, forming a homeless highway in and out of the city.

To understand more about how homeless people in more remote areas in Santa Cruz County are regulated and policed, I conducted three separate ride-alongs with police officers during my two visits to Santa Cruz. None of them said they would enter remote camping areas alone. One officer explained, "People are going to be running from you automatically and there are needles, so it's kind of dangerous." In an extended interview with John, a homeless man in his early fifties who was sleeping under a levee, he described, "I've done it all, gone up in the Poganip, but you know, if the rangers know where you're at they just come back and they tear your stuff up. They don't even give you a notice anymore; they just trash your stuff." When I asked him about the types of camps set up there, he replied "Do they build shacks up there? Yeah, some of them do but you gotta go way up there or the rangers will get you." In comparison, when John lived in a vehicle, he said, "They don't harass you too much, but they want to know where you're at." John never spent much time in the shelters. "They want to pick the cream of the crop. It's not like the salvage business—where you have to take all of it, you can't pick through it. Now that's what they're doing, they're picking through it, getting what they want and the rest is trash and they treat them like trash. It upsets me."

Interview data and PIT count data demonstrate that the number of unsheltered people camping in the greenbelt areas that surround the city is an overwhelming majority of the overall population. This makes entry-level service provision that much more important in offering basic services and a possible transition. The role of transitional shelter, permanent supportive housing, and affordable housing is also key in offering and sustaining transition. The problem of unsheltered homelessness in Santa Cruz is compounded by the stringent entry requirements of most shelter programs. When I asked the director of the only emergency shelter in Santa Cruz, "If I was a 45 year-old single man, where could I sleep tonight?" he responded, "If you have a disabling condition, we might be able to prioritize you into the River Street Shelter or the ISSP [Interfaith Satellite Shelter Program].[4] If it was a pressing thing, we might be able to triage you, but if you're an average Joe, you're in the greenbelts."

Unlike Sonoma County, Santa Cruz County does not offer any emergency shelter beds on a year-round basis, so individuals seeking emergency services need to do so between November and March, when temporary winter shelters are available. This allows a short window of time during which individuals and families must either move to some form of transitional or permanent housing or go without shelter. The transitional housing available in Santa Cruz offers a twenty-four month period during which individuals and families must become self-sufficient. In both emergency and transitional programs, the need exceeds the available shelter beds.

Santa Cruz County seems mired in confusion regarding how to address the staggering numbers of unsheltered homeless people. The county is also seen as a place to embrace alternative lifestyles, so the question of whether homeless people should simply be left alone is a serious one. Shelters and services are organized to provide basic emergency care, but transitional and permanent housing are more difficult to access. Similarly, aside from regulation and enforcement, there is not a coordinated or consistent street outreach team, which would seem a needed first step in reaching the unsheltered homeless population.

Santa Barbara County

Framed by the Channel Islands and Pacific Ocean to the south and Santa Ynez Mountains to the north, the city of Santa Barbara is the second most populous city in Santa Barbara County and without a doubt the most famous. Santa Maria is the largest city, north of Santa Barbara and ten miles from the coast. It is known as home to both agriculture and aerospace industries. The third most populous city is Lompoc, located west of Santa Maria and inland from Vandenberg Air Force Base. These three cities host the majority of the county's homeless population. The region referred to as the "south coast" includes the city of Santa Barbara and the unincorporated area in the south county, as well as Isla Vista, Goleta, and Carpinteria, all of which are located just north and south of Santa Barbara. The county also is home to the University of California–Santa Barbara. Like Sonoma and Santa Cruz counties, Santa Barbara County is a diverse area both geographically and demographically and has a substantial unsheltered homeless population.

Santa Barbara has the least sophisticated PIT count of the three counties. In addition to the official numbers submitted to HUD as part of the CoC application, the 2005 and 2007 counts were summarized in a one-page memo. Instead of a street-by-street count and/or interview component, experts were relied on for estimates of the number of homeless people on the street. There was no tally sheet to standardize data collection for the 2007 count and no specific guidelines in place for recording observable characteristics. According to the memo, a total of 1,696 people were counted in 2007, with the majority on the south coast (54 percent) and in the cities of Santa Maria (35 percent) and Lompoc (11 percent). Although both the sheltered and unsheltered populations are included in these percentages, the memo notes that 248 people were found living in vehicles on the south coast.

In contrast with these findings, the report submitted to HUD as part of the 2007 application for the CoC indicates that there were 4,253 homeless people, more than half of whom were unsheltered, a discrepancy of 2,557 people. In terms of subpopulations, 259 people were reported as chronically homeless. How these estimates were determined, why there is such a large discrepancy between the PIT count and HUD reported figures, and how the number of chronically homeless people was estimated is unclear, even according to local policy experts and CoC officials. Not only is the difference in numbers daunting, it also demonstrates how a lack of oversight can lead to over- or undercounting, which affects federal funding levels and the overall planning process.

The lack of detail in Santa Barbara's PIT count makes it almost impossible to gather information on any of the subpopulations of interest, to assess the locations or demographics of the homeless population, and in turn, to target needed services. Instead, the count is driven by the desire to enumerate populations considered problematic, like those living in vehicles in Santa Barbara, and those living in motels in Santa Maria. Focusing on populations considered problematic and providing an expert-driven approach to the PIT count are both strategies that HUD cautions against because they don't give an accurate profile of the overall homeless population.

Collecting data on homeless people is always a challenge, but the attempts made in Sonoma and Santa Cruz counties are comparably sophisticated in terms of breadth and depth. Both include significant mobilization of resources and a survey and interview component. The 2009 and 2011 counts in Santa Barbara were more organized and were done with the assistance of the nonprofit organization Common Ground. The 2011 count employed the 100,000 Homes Campaign Registry Week method.[5] Volunteers were trained in using the vulnerability index to assess health needs and to prioritize the street homeless population for housing. The 2011 count found 1,563 people overall, and 1,143 of them completed surveys. The sheltered population comprised only one-third of the total, with 29 percent on the street and 15 percent in vehicles. The vast majority (79 percent) were considered vulnerable with high mortality risk. Ideally these findings can inform the overall housing goals for the county. The more detailed count completed in 2011 shows promise in offering a more accurate profile of the homeless community from which to base policy and planning efforts.

Santa Barbara's ten-year plan focuses solely on the chronic homeless population because of resource consumption. The plan is predicated on the assumption that chronically homeless people comprise 10 to 15 percent of the overall population but consume more than 50 percent of the resources. The plan also assumes that helping this segment of the homeless population will have a "positive ripple effect," meaning that better services and additional funding created through the plan's implementation will trickle up to address the needs of all homeless people. Written in 2006, the plan uses estimates of the expense of providing health care and legal services for homeless people, including citations and jail time. Unfortunately, these data were not collected according to subpopulation data and therefore do not separate chronic homelessness from other forms of homelessness. They are also not tied to the PIT count, which, despite its limitations, estimates that 945 people were chronically homeless within the county.

To end chronic homelessness, the plan's focus areas include prevention, outreach, supportive housing, income reinforcing supports, a financing plan, and implementation structure. Implementing this plan requires a massive mobilization of human and capital resources as well as political will. Three teams designed to focus on transition, outreach, and integrated services are proposed as well as five new staff positions and a new nonprofit organization. Despite the resources needed for personnel alone, when I asked one of the plan's authors about funding, he told me, "To be honest, right now, there is no fundraising plan. It's easier to get things done in north county, where it's cheaper to build." Despite several successful housing projects that target specific populations of homeless people, without a fundraising plan or an attempt to calibrate data collection with services and housing, the viability of ending chronic homelessness is seriously called into question.

A Qualitative Profile

Santa Barbara County's approach to homelessness is polarized between offering services as rarified as an organic soup kitchen to aggressively policing those on the streets and in vehicles. Part of the reason for this is that the county's understanding of homelessness is driven by the immediate concerns of business owners and law enforcement on one side, and by homeless people and advocates on the other. Hot-button issues, as covered in previous chapters, include specific populations as well as increased rights and privileges for homeless people, like the right to sleep. Because the county's understanding of homelessness is driven by these concerns rather than organized data collection, it is difficult to track population changes and address service needs.

The culture of the streets in Santa Barbara is vibrant, dating back to the 1940s, when the first jungle community rose to prominence. It includes several grassroots organizations that argue for the rights of homeless people. There is also virulent anti-homeless sentiment that involves citizen complaint as well as aggressive enforcement. Over the years, Santa Barbara's business owners have mobilized both formally and informally to prohibit homeless people from occupying the city's more prominent tourist venues. Although this resulted in several anti-homeless ordinances, it also resulted in the creation of the city's first emergency shelter for homeless people, opened in 1999, once again demonstrating the provisional and punitive sides of regulation. While some business owners provide for homeless people by offering goods and services, complaints by business owners, citizens, and tourists also drive anti-homeless regulation.

To enforce anti-homeless ordinances, as discussed in Chapter 4, the city's police department has a Tactical Patrol Force comprised of one sergeant and four officers, specifically dedicated to the regulation of street crimes and "nuisance issues." Founded in 1983, the Tactical Patrol Force works with the downtown business community to reduce the visible signs of street crime as well as actual occurrences. Tactical Patrol officers boast that they know "everyone on their beat from the merchants to the lowest down-and-out transients." They are also one of the highest producing units of the police department, as indicated by the number of citations and arrests. Their primary mode of transportation is by bicycle, to maximize their effectiveness in making arrests related to street crime and "selective enforcement operations." Among these are conducting sweeps and regulating those living in vehicles.

In other parts of the county, problematic populations include those living in motels and squatting in foreclosed houses. The city of Santa Maria focuses on the population of people living in motels who are homeless. During a ride-along with an officer in Santa Maria, we passed a dilapidated old motel and he said, "See this motel? There's not one normal human being in this motel. These are all sex registrants. They cater to sex registrants because of Megan's Law. They're one of the few that are outside of the radius of the schools. Are you aware of that?" Intimating an overlap between sex offenders and homeless people, he said, "That's where a lot of transients stay." Although it is unclear what percentage of those living in motels as sex registrants are homeless, motels are one of the only sources of year-round housing that is affordable for someone on SSI or SSDI. In 2009, the lowest priced motel in Santa Maria was charging $550 per month.

Although Santa Maria also has its share of unsheltered homeless people living on the streets, only those in heavily trafficked areas are a problem for law enforcement. The same officer quoted above told me that "our partners made this little pact that we're going to start harassing them, I guess. And we said, hey, we're not tolerating you guys—you guys gotta get out of here. But some of them are really rational. They're like 'where do I go' and we tell them this is the nice part of town and you guys have all this trash and you're laying around so what do you expect?" He also said that he understood that some of those he confronted were congregating around the recycling center, which served as their sole source of income. "How do you argue with them?" he asked.

Lompoc also struggles to keep its one emergency shelter open, which means that homeless people either seek shelter in Santa Maria or other parts of the county, or remain unsheltered and in various forms of makeshift housing. One officer I rode along with took me to two houses that were known as homeless squats. Although we did not find anyone inside, the houses had missing windows and doors, peeling paint, and overgrown grass. Forty-ounce beer bottles littered the floors, and all of the four rooms in one of the houses had sleeping bags on the floor and possessions strewn about. "Foreclosures house homeless people," he offered, "but they really have nothing to do with homelessness. Do you think any of them ever owned a house?"

The most substantial homeless population, according to service providers, politicians, and homeless people, is located in the city of Santa Barbara. The services for homeless people are located accordingly, with fewer in Santa Maria, Lompoc, and the more rural areas of the county. In an interview with Ken Williams, who worked for four decades as a social worker for the Department of Social Services in Santa Barbara, he noted the irony of the name "emergency shelter" for shelters that only accept families or those who are employed. He also expressed frustration with the city's one emergency shelter, both because it was not open on a year-round basis and because leaders were reticent to reallocate thirty beds to target those recovering from illness. Given the size of the homeless population in Santa Barbara County, the number of deaths recorded per year,[6] and the number who remain unsheltered, low-barrier services would seem to be a key priority, along with provisions for medical needs.

Affordable housing is also a primary need in Santa Barbara County, where the median annual income is over $70,000. Homeless people are often priced out of low-income housing, making vehicle living, the streets, and the shelters more viable alternatives. In addition to shelter, Santa Barbara's nonprofit organizations provide needed services and support for homeless advocacy efforts. Within one year, they funded a series of classes at the city's emergency shelter, supported research and data collection on anti-homeless ordinances, offered direct support to homeless people interested in organizing, and funded the Safe Parking Program outlined previously. Advocates also argue tirelessly for the rights of homeless people at meetings of both the Santa Barbara City Council and County Board of Supervisors. These efforts have resulted in some truly innovative programs that focus on specific segments of the homeless population as well as overall well-being.

The Committee for Social Justice, affiliated with the Legal Defense Center, is one of the most vocal and long-standing advocacy organizations in Santa Barbara. It was primarily responsible for bringing the Safe Parking Program to fruition and for advocating for the legal right to sleep in a vehicle. Committee members work closely with homeless people and encourage them to organize their own programs and nonprofits to argue for increased rights and privileges. Homes on Wheels is one such organization, formed by two women living in their vehicles. They are the same two women who served on the Task Force on Vehicle Dwelling discussed in the previous chapter. This organization achieved nonprofit status and attracted one year of foundation funding to "address the needs and concerns of the vehicle population." Homes on Wheels rented space in a historic building downtown and invited people living in their vehicles to drop in and voice their concerns. Within one month, the organization received complaints from other tenants in the building, indicating that the appearance and behavior of its clients was disrupting business. Losing its office meant a loss of status, and Homes on Wheels struggled from that point forward to identify a focus and method for organizing its constituents.

The culture of the streets in Santa Barbara is not unfamiliar with protest and advocacy, yet it is often the "usual suspects" who are called upon to represent the face of homelessness. Not only are a select few individuals unable to represent the diverse experiences of the homeless population but they also obfuscate the need to perform accurate, informed, and organized data collection. Preliminary data from the PIT count along with a qualitative profile of Santa Barbara show that unsheltered homeless people need affordable housing and programs to serve those who are mentally ill or addicted to drugs and/or alcohol. They also show that homeless people are in dire need of year-round shelter with adequate support services.

The current cost of owning and operating the city's one emergency shelter has mandated that the city also provide transitional shelter, where guests contribute one-third of their income. Moving toward transitional shelter forces the issue of documented success, and limited stays become par for the course. On a visit to one of the city's transitional shelters, a staff member indicated, "We have a high success rate of people we place into permanent housing, but you have to be careful about what *success* means. Sometimes it means that if you can't transition, you're out."

Conclusion

Exploring the methodology and findings of the PIT counts for Sonoma, Santa Cruz, and Santa Barbara counties shows a descending-order view of the coordination of homeless services. Sonoma County has the most comprehensive planning process in terms of the qualitative and quantitative components of the PIT count, as well as its coordination with the CoC and the ten-year plan. The county also has the newest housing stock and most affordable housing overall. And Sonoma is the only county with a year-round emergency shelter. In comparison, Santa Cruz and Santa Barbara counties struggle with more expensive housing markets, older housing stock, competing special needs groups, and dense downtown areas. The PIT count conducted in Santa Cruz offers a limited qualitative profile of homeless people and service needs, as the number interviewed represents a small fraction of the overall population. Santa Barbara's PIT count offers only a vague, nuisance-driven assessment of the number of homeless people countywide, and virtually no exploration of demographics or service needs.

Although people living in vehicles feature prominently as part of the unsheltered homeless population, there is virtually no qualitative data collected on them. The quantitative data that is collected is cursory and regulation driven, particularly in Santa Barbara. Examining the landscape of data collection and CoC planning efforts for unsheltered homeless people puts vehicle living into perspective as a form of homelessness lumped into the "unsheltered" category. Without an understanding of the demographic breakdown of the unsheltered homeless population, what housing solutions they employ, or how ready they are to transition into permanent housing, offering outreach services is futile. Yet the mere size of the unsheltered population in each of the three counties demands attention and action. As previous chapters show, people living in vehicles have different service needs than people living on the street. They also have greater resources over those in the shelters or on the streets. In many counties, this means that they are not the focus of regulation. Yet their service needs remain unaddressed.

Although this book focuses on people living in their vehicles, examining the PIT counts in all three counties yields detailed information on unsheltered homeless people and the policies and planning efforts designed to serve them. Connecting information from the PIT counts with ten-year plans is a way of assessing how data gathering is used to inform policy and practice. Examining PIT counts over time shows that the unsheltered homeless population is a moving target and that the methodology employed in the PIT counts varies widely. As this analysis demonstrates, the numbers of homeless people in a given category can change dramatically from count to count, necessitating ongoing calibration of the ten-year plan. Without coordination of data gathering and planning efforts, counties do not know how many people need services or what types of services are most needed. If changing methodology produces different percentages of unsheltered homeless people, as was the case in Sonoma and Santa Cruz counties, planning efforts must be reorganized accordingly and on an ongoing basis.

The focus on specific populations of homeless people is not only cautioned against in the *HUD Guide to Counting Unsheltered Homeless People* but is also typically regulation rather than service driven. As is the case with people living in their vehicles in Santa Barbara, regulation is not only punitive. It can lead to the creation of specific programs and services. Yet focusing on one population does not ensure the coordination of services for all. The argument for housing unsheltered homeless people is that they consume the bulk of service dollars, so housing them is less expensive than leaving them on the street. Although devoid of moral implications or concerns, this argument has gained traction with communities nationwide, and in the case of Santa Barbara, it is what drives the county's ten-year plan. Even if Santa Barbara County was able to end chronic homelessness through offering transitional and permanent housing—which is doubtful for reasons previously indicated—how would the rest of the homeless population make the transition, and how would the county serve those who find themselves newly homeless?

Focusing on unsheltered homeless people and entry-level services shows the need for flexible service plans and client control and participation. Outreach and emergency shelter are the beginning of the ladder-like CoC that ideally transitions homeless people into permanent housing. Combining the Housing First approach to offering consumer driven, low demand housing with the CoC approach of offering a continuum of services is a more measured mode of service provision. Offering intake services that triage people according to need has also been piloted in several communities with documented success. This approach understands that homeless people are at different stages of housing and service readiness, both in terms of what services they need and in in terms of what they can manage and sustain in the long term. Sonoma County has moved closer to this model of service provision than Santa Cruz and Santa Barbara counties and has shown the most impressive results.

Notes

[1] 2011 PIT count estimates reveal that California is one of five states with the highest percentage of unsheltered homeless people, at 62.7 percent. The other four states are Wyoming (81.2 percent), Louisiana (63.4 percent), Florida (63.3 percent), and Oregon (59.4 percent). California is also one of five states that account for half of the nation's total homeless population. These five states are California (21.4 percent), New York (10.0 percent), Florida (8.9 percent),

Texas (5.8 percent), and Georgia (3.3 percent). The prevalence of unsheltered homeless people and the sheer volume of the unsheltered homeless population can be read in two ways: (1) California has a huge problem, or (2) California has the potential to spearhead the development of effective service delivery for unsheltered homeless people.

[2] Medi-Cal is California's Medicaid program designed for low-income people of all ages. It is a government-sponsored program, and coverage varies from state to state. It differs from Medicare, which is a federal program that primarily serves people age 65 and over, although there are provisions for younger people with qualifying disabilities. CalWORKS is a welfare program run by county welfare departments to assist families by offering cash and services. All three programs have specific eligibility requirements and distribute variable benefits. Homeless people often need assistance in determining which program best suits their needs and in keeping up with the requisite paperwork.

[3] Section 5150 of the California Welfare and Institutions Code allows qualified medical and psychiatric professionals to involuntary commit people to institutions who pose an immediate threat to themselves and/or others or who are deemed gravely disabled. The duration of the hold is typically seventy-two hours, after which they are evaluated and may be offered voluntary admission to another facility.

[4] The Interfaith Satellite Shelter Program (ISSP) provides space on church floors for approximately forty homeless individuals per night. Those wishing to access these spaces are given a voucher and told to report to a central location. They are then bused to the participating churches.

[5] The US Interagency Council on Homelessness is partnering with the 100,000 Homes campaign to help communities implement Opening Doors, the federal strategic plan to end chronic and veteran homelessness by 2015 and family and youth homelessness by 2020. The registry week method is part of the 100,000 Homes campaign and can be used as a supplement to the PIT count, although it typically occurs over several days. The registry week method uses a "vulnerability index" survey that asks social, demographic, and health questions. Members of the homeless community are identified by name when they consent to sharing this information. Implementing a registry week method into the PIT count takes several weeks of planning prior to the count and a greater commitment of resources than many communities typically mobilize. The primary benefit of this method is that it assists communities in reaching measurable housing goals that target the most difficult-to-serve members of the homeless community (see www.100khomes.org and http://100khomes.org/sites/default/files/images/Registry%20Week%20PIT%20Integration%20Toolkit_FINAL.pdf for additional information).

[6] Ken Williams documents the number and causes of homeless deaths per year. Causes range from hypothermia to violence, and the numbers are startling, at thirty-two in 2010 (see http://www.noozhawk.com/ken_williams/).

7

When Beggars Become Choosers

RV living is not a new phenomenon. It has made peripheral mention in research on homelessness since it abounded in response to the crisis in the 1980s. Yet it has never been differentiated from other types of housing for homeless people. This exploration of vehicle living has focused on three primary issues: (1) vehicle living as an alternative to shelter and street living, (2) the cycle of regulation and resistance that likens vehicle living to other forms of homelessness, and (3) data collection procedures that inform policy responses directed to serving unsheltered homeless people. This concluding chapter examines these issues in detail as they help situate vehicle living along a continuum of housing solutions.

The resources that vehicle living provides in comparison with other forms of housing are numerous. Vehicle owners prefer their vehicles over shelter or street settings for reasons that seem obvious: (1) shelters force adherence to rules, behavioral scrutiny, and substandard living conditions, (2) the streets are risky for people and possessions, and (3) vehicles offer more privacy, safety, and autonomy. The fact that vehicle living offers resources that outshine apartment living is more surprising. Like shelter living, apartment living requires adherence to rules, including a limit on pets, that is a barrier for some people living in their vehicles. It also requires negotiation with landlords, upkeep of the apartment, and managing friends, neighbors, and the neighborhood. RVers who choose to remain in their vehicles retain a degree of mobility and control over their lives and circumstances that is over and above what even those in apartments enjoy, despite issues of relative comfort. Clearly, apartment living is not an option for many people living in their vehicles for reasons that are primarily economic but also include addiction and mental illness. Vehicle living is unique in comparison with street and shelter living, and apartment rentals, as it allows for legal ownership. Although this requires negotiating the initial purchase and ongoing maintenance of the vehicle, legal ownership offers an unprecedented degree of protection and a means to resist regulation. Yet vehicle living is still pursued as a problem needing a solution that involves enforcement.

Part of the reason for this is that being homeless mars vehicle living in the same way it does other housing solutions. As is the case with traditional home ownership, the "identity" of the vehicle and that of the occupant tend to blur, such that one is associated with the other (Urry 2002; Meyer 1987). Once homeless, in other words, anything you do and anywhere you live is suspect. The regulation strategies used to constrain the occupation of public space and various behaviors associated with homelessness are numerous. Resistance is the counter to regulation, as it involves modes of survival, including occupying public space, and arguing for rights and privileges that regulation strategies attempt to circumscribe.

Why is the combination of homelessness and vehicle living so threatening? One of the reasons is the convergence of poverty, identity, and housing choice. Homeless people either fail to meet societal goals, particularly the accumulation of wealth, or reject them entirely. Either way, they symbolize an affront to the values we uphold or to our own success in achieving those goals. There is a distrust of those not participating in the formal economy, or not doing so to the degree that would allow them to become invisible. The "what's wrong with you?" question looms large in confrontations with homeless people. How could they abdicate the responsibility that goes with established home ownership or apartment rentals? There must be something morally wrong or at least suspect about those who live this lifestyle—they must be addicted, mentally ill, antisocial, or sociopathic. Ethnographic work that pursues examples of homeless people who are intelligent, employable, and "just like us" has endured criticism as have works that valorize mere survival over social change.

Part of the understanding of homeless people as pathology-ridden is place dependent. As I have argued throughout this book, being in one's proper place has spatial as well as behavioral implications. Being in a shelter, complying with the rules, acting deferent, admitting and seeking treatment for addiction or mental illness, or simply admitting that homelessness is wrong are all seen as signs that a homeless person is getting her life together. By contrast, homeless people who sleep outside and in makeshift settings, who panhandle or recycle to pay for daily expenses, and who patently refuse shelter or other forms of assistance or service are seen as morally and legally suspect. Yet as many books on homeless resistance attest (Wright 1997; Wagner 1993), understanding housing choices from a homeless person's perspective makes them not only understandable but logical.

Addressing the logic of housing choices for homeless people is particularly relevant in California, where the majority of homeless people statewide go unsheltered. California's high housing costs, its tourist market, and the fact that many of its homeless shelters are open only during the winter months have resulted in a convergence of poverty and tourism in prime urban areas. Because regulating homeless people is typically done in public spaces, California wages a daily war over the right to its streets, parks, and beaches. Creating or stepping up enforcement measures is one way of moving homeless people out of certain areas or containing them in jails or emergency shelters. Offering services and programs is a similar attempt to curtail their visibility in public and behaviors associated with homelessness, yet, it ideally offers a point of transition.

Regulation

Regulation strategies that apply to homeless people include behaviors associated with being homeless and range from life-sustaining activities to the occupation of public spaces to aggressive panhandling. Selectively enforcing the law to target homeless people and treating them as noncitizens in the process, or not treating them according to due process, are other forms of regulation that set homeless people apart and mark them as targets. Applying regulation strategies to homeless people living in vehicles also involves selective enforcement—ticketing some vehicles and not others. Yet, regulating activities associated with a life in public is more difficult. While it may be illegal to sleep in one's vehicle, proving it is another matter. To pursue vehicle living as a punishable offense trades on common understandings of what is logical and what a reasonable person would do if confronted with homelessness.

Legal ownership and a private space in which to conduct otherwise public activities are two of the marked differences between homeless people on the street versus those in vehicles. These resources are a central feature of what sets vehicle living apart from other housing solutions. Yet like chronically homeless people, RVers remain vulnerable to repeat ticketing, forcing them to remain in constant motion to avoid citation. The expense of this not only cuts into survival needs but jeopardizes long-term ownership of the vehicle. When vehicles are ticketed and towed, owners frequently lose all of their possessions, as they lack the funds to pay the ticket as well as impound and storage fees. Police officers and tow yards will sometimes allow access to the vehicle, but not always. Vehicle owners therefore face similar although less constant vulnerability, in terms of their possessions, that homeless people in other makeshifts experience. The alternative to vehicle living that is put forward by city commissioners, lawyers, and public officials in the arena of regulation is either apartment living, shelter living, or in some cases, the street.

Offering shelters as an alternative to vehicle living suggests that RVers not only have the inclination to pursue them but that they will do so on a relatively constant basis. To avoid citation and sleep in one's RV in Santa Barbara means moving it every three hours, during the hours of 2 a.m. and 6 a.m., and pursuing shelter accommodations nightly. RVers who are able to perform these activities are less likely to receive citations or, if they do receive them, are more likely to be able to fight them successfully. In addition to the shelters available to homeless people, Santa Barbara created a program to provide nightly parking and case management for RVers. Examining the inner workings of this program sheds light on the more provisional aspects of regulation. Designed to go hand-in-hand with additional restrictions of RV use and stepped up enforcement policies, the Safe Parking Program is a provision for some and for others, a trap.

Examining the differences between homeless people who are willing to participate in a program and those who are not does two things. First, it underscores the need to adhere to program guidelines as a condition of service; and second, it shows the complex issues people living in their vehicles may face, including addiction and mental illness. The second issue is particularly poignant as it is similar to what homeless people seeking apartments may also face. This underscores the still underdeveloped sense of the ongoing services many homeless people need once they are housed. The Safe Parking Program also draws attention to the question of whether homeless people need or want to be in a "program." This question is a central feature of both regulation and resistance. Posed differently, it asks: should people be allowed to remain homeless, or is it a lifestyle that is fundamentally wrong, dangerous, morally suspect, or simply needing correction?

People living in their vehicles are technically part of the unsheltered homeless population because although many vehicles are designed to be lived in, they were intended for temporary rather than permanent use. The funding and services that communities receive to house and otherwise serve unsheltered homeless people depend on an accurate count that assesses need as well as numbers. As Chapter 6 demonstrates, this information is particularly difficult to gather, resulting in over- or undercounts, an emphasis on populations deemed problematic, or simply setting unrealistic long-term goals. Yet the issue that goes unaddressed is that people living in their vehicles do not necessarily consider themselves homeless, will not necessarily submit to services or a program, and do not necessarily see anything wrong with living in their vehicles permanently. So even with accurate numbers, a qualitative profile is needed to begin to address service needs.

Resistance

Putting homeless resistance into historical perspective shows that the widespread mobilization that occurred in the 1980s (Snow, Soule, and Cress 2005) has largely been muted. In the late 1980s and beyond, "compassion fatigue" rendered homelessness an expected part of the urban landscape. Yet the scope of the problem has not diminished enough to warrant a lack of attention. David Wagner and Jennifer Goodman (2012, 5) ask, "How is it that interest in social problems such as homelessness can rise and fall so rapidly and often with no relation to the extent of the problem?" Instead of focusing on social change, "homelessness" has become associated with a group of people rather than with poverty or housing instability. Efforts to enumerate the homeless population, a key feature of receiving federal funding, further obscure the underlying causes of homelessness and instead focus on expanding welfare bureaucracy (Bogard 2001).

Forms of resistance enacted by homeless people are short-lived because they involve the occupation of public spaces or the sanctioning of public activities. Homeless people also typically lack the resources and political clout to manage long-term protest and advocacy. In some cities, the lack of available shelter has forced the allowance of public sleeping, with hourly and spatial restrictions (Wakin 2008). Ultimately, when faced with the life-threatening issues that anti-homeless regulation poses, mere existence seems a form of resistance. Remaining visible in public spaces and refusing to submit to shelters are the most common forms of resistance to the idea that homeless people belong in shelters and are not entitled to the same rights afforded housed citizens (Feldman 2004). These are relatively meager gains when compared with organized forms of resistance and protest that focus on social change.

Examining how RVers evaluate the vehicle as a housing solution shows that they value safety, privacy, autonomy, and mobility and that they view shelters and in some cases apartments as impinging on these resources. Remaining in the vehicle and enacting various survival strategies to avoid regulation is a classic tactical form of resistance. Yet, what is it that RVers and their advocates truly want? Advocacy in Santa

Barbara, relative to the RV population, is comprised of a very small group of people willing to pursue citations for sleeping and camping and eventually oversee the creation of the Safe Parking Program. Legal advocacy was successful in overturning sleeping and camping citations but ultimately resulted in stepped up restrictions relating to daily and nightly use of the vehicle. In addition, pursuing these cases as vehicle code issues rather than misdemeanor offenses meant that RVers could no longer contest the citations using legal counsel but had to pay them first and contest them in writing afterwards.

While the Safe Parking Program was created to offer safe nightly parking for people living in their vehicles, it imposed rules and restrictions similar to what shelters impose. For some people, the rules were welcomed and for others, they were intolerable. Ironically, the program was set up to resist punitive regulation yet it also imposed regulation strategies that those who remain parked on city streets resist. This underscores the dynamic nature of regulation and resistance. Some form of regulation typically accompanies any form of service. Offering service without any requirements is rare and often jeopardizes the sustainability of what is provided. Yet, is resistance without the backlash of regulation realistic? Would it mean sanctioning street homelessness?

Examining the unsheltered homeless populations in three California counties shows that street homelessness is prevalent and is often accompanied by addiction and mental illness, in addition to violence and chronic health problems. Although not explicitly sanctioned in any of the three counties, the least punitive county is Santa Cruz. This would doubtlessly be surprising to homeless people in Santa Cruz because of the anti-homeless ordinances they continually protest. Nevertheless, with a majority of the homeless population without shelter of any kind, the county has developed a visible and palpable culture of the streets. Unsheltered homeless people in Santa Cruz can receive emergency services, but there are few emergency beds available, they are only open on a seasonal basis, and outreach services and transitional housing are scarce, at best.

Resistance activities in Santa Cruz fall flat, both because they are tolerated as part of the culture and because regulation typically targets the central downtown area. In Santa Cruz, as elsewhere, tourist areas are almost universally understood as zones of regulation. Resistance is therefore typically enacted in the greenbelts and involves developing camps and subsisting in a marginal, hidden environment. Ironically, provisional regulation in the form of shelter is also typically located away from central city areas. If survival and avoiding shelters are seen as forms of resistance, then Santa Cruz's homeless population is the most successful. This does not minimize the troubling issues that are prevalent among unsheltered homeless people; rather, it pushes the question of how to break the cycle of regulation and resistance.

Future Directions

Examining the creation of the Safe Parking Program as well as the planning efforts in three California counties brings several issues to light: (1) homeless people need to be participants in policy and planning efforts designed to serve them, (2) outreach and emergency services for unsheltered homeless people still serve as a first point of contact, (3) prior to establishing permanent housing, and once placed, homeless people often need additional services and supports. These issues apply to vehicle owners as well as other subsets of the unsheltered homeless population, and they resonate with both the Housing First and CoC models of service provision. They also resonate with the idea of street identities and creative resistance that Jason Wasserman and Jeffrey Clair (2010) discuss.

Creative resistance and street identities are ways of carving normalcy out of a stigmatized existence. Survival in the shelter often means keeping to oneself and not drawing attention to one's activities. Street living, by contrast, allows for a wider variety of personalities and expression without the fear of conflict prevalent in congregate shelters (Wasserman and Clair 2010). Vehicles not only allow freedom of expression without backlash, but also a private space in which to develop and preserve a sense of self-esteem. Coupling this with legal ownership of the vehicle makes it a viable, albeit low-income, form of housing. Focusing on the services people need to access to maintain vehicle living while pursuing permanent housing is one way of breaking the cycle of regulation and resistance. It takes the emphasis off of public space restrictions and focuses on stability and access to low-barrier services.

Housing First is often misunderstood as suggesting that homeless people simply need housing without additional services. In actuality, this approach says that homeless people need to be treated as consumers rather than welfare cases (Stefancic et al. 2012). Their preferences, in other words, and their service needs need to be taken into account as something they ask for rather than something that is foisted upon them as a condition of shelter. Placing people in housing while offering case management, detox, or other services is not only less expensive than leaving them on the street but also treats them as active agents with preferences and choices. In this sense, this approach is unique. Involving homeless people in policy decisions and in running programs and services is a part of the philosophy of Housing First and is also espoused by several innovative programs, including several shelters and food pantries in Sonoma County. It is also becoming part of data gathering efforts like the 100,000 Homes campaign, which emphasizes the need to talk directly with homeless people about their service needs. Creating a culture of inclusion and success from a culture of the streets is challenging, yet including homeless people as part of the community of respected and respectable citizens is desirable. This can be transformative for both the server and the served.

Although permanent housing is a way of ending homelessness, finding enough permanent or even transitional housing for homeless people is a daunting task. This is particularly true in the counties under study, which have overwhelming numbers of unsheltered homeless people, expensive housing markets, and competing low-income groups. Ending chronic homelessness begins with a first point of contact. Outreach services for homeless people living on the street involve the most daunting, grueling work. As a result they are typically sporadic, enforcement driven, or otherwise punitive. Emergency shelters and their associated services are also a first point of contact for unsheltered homeless people. This presents a unique opportunity for transition, depending on the services offered and the overall approach to emergency service. Suggesting that outreach and emergency services need exploration does not forego the ultimate goal of providing permanent housing. It recognizes that a range of options, a lateral rather than a step-wise CoC, needs to be in place to meet the diverse needs of homeless people.

Exploring vehicle living through the lens of regulation and resistance demonstrates the problematic intersection of stigma and identity in the realm of public space. It is a dynamic that applies to other forms of unsheltered homelessness, particularly street-level makeshifts. Examining the rise of vehicle living as a problem in Santa Barbara not only shows how this dynamic is set off but underscores the extent to which vehicles remain part of the "hidden homeless" population. Legal ownership means that people living in their vehicles can avoid regulation, in part, breaking the cycle. Advocacy efforts in Santa Barbara, the only county to specifically target people living in vehicles, also resulted in some public space provisions including but not limited to the Safe Parking Program. This exploration of vehicle living sets it against a landscape of entry-level service provision and policy and planning efforts that struggle to understand service and housing needs. The resources that vehicle living offers are transformative for homeless people. At minimum, they allow status within an intra-homeless hierarchy and a safe, private living space. They also have the transformative potential of offering privacy, mobility, and choice for people who are otherwise homeless.

References

Agnew, J. 1982. "Home Ownership and Identity in Capitalist Societies." Pp. 60-97 in *Housing and Identity: Cross-Cultural Perspectives,* ed. J. Duncan. New York: Holmes and Meier.

Aldrich, D., and K. Crook. 2008. "Strong Civil Society as a Double-Edged Sword: Siting Trailers in Post Katrina New Orleans." *Political Research Quarterly* 61 (3): 379–389.

Anderson, N. 1923. *The Hobo: The Sociology of the Homeless Man.* Chicago: University of Chicago Press.

Associated Press. 2010. "New Orleans Moves to Get Rid of Last FEMA Trailers." *USA Today,* December 31.

Bahr, H. 1970. *Disaffiliated Man: Essays and Bibliography on Skid row, Vagrancy, and Outsiders.* Toronto: University of Toronto Press.

Bahr. H. 1973. *Skid Row: An Introduction to Disaffiliation.* New York: Oxford University Press.

Bahr, H., and T. Caplow. 1973. *Old Men Drunk and Sober.* New York: New York University Press.

Baxter, E., and K. Hopper. 1981. "Private Lives/Public Spaces: Homeless Adults on the Streets of New York City." New York: Community Service Society.

Becker, H. 1971. *Labeling Deviant Behavior: Its Sociological Implications.* New York: Harper and Row.

Bennett, S. 1995. "No relief but upon the Terms of Coming into the House–Controlled Spaces, Invisible Disentitlements, and Homelessness in an Urban Shelter Setting." *Yale Law Journal* 104 (8): 2157–2122.

Blasi, G. 1994. "And We Are Not Seen: Ideological and Political Barriers to Understanding Homelessness." *American Behavioral Scientist* 37 (4): 563–586.

Bogard, C. 2001. "Advocacy and Enumeration: Counting Homeless People in a Suburban Community." *American Behavioral Scientist* 45 (1): 105–120.

Bogue, D. 1963. *Skid Row in American Cities.* Chicago: Community and Family Study Center, University of Chicago.

Bratt, R. G. 2003. "Housing for Very Low-Income Households: The Record of President Clinton, 1993–2000." *Housing Studies* 18 (4): 607–635.

Brunker, M. 2006. "Are FEMA Trailers Toxic Tin Cans?" *msnbc.com*, July 25, 2006, accessed December 3, 2012. http://www.msnbc.msn.com/id/14011193/ns/us_news-katrina_the_long_road_back/t/are-fema-trailers-toxic-tin-cans/.

Burgess, E. W. 1925. "The Growth of the City: An Introduction to a Research Project." Pp. 85–97 in *Urban Ecology*, vol. 18, eds. J. M. Marzluff et al. Publication of the American Sociological Society.

Burkhart, B., P. Noyes, and A. Arieff. 2002. *Trailer Travel: A Visual History of Mobile America.* Salt Lake City: Gibbs Smith.

Burt, M. R., and B. Cohen. 1989. *America's Homeless: Numbers, Characteristics, and Programs that Serve Them.* Washington, DC: Urban Institute Press.

Burt, M. R., L. Y. Aron, E. Lee, and J. Valente. 2001. *Helping America's Homeless: Emergency Shelter or Affordable Housing.* Washington, DC: Urban Institute Press.

Carr, L. 1994. "The Can't Move–Must Move Contradiction: A Case Study of Displacement of the Poor and Social Stress." *Journal of Social Distress and the Homeless* 3: 185–201.

Chawkins, S. 2008. "Homeless Find Haven in Their Vehicles." *Los Angeles Times.* January 13.

Clark, C. D., and C. E. Wilcox. 1938. "The House Trailer Movement." *Sociology and Social Research* 22 (6): 503–519.

Cole, R. 1991. "Participant Observer Research: An Activist Role." Pp. 159–166 in *Participatory Action Research,* ed. W. Foote Whyte. London: Sage Publications.

Counts, D. A. and D. R. Counts. 1992. "They're My Family Now: The Creation of Community among RVers." *Anthropologica* 34: 153–182.

Cress, D., and D. Snow. 1996. "Mobilization at the Margins: Resources, Benefactors, and the Viability of Homeless Social Movement Organizations." *American Sociological Review* 61: 1089–1109.

Cresswell, T. 2001. *The Tramp in America.* London: Reaktion Books.

Crowley. S. 2003. "The Affordable Housing Crisis: Residential Mobility of Poor Families and School Mobility of Poor Children." *Journal of Negro Education* 72 (1): 22–38.

Cuba, L., and D. M. Hummon. 1993. "A Place to Call Home: Identification with Dwelling, Community, and Region." *Sociological Quarterly* 34 (1): 111–131.

Culhane, D. P., and R. Kuhn. 1998. "Patterns and Determinants of Public Shelter Utilization among Homeless Adults in New York City and Philadelphia." *Journal of Policy Analysis and Management* 17 (1): 23–43.

DaCosta Nunez, R. 1994. *Hopes, Dreams, and Promise: The Future of Homeless Children in America.* New York: Institute for Children and Poverty.

Danielson, C., and J. A. Klerman. 2008. "Did Welfare Reform Cause the Caseload Decline?" *Social Service Review* 82 (4): 703–730.

Davis, B., and V. Bali. 2008. "Examining the Role of Race, NIMBY, and Local Politics in FEMA Trailer Park Placement." *Social Science Quarterly* 85 (5): 1175–1194.

Dear, M. 1992. "Understanding and Overcoming the NIMBY Syndrome." *Journal of the American Planning Association* 58 (3): 288–307.

Dear, M., and Wolch, J. 1987. *Landscapes of Despair.* Princeton, NJ: Princeton University Press.

DeCerteau, M. 1984. *The Practice of Everyday Life.* Berkeley: University of California Press.

DePastino, T. 2003. *Citizen Hobo: How a Century of Homelessness Shaped America.* Chicago: Chicago University Press.

DiFazio, W. 2006. *Ordinary Poverty: A Little Food and Cold Storage.* Philadelphia: Temple University Press.
Dordick, G. 1997. *Something Left to Lose: Personal Relations and Survival among New York's Homeless.* Philadelphia: Temple University Press.
Dreier, P. 2004. "Reagan's Legacy: Homelessness in America." *Shelterforce Online* (135) May/June 2004, accessed July 18, 2011. http://www.nhi.org/online/issues/135/reagan.html.
Duneier, M. 1999. *Sidewalk.* New York: Farrar, Straus, and Giroux.
Dyson, M. E. 2005. *Come Hell or High Water: Hurricane Katrina and the Color of Disaster.* New York: Basic Civitas Books.
Ellickson, R. C. 2001. "Controlling Chronic Misconduct in City Spaces: Of Panhandlers, Skid Rows, and Public-Space Zoning." Pp. 19–30 in *The Legal Geographies Reader*, eds. N. Blomley, D. Delaney, and R. T. Ford. Oxford: Blackwell Publishers.
Emerson, R. M. 2001. *Contemporary Field Research: Perspectives and Formulations,* 2nd ed. Long Grove, IL: Waveland Press.
Feldman, L. 2004. *Citizens without Shelter.* Ithaca, NY: Cornell University Press.
Federal Emergency Management Agency. 2005. "Frequently Requested National Statistics Hurricane Katrina—One Year Later." Accessed October 1, 2012. http://www.fema.gov/hazard/hurricane/2005katrina/anniversary factsheet.shtm.
Fetterman, D. M. 1991. "A Walk through the Wilderness: Learning to Find Your Way." Pp. 87–97 in *Experiencing Fieldwork,* eds. W. B. Shaffir and R. A. Stebbins. London: Sage Publications.
Flynn, K. 2008. *The New Deal.* Salt Lake City: Gibbs Smith.
Foote Whyte, W., D. Greenwood, and P. Lazes. 1991. "Participatory Action Research." Pp. 19–55 in *Participatory Action Research,* ed. W. Foote Whyte. London: Sage Publications.
Foscarinis, M. 1996. "Downward Spiral: Homelessness and Its Criminalization," *Yale Law and Policy Review* 14: 1–63.
Foster, R. 1980. "Wartime Trailer Housing in the San Francisco Bay Area," *Geographical Review (AGS)* 70: 276–290.
Friedman, B. D. 1994. "No Place Like Home: A Study of Two Homeless Shelters." *Journal of Social Distress and the Homeless* 3 (4): 321–339.
Garfinkel, H. 1956. "Conditions of Successful Degradation Ceremonies." *American Journal of Sociology* 61 (5): 420–424.
Goffman, E. 1959. *The Presentation of Self in Everyday Life.* New York: Anchor Books.
Goffman, E. 1963. *Stigma.* New York: Simon and Schuster.
Gregory, J. 1989. *American Exodus: The Dust Bowl Migration and Okie Culture in California.* New York: Oxford University Press.
Grigsby, C., D. Baumann, S. Gregorich, and C. Roberts-Gray. 1990. "Disaffiliation to Entrenchment: A Model for Understanding Homelessness." *Journal of Social Issues* 46: 141–156.
Gutierrez, T., and W. Drash. 2008."Mom Forced to Live in Car with Dogs," *CNN,* May 19.
Haggstrom, J. 1994. "The Santa Barbara Sleeping Law Controversy: A Study of the Empowerment of the Homeless." Ph.D. diss., University of California, Santa Barbara.

Hallett, R. E. 2012. *Educational Experiences of Hidden Homeless Teenagers: Living Doubled-up.* New York: Routledge.
Harmon, D. L. 2001. "American Camp Culture: A History of Recreational Vehicle Development and Leisure Camping in the United States, 1890–1960." Ph.D. diss., Iowa State University.
Herbert, S. 1997. *Policing Space: Territoriality and the Los Angeles Police Department.* Minneapolis: University of Minnesota Press.
Hoch, C., and R. Slayton. 1989. *New Homeless and Old.* Philadelphia: Temple University Press.
Hombs, M. E., and M. Snyder. 1982. *Homelessness in America: A Forced March to Nowhere.* Washington, DC: Community for Creative Non-Violence.
Hopper, K. 2003. *Reckoning with Homelessness.* New York: Cornell University.
Hopper, K., E. Susser, and S. Conover. 1985. "Economies of Makeshift: Deindustrialization and Homelessness in New York City." *Urban Anthropology* 14 (1-3): 183–236.
Hurley, A. 2001. *Diners, Bowling Alleys, and Trailer Parks: Chasing the American Dream in Postwar Consumer Culture.* New York: Basic Books.
Industrial Workers of the World. 1905. Preamble to the 1905 Constitution. Accessed March 13, 2013, http://xroads.virginia.edu/~MA05/cline/preamble.htm.
Jensen, B. 2005. "Program Pioneering Housing First Is Catching on across the Country." *Chronicle of Philanthropy,* August 18, 2005, accessed January 1, 2011. http://philanthropy.com/article/Program-Pioneering-Housing/56080/.
Joniak, E. 2005. "Exclusionary Practices and the Delegitimization of Client Voice: How Staff Create, Sustain, and Escalate Conflict in a Drop-in Center for Street Kids." *American Behavioral Scientist* 48 (8): 961–988.
Jorgensen, D. L. 1989. *Participant Observation: A Methodology for Human Studies.* Applied Social Research Methods Series, Vol. 15. Newbury Park, CA: Sage Publications.
Kelling, G. L., and C. M. Coles. 1996. *Fixing Broken Windows.* New York: Martin Kessler Books.
Kesey, K. 1962. *One Flew Over the Cuckoo's Nest.* New York: Viking Press and Signet Books.
Kim, M. M., and J. D. Ford. 2006. "Trauma and Post-Traumatic Stress among Homeless Men: A Review of Current Research." *Journal of Aggression, Maltreatment, and Trauma* 13 (2): 1–22.
Kusmer, K. 2002. *Down and Out, On the Road: The Homeless in American History.* Oxford: Oxford University Press.
Link, B., J. Phelan, M. Bresnahan, A. Stueve, R. Moore, and E. Susser. 1995. "Life-Time and Five-Year Prevalence of Homelessness in the United States: New Evidence on an Old Debate." *American Journal of Orthopsychiatry* 65 (3): 347–354.
Lofland, J., D. Snow, L. Anderson, and L. Lofland. 2006. *Analyzing Social Settings: A Guide to Qualitative Observation and Analysis.* Belmont, CA: Wadsworth/Thomson Learning.
Lott, B, and K. Webster. 2006. "Carry the Banner Where It Can Be Seen: Small Wins for Social Justice." *Social Justice Research* 19 (1): 123–134.
Marcuse, P. 1988. "Neutralizing Homelessness." *Socialist Review* 19 (1): 69–96.

Maher, N. M. 2008. *Nature's New Deal*. Oxford: Oxford University Press.

Marin, P. 1995. *Freedom and Its Discontents*. South Royalton, VT: Steerforth Press.

McChesney, K. Y. 1990. "Family Homelessness: A Systemic Problem." *Journal of Social Issues* 46 (4): 191–205.

Melnitzer, S. B. 2007. "Marginalization and the Homeless: A Prescriptive Analysis." *Journal of Social Distress and the Homeless* 16 (3): 193–220.

Meyer, C. J. 1987. "Stress: There's No Place Like a First Home." *Family Relations* 36: 198–203.

Mitchell, D. 2001. "The Annihilation of Space by Law: The Roots and Implications of Anti-Homeless Laws in the United States." Pp. 6–18 in *The Legal Geographies Reader,* eds. N. Blomley, D. Delaney, and R. T. Ford. Oxford: Blackwell Publishers.

Mitchell, D. 2003. *The Right to the City*. New York: Guilford Press.

Morton, M. 1995. *The Tunnel*. New Haven, CT: Yale University Press.

National Alliance to End Homelessness. 2011. FY 2012 Appropriations: HUD's Homeless Assistance Grants. http://onefamilyinc.files.wordpress.com/2011/08/policy-one-pager.pdf.

National Coalition for the Homeless. 2006. McKinney-Vento Act NCH Fact Sheet #18. http://www.nationalhomeless.org/publications/facts/McKinney.pdf.

National Coalition for the Homeless. 2007. *A Dream Denied: The Criminalization of Homelessness in U.S. Cities.* http://www.national homeless.org/publications/facts/criminalization.html.

National Coalition for the Homeless. 2009. *How Many People Experience Homelessness?* http://www.nationalhomeless.org/factsheets/How_Many.Html.

National Law Center on Homelessness and Poverty. 1991. *Go Directly to Jail: A Report Analyzing Local Anti-Homeless Ordinances*. Available from National Law Center on Homelessness and Poverty, 1411 K Street NW, Suite 1400, Washington, DC 20005.

National Law Center on Homelessness and Poverty. 2002. *Combating the Criminalization of Homelessness: A Guide to Understand and Prevent Legislation that Criminalizes Life-Sustaining Activities*. Washington, DC: National Law Center on Homelessness and Poverty.

National Law Center on Homelessness and Poverty and the National Coalition for the Homeless. 2009. *Homes not Handcuffs: The Criminalization of Homelessness in US Cities*. Washington, DC: National Law Center on Homelessness and Poverty and the National Coalition for the Homeless.

National Low Income Housing Coalition. 2012. *Out of Reach 2012: America's Forgotten Housing Crisis*. Washington, DC: National Low Income Housing Coalition.

Oyserman, D., and J. K. Swim. 2001. "Stigma: An Insider's View." *Journal of Social Issues* 57 (1): 1–14.

Ozawa, M. N., and H. S. Yoon. 2005. "'Leavers' from TANF and AFDC: How Do They Fare Economically." *Social Work* 50 (3): 239–249.

Padgett, D. K., L. Gulcur, and S. Tsemberis. 2006. "Housing First Services for People Who Are Homeless with Co-Occurring Serious Mental Illness and Substance Abuse." *Research on Social Work Practice* 16 (1): 74–83.

Park, R. 1967. "The Mind of the Hobo: Reflections upon the Relation between Mentality and Locomotion." Pp. 156–160 in *The City,* eds. R. E. Park, and E. W. Burgess. Chicago: University of Chicago Press.

Pearson, C., A. E. Montgomery, and G. Locke. 2009. "Housing Stability among Homeless Individuals with Serious Mental Illness Participating in Housing First Programs." *Journal of Community Psychology* 37 (3): 404–417.

Phillips, A., and S. Hamilton. 1996. "Huts for the Homeless: A Low-Technology Approach for Squatters in Atlanta, Georgia." Pp. 81–103 in *There's No Place Like Home,* ed. A. L. Dehavenon. Westport, CT: Bergin and Garvey.

Piven, F. F., and R. A. Cloward. 1993. *Regulating the Poor: The Functions of Public Welfare.* New York: Vintage Books.

Quigley, J. M., S. Raphael, and E. Smolensky. 2001. "Homelessness in America, Homeless in California." *Review of Economics and Statistics* 83 (1): 37–51.

Roberts, J. J. 2004. *How to Increase Homelessness.* Loyalpublishing.com.

Rosenthal, R. 1994. *Homeless in Paradise: A Map of the Terrain.* Philadelphia: Temple University Press.

Rossi, P. H. 1989. *Down and Out in America: The Origins of Homelessness.* Chicago: University of Chicago Press.

Ruddick, S. 1996. *Young and Homeless in Hollywood.* New York: Routledge.

Santa Barbara County. 2006. County Statistical Profile. http://www.county ofsb.org/ceo/pdf/budget/0708/Sectionb.pdf.

Sermons, M. W., and P. Witte. 2011. "State of Homelessness in America." Washington, DC: National Alliance to End Homelessness, Homelessness Research Institute.

Shaw, C. R. 1966. *The Jack-Roller: A Delinquent Boy's Own Story.* Chicago: University of Chicago Press.

Shinn, M, C. Gillespie. 1994. "The Roles of Housing and Poverty in the Origins of Homelessness." *American Behavioral Scientist* 37 (4): 505-522.

Snow, D., L. Anderson, T. Quist, and D. Cress. 1996. "Material Survival Strategies on the Street: Homeless People as *Bricoleurs."* Pp. 86–96 in *Homelessness in America,* ed. J. Baumohl. Phoenix, AZ: Oryx Press.

Snow, D., and L. Anderson. 1987. "Identity Work among the Homeless: The Verbal Construction and Avowal of Personal Identities." *American Journal of Sociology* 92 (6): 1336–1371.

Snow, D., and L. Anderson. 1993. *Down on Their Luck: A Study of Homeless Street People.* Berkeley: University of California Press.

Snow, D., S. Soule, and D. Cress. "Identifying the Precipitants of Homeless Protest across 17 US Cities, 1980 to 1990." *Social Forces* 83 (3): 1183–1210.

Solenberger, A. W. 1911. *One Thousand Homeless Men: A Study of Original Records (1911).* Philadelphia: Russell Sage Foundation.

Southard, P. A. 1998. "Looking for Sanctuary: Staying on Publicly Owned Lands as a Response to Homelessness." Ph.D. diss., University of Oregon.

Spradley, J. P. 2000. *You Owe Yourself a Drunk: An Ethnography of Urban Nomads.* Long Grove, IL: Waveland Press.

Stefancic, A., L. Hul, C. Gillespie, J. Jost, S. Tsemberis, and H. Jones. 2012. "Reconciling Alternative to Incarceration and Treatment Mandates with a Consumer Choice Housing First Model: A Qualitative Study of Individuals

with Psychiatric Disabilities." *Journal of Forensic Psychology Practice* 12 (4): 382–408.
Stein, J. 2003. "The Real Face of Homelessness." *Time Magazine World*, January 13, 2003, accessed November 15, 2011. http://www.time.com/time/magazine/article/0,9171,407358,00.html.
Sutherland, E. H., and H. L. Locke. 1936. *Twenty Thousand Homeless Men.* Chicago: J. P. Lippincott.
Thornburg, D. A. 1991. *Galloping Bungalows: The Rise and Decline of the American House Trailer.* Hamden, CT: Archon Books.
Tietz, J. 2012. "The Sharp, Sudden Decline of America's Middle Class." *Rolling Stone,* June 25. http://www.rollingstone.com/culture/news/the-sharp-sudden-decline-of-americas-middle-class-20120622.
Toth, J. 1993. *The Mole People.* Chicago: Chicago Review Press.
Tsemberis, S., L. Gulcur, and M. Nakae. 2004. "Housing First, Consumer Choice, and Harm Reduction for Homeless Individuals with a Dual Diagnosis." *American Journal of Public Health* 94 (4): 651–656.
United States Department of Housing and Urban Development. 2004. A Guide to Counting Unsheltered Homeless People. Washington, DC: Office of Community Planning and Development.
United States Department of Housing and Urban Development. 2008. A Guide to Counting Unsheltered Homeless People. Washington, DC: Office of Community Planning and Development.
United States Department of Housing and Urban Development. 2011. Annual Homeless Assessment Report to Congress. Washington, DC: Office of Community Planning and Development.
United States Interagency Council on Homelessness. 2010. *Opening Doors: Federal Strategic Plan to Prevent and End Homelessness.* Washington, DC: US Interagency Council on Homelessness.
United States Census Bureau. 2010. State & County Quickfacts. http://quickfacts.census.gov/qfd/states/06000.html.
Urbina, I. 2006. "Keeping It Secret as the Family Car Becomes a Home." *New York Times*, April 2.
Urry, J. 2002. *Inhabiting the Car.* Accessed January 2004, http://www.comp.lancs.ac.uk/sociology/soc102ju.htm.
Van Maanen, J. 2006. "The Asshole." Pp. 304–325 in *The Police and Society, Touchstone Readings,* ed. V. Kappeler. Long Grove, IL: Waveland Press.
Veness. A. 1993. "Neither Homed nor Homeless: Contested Definitions and the Personal Worlds of the Poor." *Political Geography* 12 (4): 319–340.
Wagner, D. 1993. *Checkerboard Square: Culture and Resistance in a Homeless Community.* Boulder, CO: Westview Press.
Wagner, D., and M. Cohen. 1991. "The Power of the People: Homeless Protesters in the Aftermath of Social Movement Participation." *Social Problems* 38 (4): 543–561.
Wagner, D., and J. B. Gilman. 2012. *Confronting Homelessness: Poverty, Politics, and the Failure of Social Policy.* Boulder, CO: Lynne Reinner Publishers.
Wakin, M. 2005. "Not Sheltered, Not Homeless: RVs as Makeshifts." *American Behavioral Scientist* 48 (8): 1013–1033.
Wakin, M. 2008. "Using Vehicles to Challenge Antisleeping Ordinances." *City and Community* 7 (4): 309–329.

Wallis, A. D. 1991. *Wheel Estate: The Rise and Decline of Mobile Homes.* Baltimore: Johns Hopkins University Press.

Wasserman, J. A., and J. M. Clair. 2010. *At Home on the Street: People, Poverty, and a Hidden Culture of Homelessness.* Boulder, CO: Lynne Reinner Publishers.

Waterhouse, C. 2009. "Failed Plans and Planned Failures: The Lower Ninth Ward, Hurricane Katrina, and the Continuing Story of Environmental Injustice." Pp. 156–182 in *Hurricane Katrina: America's Unnatural Disaster,* eds. J. I. Levitt and M. C. Whitaker. Lincoln: University of Nebraska Press.

Weinreb, L. and P. H. Rossi. 1995. "The American Homeless Family Shelter 'System.'" *Social Service Review* 69 (1): 86–107.

White, R. B. 2000. *Home on the Road: The Motor Home in America.* Washington, DC: Smithsonian Institution Press.

Wolch, J. R. 1995. "Inside/Outside: The Dialectics of Homelessness." Pp. 77–90 in *Populations at risk in America,* eds. G. J. Demko and M. C. Jackson. Boulder, CO: Westview Press.

Wolch, J., and M. Dear. 1993. *Malign Neglect.* San Francisco: Jossey-Bass.

Wolfe, T .1968. *The Electric Kool-Aid Acid Test.* New York: Farrar, Strauss, and Giroux.

Wood, D. F. 2002. *RVs and Campers, 1900–2000.* Hudson, WI: Iconografix.

Wong, Y. I., J. M. Park, and H. Nemon. 2006. "Homeless Service Delivery in the Context of the Continuum of Care." *Administration in Social Work* 30 (1): 67–94.

Wright, T. 1995. "Tranquility City: Self-Organization, Protest, and Collective Gains within a Chicago Homeless Encampment." Pp. 37–68 in *Marginal Spaces,* ed. M. P. Smith. New Brunswick, NJ: Transaction.

Wright, T. 1997. *Out of Place: Homeless Mobilizations, Subcities, and Contested Landscapes.* Albany: State University of New York Press.

Wright, T., and A. Vermund. 1996. "Suburban Homelessness and Social Space: Strategies of Authority and Local Resistance in Orange County, California." Pp. 121–143 in *There's No Place Like Home,* ed. A. L. Dehavenon. London: Bergin and Garvey.

Wright, D. 2001. *How to Buy an RV and Save Thousands.* Elkhart, IN: Cottage Publications.

Index

AIDS, 35; AIDS/HIV, 20n9, 134, 146
Aid to Families with Dependent Children (AFDC), 36
Anderson, Leon, 12-13, 15
Anderson, Nels, 23-24
Anti-homeless, 9, 12, 152, 159; anti-homeless laws, 9, 19n8, 74
Anti-homeless ordinances, 11, 16-17, 91, 151-152, 159-161, 172
Anti-homeless regulation, 11-14, 46, 131, 159, 171
Applied Survey Research (ASR), 136, 150
Auto camping, 16, 22, 25-27, 59; auto campers, 22-23
Becker, Howard, 12
Bowery, NYC, 31; see also skid row
Bravery in the field, 18n3
Broken windows, 15
Burgess, Ernest, 23
California, 4-5, 8, 10-11, 16, 19n4, 25-26, 29, 42, 43, 44n6, 45, 50, 52, 55, 71, 71n1, 111, 126, 128-129, 131-132, 136, 144, 147, 164, 165n1, 165n2, 165n3, 169, 172-173; California Supreme Court, 86; Dust Bowl immigrants, 25-26; highway patrol, 136; housing market, 55, 128, 169; legal decisions and cases, 92; Medicaid program, 165n2; shelter restrictions, 11; trailer park citing 29; unsheltered homeless people, 126, 169; vehicle code, 91; vehicle living, 4; vehicle registration, 71n1; Welfare and Institutions Code, 165n3; see also Santa Barbara; Santa Cruz; Santa Rosa; and Sonoma
CalWORKS, 148, 165n2
Channel Counties Legal Services Association, 2
Chicago's main stem, 28; West Madison Street, 24, 31; see also skid row; hobohemia
Chicago School (sociology), 23
Chronic health problems, 148, 172
Chronic pain, 61
Chronic homelessness, 7, 20n9, 36-38, 73, 76, 137, 146, 157-159, 164, 165n5, 169, 174
Civilian Conservation Corps (CCC), 28
Committee for Social Justice, 56, 86, 93-94, 99, 161
Committee on the Shelterless (COTS), 140-141
Continuum of Care (CoC), 8, 35-36, 97-98, 125-127, 131, 157, 163-164, 173-174; Continuum of Care Application, 157; Continuum of Care Action Plan, 133; Continuum of Care Planning Group, 136-137
Criminalization, 9-10, 19, 20n8, 53
DePastino, Todd, 23-25
Digital audio recording, 5; digital photographs, 47
Dordick, Gwendolyn, 10, 13, 18n3, 98
Doubled up, 7, 8, 43n6, 133, 137
Duneier, Mitchell, 4, 15
Dust Bowl, 26, 39
Environmental racism, 39
Ethnographic research, 1; ethnography, 7

Farm workers, 26, 129-130
Federal Emergency Management Agency (FEMA), 38-39, 43n4
Federal Strategic Plan to Prevent and End Homelessness; see Opening Doors
Federal Housing Authority (FHA), 29
Federal Transient Service (FTS), 28
Field notes, 5, 95n1
Fig Tree, 41, 46; Moreton Bay Fig Tree, 1
General relief (GR), 3, 49; general assistance (GA), 148
GI Bill of rights, 29
Goffman, Erving, 7, 12-13
Great Depression, 25
Hegemony, 43n2
Hidden homeless, 8, 174
Hobohemia, 23-24, 30-31
Hoboes, 24, 26-27, 30-31; hobo college, 23
Home guard, 28
Homeless and homelessness, 8-11, 13-15, 21-22, 25, 28, 34-38, 42, 45, 47-49, 58, 62n7, 62-64, 68-69, 73, 75, 78, 80-81, 84, 88, 94, 97, 110, 116, 119, 121, 122n2, 126-127, 133-134, 137, 139-140, 142-145, 147-149, 151-153, 155-158
Homeless assistance, 7-8, 35, 37, 126-127
Homeless community, 5, 17, 21, 41, 60, 67, 122n2, 125, 137-138, 143, 145, 148, 150, 154
Homeless families, 36, 38, 137, 149; homeless parents, 10, 63; homeless children/youth, 38, 63, 137
Homeless people, 3-18, 19n5, 19n6, 19n7, 20n8, 20n9, 20n10, 20n11, 21-23, 26, 28, 31-32, 34-37, 40-42, 45-47, 50, 51-54, 59, 61, 63, 67, 70, 72n4, 72n7, 73-79, 81-85, 89, 94-95, 95n1, 97-99, 104-110, 121, 123n6, 123n7, 125-138, 140, 143-153, 155-165, 167-175; homeless camps and campers, 95n1, 154; homeless court, 152; homeless defendants, 6; homeless prevention, 137, 150
Homeless population, 6-8, 17-18, 28, 35, 37, 40, 102, 121, 132, 136
Homeless services, 19n5, 37, 46, 54, 70, 120-121, 140, 144, 152; homeless service providers, 19n4, 101; homeless service occupations, 105
Homeless shelter, 1, 18n2, 46, 51, 88, 128, 140, 143-144
Homeless Emergency and Rapid Transition to Housing Act (HEARTH), 37
Homeless Management Information System (HMIS), 19n5
Homeless Outreach Coordinator, 6, 104, 107, 119, 122n3
Homeless People's Association (HPA), 41
Homeless United for Friendship and Freedom (HUFF), 151
Hoovervilles, 25
Hopper, Kim, 10-11, 20n10
Housing First, 37, 54, 97-98, 125, 128, 164, 173-174
HUD; see United States Department of Housing and Urban Development
Hurricane Katrina, 38-39, 43n4
Identity work, 12-13; Identity talk, 12-13
Industrial Workers of the World (IWW), 24
Interfaith Satellite Shelter Program (ISSP), 165n4
International Brotherhood Welfare Association (IBWA), 24
Interviews, 5, 49, 72n7, 116, 140, 146
Jungle, 19n3, 41, 43n5, 69, 159
Kampgrounds of America (KOA), 33
Labeling, 15, 69-70, 75
Lillian Child, 40, 43n5

Index 187

Linear residential treatment model (LRT), 36, 97-98
Louie, 1-3, 5, 18n1, 52-58, 61, 66-70, 113, 123n6
Lyn, 55-56, 60, 62, 65-66, 98
Main stem, 24-25, 28; see also skid row; hobohemia
Makeshifts, 4-5, 14, 19n3, 70, 170, 174
Makeshift housing, 4, 13, 15, 19n6, 42, 161
Makeshift living, 11, 14, 32, 42
Makeshift camping, 25
Marx, Karl, 21
Master status, 15
McKinney-Vento Homeless Assistance Act, 35
Minneapolis Gateway area, 32; see also skid row
Mobile home, 30, 38-39
Mobile Home Manufacturers Association, 30
Moreton Bay Fig Tree; see Fig Tree
Motor home, 3, 21, 30, 33-34, 42, 61, 68; motor home parks, 70
New Deal, 26-29
"New" homeless, 22
National Coalition for the Homeless, 4, 8-9, 35
National Committee on Care of Transient and Homeless, 27
National Law Center on Homelessness and Poverty, 1, 9, 13
Nonprofit, 94, 100, 102-104; nonprofit advocates, 6
Not in my backyard (NIMBY), 1, 18n2, 38, 42, 73, 98, 128
Opening Doors (Federal Strategic Plan to Prevent and End Homelessness), 37, 165n5
Panhandling, 19n8, 59, 82, 99, 149, 152-153, 169; spanging, 82
Park, Robert, 23
Participatory Action Research (PAR), 6
Pickup camper, 32-33, 56, 62, 116

Placemaking, 12, 14
Point in Time (PIT) Count, 6-8, 18, 19n6, 20n9, 37, 125-128, 131-132, 162-164, 164n1, 165n5; homeless census, 136; homeless street counts, 19n4; in Sonoma County, 132, 134-137, 143; in Santa Cruz County, 144-150, 156; in Santa Barbara County, 157-159, 162
Post-traumatic stress disorder (PTSD), 61-62, 69, 114-115, 148
Psychiatric health facility (PHF, Puff Unit), 112
Racism; see environmental racism
Rapid re-housing, 125
Recreational Vehicle Institute, 30
Regulation, 4-5, 9-11, 13-18, 19n7, 41-42, 45-48, 53, 59, 64, 69-70, 73, 79-80, 85, 91, 94-95, 96n3, 97-99, 117, 121, 122n5, 125, 131, 151, 153, 156, 159-160, 163-164, 167-174
Regulation-resistance dynamic, 4, 16, 18, 72, 130, 167-174
Representative Payee, 3, 18n1, 72n6
Resistance, 4, 5, 11-14, 17-18, 42, 45, 53, 91, 98, 168, 171-174
Rosenthal, Robert, 40-41
Rubber tramps, 69; see also trailerites
Safe Parking Program, 6, 17, 99-121, 122n2, 122n3, 123n7, 161, 170, 172-174
Salvation Army (Sally), 51, 52, 104, 109
Santa Barbara, 1, 5-6, 16, 17, 40-41, 43n5, 45-46, 49-54, 57, 59, 63, 66-70, 71n1, 72n5, 77, 81-83, 88, 90-91, 93, 95n1, 96n3, 99-100, 102, 107, 110-111, 117-119, 122n2, 125, 129-132, 157-159, 161-164, 170, 174; population density, 130-131; Santa Barbara Housing Authority, 89; Santa Barbara Municipal Code,

91; Santa Barbara Municipal Court, 86; Santa Barbara Surf Club, 123; ten-year plan, 158
Santa Barbara City Council, 6, 81, 85, 93, 99-102, 161
Santa Barbara County Board of Supervisors, 6, 93, 99-100, 161
Santa Barbara Police Department, 71n1, 77, 100, 122n5
Santa Cruz, 50, 83, 131, 144, 149, 151-156; Santa Cruz Municipal Code, 153
Santa Cruz City Council, 151-152
Santa Cruz County, 5-6, 16-17, 77, 82-83, 94, 95n1, 125, 129-131, 144-151, 153-158, 162-164, 172; unsheltered homeless, 132
Santa Rosa, 84, 129-132, 136, 138-141
Seattle, Washington, Pioneer Square, 20n11, 24, 31; see also skid row
Seven subpopulations (required by HUD), 20n9, 133-134, 145-146
Shelterization, 9-11, 19n7, 53, 70
Single Rent Occupancy (SRO), 31, 54, 93, 102
Skid row, 16, 20n11, 22-26, 28, 31-32
Snow, David, 5, 12-13, 15-16, 171
Social legitimacy, 5, 12, 15, 18
Social Security, 18n1, 71n3
Sonoma County, 6, 16-17, 77, 81-82, 94, 95n1, 125, 128, 131-138, 141, 143-145, 147-150, 156-158, 162-164, 174
Stigma, 9, 11-13, 16, 19n6, 35, 40, 42, 45, 62-64, 104, 107, 115, 121, 173-174
Supplemental Security Income (SSI), 2-3, 10, 40, 49, 55-57, 59, 66, 68-69, 71n3, 72n6, 79, 90, 128-129, 136, 139, 142, 148, 160
Supplemental Security Disability Income (SSDI), 49, 68-69, 71n3, 136, 141, 148, 160

Sweeps, 9, 13, 41, 74, 111, 127, 136, 142-143, 160
Temporary Assistance to Needy Families (TANF), 36, 136
The Great Depression, 25
Tin can tourists, 22, 43n1
Trailer Coach Manufacturers Association, 30
Trailerites, 27
Transient, 23, 27-28, 49, 77-78, 80, 83, 160
University of California, 144, 157
United States Department of Housing and Urban Development (HUD) 7-8, 19n4, 20n9, 72n5, 125, 127, 133-134, 136, 145-146, 150, 157-158; HUD Guide to Counting Unsheltered Homeless People, 133, 164
United States Interagency Council on Homelessness (USICH), 37
Unsheltered homeless, 8, 17-18, 125, 133, 146
Vehicle counts, 5, 92
Veterans, 20n9, 29, 35, 38, 43n5, 51, 137, 141, 143, 146, 152
Veterans Administration (VA), 37
Wagner, David, 10-11, 14, 35-36, 53-54, 98, 126, 168, 171
Winnebagos, 21
World War I, 28
World War II, 28-29, 39
Wright, Talmadge, 4, 9, 14, 98, 16

About the Book

Privacy, mobility, dignity—living in a vehicle offers many advantages over life in a shelter or on the street. Michele Wakin broadens our understanding of homelessness by exploring the growing phenomenon of vehicle living and how it differs from other forms of makeshift housing.

Incorporating both quantitative data and ethnographic work in California, Wakin takes us into the lives of those who call a car, truck, or RV home. She probes the forces that pushed them out of traditional housing, their unique strengths and vulnerabilities in navigating everyday life, and their complex relationships with local communities, law enforcement, and social service providers. Her analysis of this overlooked population illuminates the dynamics that make it so hard to break the cycle of regulation and resistance that impedes the escape from poverty.

Michele Wakin is executive director of the Institute for Social Justice and associate professor of sociology at Bridgewater State University.